The Agile Team Handbook

Second Edition

Putting Scrum To Work For Your Team

Jan Beaver

Many of the designations used by manufacturers and sellers to distinguish their products are claimed as trademarks. Where these designations appear in this book and the author was aware of a trademark claim, the designations have been printed in initial capital letters, all capital letters, or with appropriate registration marks.

The author has taken care in the preparation of this document, but makes no expressed or implied warranty of any kind and assumes no responsibility for errors or omissions. No liability is assumed for incidental or consequential damages in connection with or arising out of the use of the information contained herein.

Copyright © 2017 Jan Beaver

All rights reserved.

Printed in the United States of America.

No part of this publication may be reproduced, stored in a retrieval system, or transmitted, in any form, or by any means, electronic, mechanical, photocopying, recording, or otherwise, without the prior consent of the copyright holder.

ISBN-10: 1973714337

ISBN-13: 978-1973714330

Table of Contents

Table of Contents i
Preface vii
Acknowledgements ix
About The Author xi
Introduction xiii
    Organization xiv
    To Scrum Or Not To Scrum? xiv
    A Word About Words xiv
    About The Layout xv
    Let's Go! xvi
Chapter 1 Agile Origins and Overview 1
    Process Control Models 1
        Defined Process Control 1
        Empirical Process Control 3
        Transparency, Inspection, Adaptation 4
        Why Bother? 5
    The Agile Manifesto 7
        Agile Manifesto Values 10
        Agile Manifesto Principles 12
    Origins of Scrum 22
        Scrum Roles 24
        Scrum Events 24
        Scrum Artifacts 25
    How Scrum Works 25
    A Cautionary Note 27
    Scrum Values 27
        Commitment 27
        Focus 27
        Openness 28
        Respect 28
        Courage 28

Table of Contents

- Trust 28
- Having Fun 28
- Make It Real 28
- Further Reading 29

Chapter 2 Scrum Roles: Scrum Master and Product Owner 31
- Scrum Master 31
  - Facilitator and Servant-leader 32
- Product Owner 33
  - Product Owner As Linchpin 34
- Not The Final Word 35
- Further Reading 35

Chapter 3 Scrum Roles: The Development Team 37
- Development Team Characteristics 38
  - Small 38
  - Dedicated Full-time to the Team and Product 39
  - Self-organizing and Self-managing 41
  - Cross-functional 42
  - The Sole Owners of Estimates and Sprint Commitments 51
  - Accountable for Developing a Quality Product at a Sustainable Pace 51
  - Responsible for Demonstrating a Potentially Shippable Product Increment at the End of Every Sprint to the Product Owner, Customers, and Stakeholders 53
  - Accountable for Team improvement 53
- Team Maturity 54
  - Forming 54
  - Storming 55
  - Norming 58
  - Performing 59
  - Beware the J-Shaped Curve 59
  - What If We Never Get Beyond Storming? 61
- A Final Word About Teams and Teamwork 62
- Teams Are Key 62
- Further Reading 62

Chapter 4 The Product Backlog 63
- Adaptive Planning 63
- What the Development Team Gets From the Product Backlog 64
- User Stories 65
  - User Story Template 65
  - An Example 66
- Some Useful Terms 67

Epic 67
Theme 68
The Three C's of a User Story 68
Card 68
Conversation 68
Confirmation 69
Where are the Details? 69
Details as Acceptance Criteria 70
Details as Definition of Done 71
Details as Smaller Stories 72
Getting to Goldilocks 73
INVEST in Your User Stories 74
Independent 74
Negotiable 74
Valuable 74
Estimable 75
Small (or Sized Appropriately) 75
Testable 76
The Product Backlog as Iceberg 76
Backlog Refinement 77
Writing User Stories 78
Wrapping Up 79
Further Reading 80

Chapter 5 Scrum Events 81
Sprint 83
Scrum Master as Facilitator 83
What If We're Not Using Scrum? 83
Sprint Planning 84
Daily Scrum/Daily Stand-up 85
The Three Questions 86
It's Daily Planning, Not Daily Status Reporting 88
Impediments 88
Backlog Refinement/Story Time 89
Estimating and Estimates 90
Relative Estimates 91
Story Points 93
Approaches to Relative Estimating 95
Spikes 102
Sprint Review 103
Sprint Retrospective 106
Wrapping Up 109

Further Reading 109

Chapter 6 Sprints **111**
　The Meaning of "Potentially Shippable" 112
　Toward a Definition of Done 112
　The Mini-waterfall Trap 114
　Technical Debt 116
　　Technical Debt and the Agile Death Spiral 116
　　The Solution: Focus on Finishing Stories 117
　　Approaches to Eliminating Technical Debt 118
　Reciprocal Commitments 119
　Changes to the Sprint Backlog 120
　Velocity 122
　What If You're Not Done? 124
　Wrapping Up 125
　Further Reading 126

Chapter 7 Sprint Planning **127**
　When Should You Do Sprint Planning? 127
　What Do You Need to Plan a Sprint? 129
　No Surprises 130
　The Sprint Goal 131
　To Commit or Not To Commit? 132
　Two Ways to Plan a Sprint 133
　　All-in-One Sprint Planning 133
　　Two-Part Sprint Planning 134
　Task Packages 136
　Managing the Sprint Backlog 137
　　Task Boards 137
　　Swarming Around Work 140
　Multitasking 141
　　A Multitasking Test 142
　A Heuristic for Task Work 143
　Wrapping Up 144
　Further Reading 144

Chapter 8 Making Progress Visible **145**
　Traditional Measures of Progress 145
　The Trouble With Burndown Charts 146
　Build-up Charts 149
　　Sprint Build-up Chart 150
　　Release Build-up Chart 151
　Organic Transparency 152

    Wrapping Up 152
    Further Reading 152

Chapter 9 Collaboration 153
    A Definition 153
    High-bandwidth Communication 154
        The Team Room 156
        Dedicated Space 158
    Communication Modes 159
        Convection Currents 159
        Osmotic Communication 160
        Drafts 160
    The Importance of Proximity 161
    Dispersed Teams and Collaboration 161
        Use Technology to Approximate Face-to-face Communication 161
        What If We're In Different Time Zones? 162
        Build Co-located Teams 163
    Wrapping Up 163
    Further Reading 164

Chapter 10 Agile Teams in the Enterprise 165
    Scaling Up To Take On Large Projects 165
    Architecture and Design 166
    Sharing the Product Backlog 167
    Component Teams 168
    Coordinating Sprints and Scrum Events 170
        Stagger Daily Scrums 170
        Synchronize Sprints 171
        The Importance of Continuous Integration 173
    Coordinating Work Across Teams 173
        Scrum of Scrums 173
    What About The Product Owner? 175
    Communities of Practice 177
    Wrapping Up 179
    Further Reading 179

Chapter 11 Implementing Scrum 181
    Scrum is Disruptive – So Find a Sponsor 181
    Train Everyone Involved 182
    Choose a Product 183
    Assemble Your Team – Product Owner, Scrum Master, Development Team Members 184
        Product Owner Hits The Ground Running 184

- Scrum Master Self-selects ... 184
- Development Team Self-selects Too ... 185
- Team Working Agreement ... 186
- Do As Little As Necessary to Get Started...And Then Get Started! ... 187
  - Refine The Product Vision ... 187
  - Generate and Refine The Initial Product Backlog ... 187
  - Plan The First Sprint and Get Started! ... 189
- Insulate the Team From Organizational Politics ... 189
- Build a Fault-Tolerant Environment ... 191
- Make It Real! ... 192
- Go Big Or Go Home? ... 192
- Now, Do It Again ... 193
- Wrapping Up ... 193
- Further Reading ... 193

Epilogue: Never Stop ... 195

References ... 197

Index ... 201

Preface

You've joined an Agile Team – congratulations! Now what? Many organizations making the transition to Agile assume that Team Members can simply learn all about Agile from others: the Scrum Master (if you're using Scrum), other Team Members, through osmosis, or some other undefined means. The truth is, Agile frameworks like Scrum or eXtreme Programming (XP) are quite simple in the abstract, consisting of just a handful of Roles, Events, Artifacts, and practices. In practice, however, Agile is exceedingly difficult. And while there are plenty of training opportunities available for Scrum Masters and Product Owners, very little attention trickles down to the true engine of any organization using or moving to Agile: the Agile Team Members.

One purpose of this handbook is to address that glaring omission. As a companion to Agile Team Training or Certified Scrum Master training, this handbook is a, well, handy resource providing guidance, practical exercises, and room for recording marginal notes and other thoughts. Detached from formal training, this handbook is designed to provide as much practical help as possible to Agile Team Members, both the freshly minted and the grizzled veterans of many product development cycles.

Another purpose of this handbook is to serve as a guide to organizational agility. Yes, the Agile framework you adopt whether Scrum or otherwise is important – but the framework itself is not the point. Using Scrum or another Agile framework puts an organization and its Teams in a great position to advance toward agility. However, practicing Scrum by rote, even if the organization and all Teams follow the rules of Scrum to the letter, in no way guarantees a successful Agile transformation. So yes, learn Scrum or XP or whatever Agile framework you choose to implement. Practice it until it becomes muscle memory. But also continuously apply Agile values and principles to move beyond the framework and its practices and into agility. Put another way, the practices are the road, not the destination.

As your guide along the Agile road, I should tell you right now why I like Scrum and why I believe it is so important to follow the rules of Scrum conscientiously. So here goes: I like Scrum because it contains all the moving parts Teams and organizations need to get started, now, today, on their Agile journey. Scrum just works, right out of the box, no modifications needed or wanted. Scrum is lightweight. Scrum is simple. But Scrum is almost always surprisingly difficult to put into practice. That's why it is so important to practice Scrum until its rhythms are reflex. When your first instinct when confronting any product development or organizational problem is to apply Scrum to find a solution, you've arrived. If your first instinct in that situation is, by contrast, to change Scrum to hide the problem, you're not ready.

And with that, let's get started. It's going to be a fast, sometimes bumpy, but always exhilarating ride!

Jan Beaver, PhD, Certified Scrum Trainer®
Laporte, CO
July 2017

Acknowledgements

I began my real, post-graduate-school career working in a small company that was doing things in a way I now recognize as proto-Agile. In 1987, there was no such thing as "Agile," yet in this company everyone helped out with functional and regression testing, everyone contributed to what today is called User Acceptance Testing (UAT) – in short, everyone basically did whatever the company needed at a given moment to be successful.

We did not work in well-defined teams nor did we have constructs that resembled the formal backlogs of Scrum or XP. But we most assuredly did employ the concept of incremental and iterative product development, with daily builds and nightly automated test runs of both hardware and software. We also worked in close contact with the business, engaging in daily conversation with sales, marketing, and the company president on what customers wanted, needed, might like, clearly didn't like, etc.

When I moved on to other jobs, I discovered – much to my shock and horror – that what I had experienced in my first real job was not that usual way of working in the technology industry. People lived and worked in specialist silos. Projects were managed in ways that made so little sense it was a running joke. "Testing" was an activity that was the exclusive domain of "testers." The relationship between "coders" and "testers" was often adversarial. The business rarely interacted with either the coding or testing arms of the company and when they did, that relationship was also generally adversarial. Indeed, sales, marketing, and executive management often saw "engineering" or "IT" as a problem to be solved, not as a partner in delivering great products to the company's customers.

I certainly haven't seen it all, but I've seen more than enough to know that a team-based environment in which there is a deep commitment to implementing Agile Values and Principles offers the greatest potential not just for success as a company, but for being a great place to work. That realization has led me to seek out opportunities to work in and with Agile organizations, first as a technical contributor and now as an Agile/Scrum trainer and coach, which is how I now earn a living.

Acknowledgements

This book is based largely on many years of personal experience training, coaching, and working in and among Agile Teams. I've learned a wide variety of lessons from the people with whom it has been both a privilege and a curse to work. I'll leave the latter appropriately nameless, but would like to mention a handful of people in the former category.

Jeff McKenna was a member of the first Scrum Team back in the early 1990s. Jeff is my Agile and Scrum mentor, personal confidant, and the one person from whom I have learned the most about Scrum and agility.

Dr. Dan Rawsthorne is a good friend and another source of practical knowledge and expertise in Scrum and agility. Dan has always gone well out of his way to talk with me and is a fun and interesting sounding board for ideas.

The late Jean Tabaka lived just down the road near Boulder, CO. Jean taught me more about communication, collaboration, and teamwork than I thought I would ever know. I miss her.

Tim Walker also lives just down the road, near Broomfield, CO. Tim introduced me to Scrum in practice and also got me started as an Agile trainer and coach. Tim is one of the finest people I know. He just instinctively understands what Agile is all about.

Finally, and most significantly, I want to acknowledge all of the people who have worked through training sessions I've facilitated; all of the people who have been willing to suspend disbelief and try ideas I've suggested while coaching their teams; and mostly the wonderful team players and team leaders I've had the privilege of working with and learning from over the last decade.

Thank you all!

About The Author

I am a jack of many trades, but definitely master of some. During my varied working life – I shrink from calling it a "career" although perhaps with sufficient reflection I can identify some themes – I have been hip-deep in virtually every aspect of the development of software products. I started out writing BASIC programs on a Commodore 64, with a cassette tape drive for storage, in the late 1970s and have followed a zigzag path through the technology stack from that point until now.

I am a self-taught technologist, from the design of RF power circuits based on my lifelong hobby of amateur radio through professional pursuits including technical writing, coding in a wide variety of languages and environments from client-side JavaScript to embedded C code on Unix platforms, designing and implementing user interfaces, and testing, testing, testing.

I now make my living training, coaching, and mentoring individuals, teams, and organizations in various Agile frameworks including Scrum, eXtreme Programming, and variations on Lean and Kanban. For the last four years I have been focused primarily on Scrum Alliance certified training (Certified Scrum Master, Certified Scrum Product Owner) in my role as a Certified Scrum Trainer®. I am a regular speaker at various Agile and Scrum conferences in the USA and elsewhere. My chief goal in all of this is to make people's lives better by improving their working conditions, their effectiveness, and the strength and capabilities of the organizations that employ them.

My formal education consists of three degrees in history, culminating in a Ph.D. The study of history is an intellectual pursuit that I simply couldn't escape despite the economics of the current era, which make such things expensive hobbies rather than viable career options. An education in the liberal arts is still extremely useful, however. Of the many things I learned, the two that I carry with me every day are the ability to think critically about any subject and a deep understanding of systems and how systems interact with one another. It was all worth it just for those two things.

About The Author

You can follow me on Twitter @jan_beaver or reach me by email at jbeaver@greyrockagile.com

Introduction

This book is for Agile Team Members. As I write this, it is the only book I know of that is devoted entirely to this absolutely vital, yet underserved segment of the Agile universe. As the entity that develops and delivers value in an organization, the team is literally the engine that drives success. Given that fact, it is a fair question to wonder why Teams have not received more direct attention from the Agile community. My intention in writing this book is to begin to fill that gap.

This book is based on my experience training, coaching, mentoring and working on Agile Teams during the last thirty years. It is based on real-world problems and issues, spectacular successes and equally spectacular failures the teams with which I have been associated have experienced. While there is some theory contained between the covers, the vast majority of the material is drawn from the down-and-dirty, daily life of teams building complex software products.

This handbook is intended for Agile Team Members of all levels of experience, from beginner to seasoned veteran. Beginners will, of course, find much more material to chew on than their deeply experienced peers, yet I believe even the latter will find valuable bits to add to their Agile bag of tricks.

If you were to distill everything on these pages down to its essence, you would find that the entire book is about teams and teamwork. I mention the importance of solid technical practices, such as Test Driven Development (TDD), continuous integration, automated testing, refactoring, etc., but that is not what this book is about. There are plenty of great sources that can help you with the technical aspects of working on an Agile Team. And really, learning new technical practices or technologies is not all that difficult for people who are already skilled in technology.

On the other hand, technical people in general find the social interaction that is the basis of teamwork something between challenging and terrifying. And since teamwork is the basis of a high-performing team, it seemed like a good subject area for this book to focus on.

Organization

This handbook begins at the highest levels of product development and process control theory, rapidly descending into the realm of the practical, day-to-day life on a development team. I find that it is extremely important for everyone on a team – and in an organization – to understand the motivating forces and theoretical bases for the specific roles, rhythms, practices, and artifacts that define the day-to-day world of working on an Agile Team. Every action Team Members engage in has a basis in some higher-level theory, value, or principle. Put another way, nothing we do when working in an Agile organization is random, capricious, or lacking in firm grounding in theory, values, principles, and knowledge gained through working.

I wrote this handbook with the intention that readers will move through it sequentially on the first reading. Try to follow that progression as much as possible as one concept builds the foundation for those that follow. After reading through once, however, there is no reason not to use this book as a quick reference to the specific roles, rhythms, practices, and artifacts of your Agile framework.

To Scrum Or Not To Scrum?

Scrum is both the most recognized Agile framework and also by far the most widely practiced, but it is not the only one nor is it necessarily the be-all end-all of agility. It is, however, a great place to start as it contains all of the moving parts you need to get your team assembled and moving quickly and purposefully. Most of the information and recommendations in this book are directed at the use of Scrum. The terminology used here is also based on the standard definition of Scrum. That said, I think you will still find value in these pages if you are implementing any team-based Agile framework. Again, this handbook is for Agile Team Members, a description that goes beyond the boundaries of any specific Agile framework.

A Word About Words

I use terminology in a fairly specific manner. I capitalize proper nouns, hence "Agile" when referring to frameworks based on the values and principles of the Agile Manifesto. Likewise, "Development Team Member" is a defined Scrum role and therefore a proper noun deserving of capitalization every bit as much as Scrum Master or Product Owner. I sometimes refer to the Development Team as the "Team" but always attempt to ensure that the context is clear. Whenever I refer to all three roles working together I use the term "Scrum Team" In addition, I have made every effort to use terminology consistently throughout.

About The Layout

I designed the physical layout of the book to leave fairly wide margins on every page. Those margins are there – and I left them completely empty – for you to use as you see fit. This is not great literature (sadly), so feel free to write notes, scribble random thoughts, draw diagrams, or simply doodle in the margins.

Another layout element that is a little unique is the lack of captions on the diagrams sprinkled throughout the text. Labeling figures seemed redundant considering that the surrounding text reinforces the visual elements and the visual elements reinforce the surrounding text. I have, as much as physically possible made sure that the text and related visual elements are on the same page or at worst on facing pages. You should never have to turn the page to see the visual element referred to in the text, although the text may carry on for a page or two beyond the reinforcing visual element.

Finally, I have made use of a simple text highlight to call out what I believe to be special information that deserves extra attention. Here are some definitions of the most common items:

> *Magician's Secret*
> Callouts in this category contain insights I have gained through years of working with, training, coaching, and mentoring Agile Teams. These are the kinds of things that often remain unsaid but are important to the topic at hand. Like a magician explaining how a particular illusion works, these items give you the lowdown on the "why" of a topic.

> *Tip*
> These items are just what they look like – quick tips to help you move forward in a specific area.

> **Try This**
> These items contain practical advice on specific things to do within your team to address an issue or to generate a particular insight.

Let's Go!

And with that, let's dive right in and get going! When I coach Agile Teams, a guiding principle I work from is to do just enough to get started *and then get started.* Only through actually working do we build knowledge, team muscle, and insight. Read on and begin – or continue – your Agile Team journey.

Chapter 1 Agile Origins and Overview

"Scrum is a framework for developing and sustaining complex products."
– *The Scrum Guide, July 2016*

Process Control Models

When we think about the ways in which people have figured out how to control process, there are really just two high-level approaches: Defined and Empirical Process Control models. Let's start with the older of the two: Defined Process Control.

Defined Process Control

In 1911, Frederick Winslow Taylor presented a paper titled *The Principles of Scientific Management*[*] to the American Society of Mechanical Engineers (ASME) annual conference. In this paper, Taylor laid the foundations for what would become the assembly line-based industrial economy of the first part of the twentieth century. Taylor proposed a system in which the company's management would supersede the knowledge of the people doing the work, replacing traditional notions of work processes with carefully measured and strictly defined work procedures discovered and honed by a new class of corporate experts: managers.

Left to their own devices, Taylor insisted, the workers would fall into patterns of inefficiency based on traditional work methods and constrained by the power of social pressure – essentially, the workers would all slow to the pace of their slowest member, rendering improvements in efficiency impossible.

To counteract this "soldiering" as it was called in that era, Taylor devised a system in which management experts would devise work rules, strictly enforce work in accordance with those rules, and then measure worker

---

[*] Taylor 1911. See the References section for complete information on all cited sources.

performance based on compliance with the rules. Managers clad in white shirts scurried around the shop floor with stopwatches and clipboards, timing every worker motion and capturing the results on their task sheets. Workers, generally clad in blue shirts, were compelled to follow the resulting work rules to the letter – to the second actually – or face being fired and replaced with someone who could perform the job in the specified time period.

The result of this system was a vast improvement in the efficiency of work results. Not only were workers held to strict time-and-task standards, the new "white-collar" managers made incremental changes to workspaces, moving frequently used tools and parts closer to the workers, for example, to reduce unnecessary motion and thereby reduce the time required to perform a sliver of a larger task.

When added together, these "scientific" improvements, based on observation, tuning of the work environment, and enforcement of work rules on the now robotic workers, produced the industrial boom of the early twentieth century.

The theoretical basis of Defined Process Control is something called *causal determinism*. The basic components of causal determinism are *up-front design, top-down planning,* and *tight control* to ensure adherence to the plan. Notice that the flow of information organizationally is from the top to the bottom, or practically speaking from management to labor. There is no place for feedback or even an expectation that information should or could flow in the reverse direction.

Any color you want, as long as it's black...
The emblematic product of the era of Defined Process Control was the Ford Model T. Henry Ford adopted Taylorism, ruling his River Rouge factory and the others in the area around Detroit, in which iron ore came in one end off the river and Model T's, all of them identical, rolled out the other end, with an iron fist. It was the world's largest factory. It was also the world's most productive factory, based on Ford's innovative moving assembly line and Taylor's scientific management.

As long as the Model T's were all black – and as long as that was all anyone wanted – Taylorism worked well, from a management perspective at least. The work itself was simple, repeatable, repetitive, and required no great skill while Ford's work rules extended far beyond the factory floor into the private lives of his employees. (Ford employed an army of what were in effect secret police agents to spy on his vast, potentially unruly workforce.) Henry Ford once famously said: "Why is it when I want to hire a pair of hands, a brain comes attached to them?" That statement captures the essence of Taylorism: the workers are there simply to follow the commands of management to the letter and not to think for themselves. The workers have nothing to contribute to the conversation.

We might still be driving black Model T's if not for the contributions of Alfred P. Sloan, who in the 1920s recognized that people were not going to be content with one choice in motorized transport. Sloan's contribution was cars in different colors, different models, and eventually, cars of the same model with different options. At that point, when the work output become variable, Taylorism started to collapse. Ford had to adapt in order to fend off competition from his new rival, Sloan's burgeoning General Motors.

Defined Process Control models are highly effective at taking advantage of economies of scale. When the work is repetitive, predictable, and subject to precise and complete control, economies of scale produce huge benefits. However, when the work is non-repetitive, unpredictable, and defeats all efforts to bring it under precise control, Defined Process Control models are ineffective and inappropriate.

Empirical Process Control

Fast-forward a few decades to the emergence of the alternative model: Empirical Process Control. It turns out that in a complex industrial world – let alone a post-industrial, knowledge-based economy such as the one we find ourselves in today – Defined Process Control simply couldn't adapt to variability in the work output. In the late 1930s, a Fellow at Bell Labs, Walter Shewhart, devised the beginnings of a process control model that would provide adaptability in the face of highly variable and increasingly complex work. Shewhart thought an approach based more broadly on the scientific method would be much more appropriate. Basically what Shewhart proposed was that work should be broken down into small batches and then fed into an endless, iterative cycle that he called Plan-Do-Study-Act or PDSA.[*]

Plan: Devise a short-term plan covering what you think you can safely predict

Do: Execute on that plan – prove that you can do some or all of what you planned to do

Study: Collect data by examining the results of what you did

---

[*] Shewhart 1939

Act: Draw conclusions based on the examination of the collected data in preparation for another planning phase, which then incorporates a small change based on the experience of the last cycle; this is the essence of what we now call Continuous Improvement

A student of Shewhart's, W. Edwards Deming, called this the Plan-Do-Check-Act (PDCA) cycle. In the Agile world, it is commonly called Plan-Do-Inspect-Adapt. It's really all the same thing, although the Inspect-Adapt terminology is current and provides a nice segue into the next section.

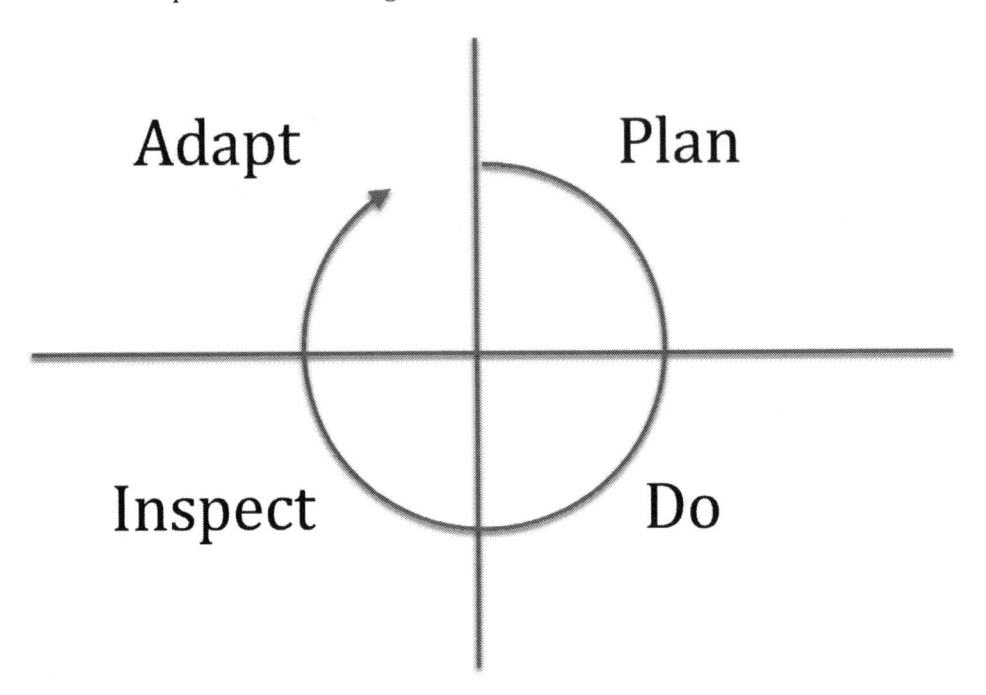

Transparency, Inspection, Adaptation

All Empirical approaches to product development, including Scrum and all other Agile frameworks, are based on three principles: Transparency, Inspection, and Adaptation.

Transparency: The moving parts of the process must be visible from the outside. Those committed to, involved in, and accountable for the results must be able to see what's going on. This means that there is a common domain language used within the process. It also means that the outward-facing, visible aspects of the process must be coherent and consistent across the organization so that interested observers can effectively and appropriately interpret its activities and results. Finally, a common, shared understanding of what "done" looks like for all pieces of work output is necessary for those who do the work and those who accept the results. A critical question to ask about any planned work is: How will you know when you're done – and how will you prove it?

Inspection: Frequent inspection of work results and evaluation of progress toward short- and long-term goals is necessary to provide the data for making appropriate decisions. Empirical Process Control demands that we make decisions based on data. Wishful thinking or fanciful notions of what ***should*** be going on are not acceptable bases for decision-making. Inspection must be frequent enough to generate the right quantity and type of data, but not so frequent that it interferes with the work.

Adaptation: It is clearly not sufficient simply to observe a process and collect data about both the process and the work results it produces. We must make use of the benefits of Transparency and Inspection so that we can adapt both the process and the work results as we learn. Adaptation is the engine of Continuous Improvement, providing opportunities to make incremental changes to the process and product so that we can improve the work results, the product, and the process by which it is produced. In keeping with the scientific method, which is the foundation for Empirical Process Control, we make small, measurable changes, observe and inspect the results, and then decide how to adapt in the next iterative cycle.

Everything we do from this point forward is directed toward upholding these three principles of Empirical Process Control.

Why Bother?

Empirical Process Control is well suited to the development of complex products. Sound familiar? It should. Turn back to the first page of this chapter and reread the quote under the chapter title. If you're not developing complex products, you probably don't need the overhead of an empirical process. A simple Defined Process Control methodology, like Waterfall, works just fine if you're making millions of identical Model T's.

The matrix shown below is based on the work of Ralph D. Stacey[*] that describes management of complexity in organizations. Model T territory is in the lower left quadrant where Requirements Agreement and Technological

---

[*] Stacey 2002. The diagram on the next page is based on a hand-drawn modification of the standard Stacey Diagram by my colleague Doug Shimp.

Certainty are high. If your product truly falls into that category, you really can employ Defined Process Control to plan the work to the last detail and then execute on the plan. On the other hand, if Agreement and Certainty are somewhere out on the *y* and *x* axes respectively, Empirical Process Control is not only your best bet for achieving success, it is your only hope.

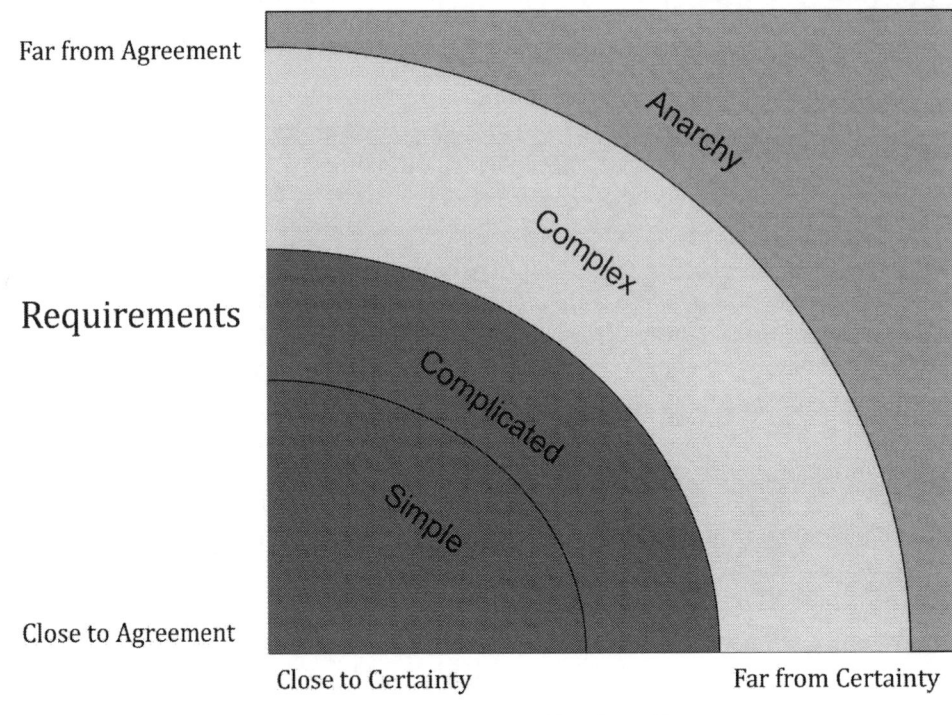

Far from Agreement

Requirements

Close to Agreement

Close to Certainty   Far from Certainty

Anarchy

Complex

Complicated

Simple

Technology

The sweet spot for Empirical Process Control in the Stacey Matrix is in the Complicated and Complex zones. Transparency, Inspection, and Adaptation provide the tools you need to manage complexity through continuous learning. In the Anarchy zone, no known process control model can guarantee a positive outcome. However, Empirical Process Control offers the ability to pull a portion of the zone of Anarchy into the Complex portion of the matrix by making astute use of short cycles of Inspection and Adaptation.

Software products in particular almost always fall into the Complicated, Complex, or Anarchy zones of the Stacey matrix. The simple fact that the work is non-repetitive, unpredictable, even creative – you are not simply duplicating work done in the past – and that both the producers and consumers of the resulting product are non-linear human beings makes software a uniquely challenging endeavor. Throw in constantly changing technologies and it's no wonder traditional defined processes, like Waterfall, have failed so miserably to produce high-quality software with the right features at the right time and at the right price.

To put the inherent complexity software development into context, I can think of no better authority than Frederick P. Brooks, Jr., who wrote:

> *"Software entities are more complex for their size than perhaps any other human construct because no two parts are alike."*[*]

Think about that for a minute – software is possibly the most complex endeavor, relative to size, that human beings have ever attempted. The fact that every part is essentially unique, or better be, makes building software a continuous act of invention and creativity. By their very nature, invention and creativity are neither repetitive, nor repeatable, nor subject to precise and complete control.

The Agile Manifesto

Okay, great. So Empirical Process Control is the way to go for complex product development. But how do we do it? Transparency, Inspection, and Adaptation sound simple, but where do we start?

These are all good questions, but before we start doing, we need to examine another set of values and principles to guide us. Enter the Manifesto for Agile Software Development, commonly known as The Agile Manifesto.

The term "Agile" in the context of software development comes from this document, which was the work of 17 real-life software development professionals over three days in February 2001. While the statement itself is brief and to the point, pay particular attention to the use of language, which is powerful. First, the text:

---

[*] Brooks 1987, p. 11

> We are uncovering better ways of developing
> software by doing it and helping others do it.
> Through this work we have come to value:
>
> **Individuals and interactions** over processes and tools
> **Working software** over comprehensive documentation
> **Customer collaboration** over contract negotiation
> **Responding to change** over following a plan
>
> That is, while there is value in the items on
> the right, we value the items on the left more.*

Notice the preamble – I have put the key phrases in bold-italic type:

> We are uncovering better ways of developing
> software ***by doing it*** and ***helping others do it.***
> ***Through this work*** we have come to value...

There is nothing speculative in this statement. The authors of the Manifesto arrived at their values not by thinking in abstract terms about how developing software might possibly be improved or imagining an ideal world in which software development would be perfect.

By contrast Winston Royce in his 1970 paper, which presented what has since become known as the Waterfall process, described a speculative process of developing large systems based on completion of a series of sequential activities.† Royce was drawing on his experience developing aerospace software projects, but he had never seen the process he described used in practice. The sequential activities Royce described are familiar to anyone who has worked on a Waterfall project:

---

* Agilemanifesto.org/
† Royce 1970

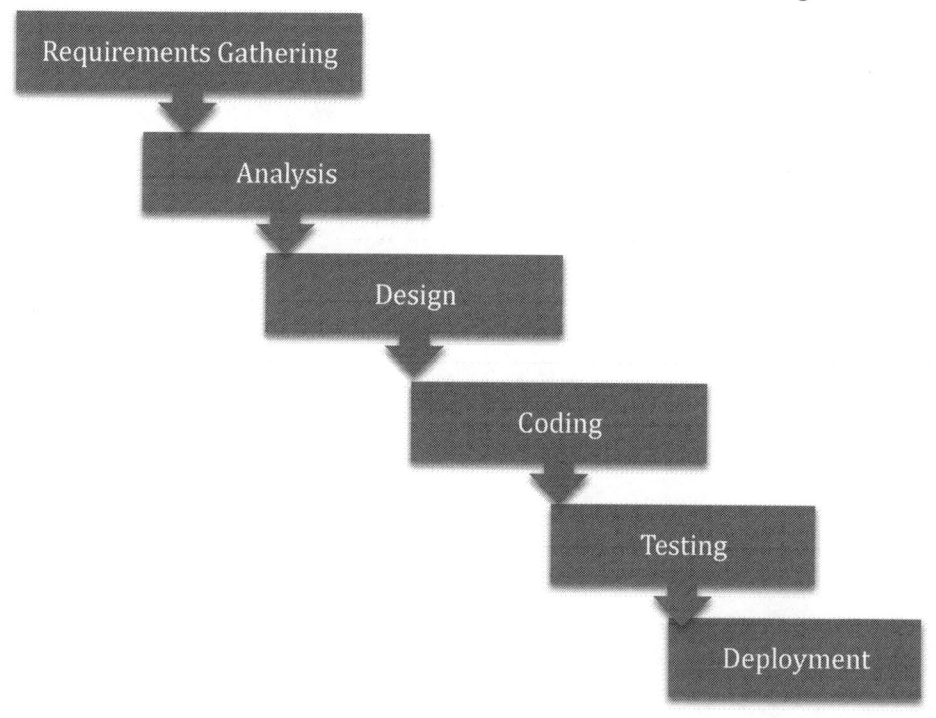

```
Requirements Gathering
    ↓
    Analysis
        ↓
        Design
            ↓
            Coding
                ↓
                Testing
                    ↓
                    Deployment
```

"I believe in this concept, but the implementation described above is risky and invites failure." – Winston Royce[*]

To his credit, Royce went on – in the very same paper – to describe an iterative process that involved customer feedback, but for some reason the risky and failure-prone sequential development process he outlined in the first couple of pages became entrenched in software development. That's another story for another day. The point here is that the authors of the Agile Manifesto were most assuredly not dreamers, imagining some perfect new world of software development. They were experienced realists with many decades of combined experience in the complex and extremely messy day-to-day world of software development.

---

[*] Royce, p. 329

Agile Manifesto Values

It is extremely important to understand what the four Agile Manifesto Values say – and do not say. Valuing the items on the left over the items on the right **does not mean** that we can simply drop process, tools, documentation, contracts, or plans. Those things still have value according to the Manifesto's authors. The key point is that, collectively and in isolation, individuals and interactions, working software, customer collaboration, and responding to change are **more valuable** in the down-and-dirty business of developing software than are the items listed on the right side of each equation.

Now, let's examine the four Values of the Agile Manifesto in more detail:

Individuals and interactions over processes and tools

Processes and tools don't write software, people do. People working together produce great products. When processes and tools help in that endeavor, which they most assuredly can, we should make use of them. The essential point here is that processes and tools must work for you, not the other way around. Too often people have become servicers of cumbersome, heavyweight, non-functional, non-productive processes and tools. Processes and tools are almost never the value proposition we are building – and they are never the customers – so put them in their proper place.

Working software over comprehensive documentation

In a traditional plan-driven environment, huge quantities of money and effort typically go into building "The Plan." The attempt to perfect the requirements, architecture, and design in advance of commencing actual work on the project has been the source of untold waste in software development over the last four decades. There are a couple of major problems with this approach. First, you will never know **less** about the project than before commencing actual work. How then does it make sense to construct a detailed plan at that point? Secondly, the investment of time, money, and effort in the planning document makes it difficult – and expensive – to change the plan as you learn by building the product. Think of it this way, once you've filled a warehouse with expensive inventory – which is exactly what that comprehensive requirements document represents – you are constrained either to use up the inventory regardless of its suitability or scrap it. Either way, you've incurred a huge amount of waste.

"So Agile teams don't write documentation at all then," you've concluded. Well, that's really not the case either. Any and all documentation that adds value to the product, including user documentation, architectural and design write-ups, UML diagrams, etc., is part of the value being delivered. The difference is that the documentation is an organic part of the ongoing work, not the end result of one phase of the development lifecycle.

When you get right down to it, working software is the only way to prove that you've accomplished anything. Remember Transparency, Inspection, and Adaptation? Do your work. Show your work. Adapt for the next cycle.

Customer collaboration over contract negotiation

The traditional process of negotiating a fixed price-scope-date contract with a customer is fraught with dishonesty and deception. Everyone on both sides of the negotiation knows the end result will not fall within the boundaries contained in the contract. The "Iron Triangle" of fixed price, scope, and delivery date is a fantasy in the realm of complex product development.

The result of this mutual self-deception is an adversarial relationship with customers in which they demand everything they can possibly think of in the hope that they'll get at least the minimum they need, while we, on the other side of the table, pad our estimates to ensure we can deliver at least enough in the end to keep the punitive clauses in the contract from kicking in.

The authors of the Agile Manifesto believed a better, more honest, and ultimately more mutually beneficial relationship results from regular collaboration with customers. If we're upholding the previous value, you know, the one about "working software," we have the basis for a real conversation with customers throughout the course of development. Customer relationships built on trust and collaboration are infinitely more successful – and profitable – than adversarial, contract-based relationships.

Responding to change over following a plan

Agile is all about being adaptable. Software development is, by its very nature, a slippery, constantly changing endeavor. Traditional plan-driven environments make use of what are commonly called "change control boards," or other change-control mechanisms whose purpose is to regulate or prevent changes in scope, direction, purpose, etc., so that the project doesn't descend into utter chaos. The problem is that attempts to prevent change result in software products that are outdated or even obsolete long before they are ever delivered. Even worse, preventing change can – and often does – produce software products that simply contain the wrong features.

A domain in which the desired end result is constantly shifting need not produce chaos, however. Agilists have long held that while Waterfall and other traditional development methodologies are *plan* driven, Agile is *planning* driven. What this means in practice is that planning is not a phase in the lifecycle of a software product; it is instead a continuous activity that begins on day one and only wraps up when the product reaches the end of its usable life, typically when it is no longer supported.

The contrast may sound subtle, but it represents a shattering mind-shift in the way we think about developing software or other complex products. Any plan is only as good as the knowledge its authors possessed at the time they constructed the plan. By definition, "the plan" becomes increasingly outdated, week-by-week, as work on the product proceeds. Why? Simple. With each passing day, we know more about the product, the technology, the customers, the market, the micro- and macroeconomic conditions into which the product will emerge, and a host of other information that we could never have anticipated when developing "the plan."

By contrast, Agile environments place little stock – and even less cost and effort – into the *plan,* concentrating instead on the ongoing activity of *planning.* Whenever we learn something new about the product and its broader ecosystem, we update the plan to reflect this newly acquired knowledge so that "the plan" remains lightweight, flexible, and subject to continuous revision as we gain new knowledge.

The specific practices that make Agile planning possible are described in detail later in this handbook. For now, keep those three principles of Empirical Process Control visible until they become muscle memory. If you adhere to Transparency, Inspection, and Adaptation in your planning, you'll be well on your way to making this Agile Manifesto Value a reality.

Agile Manifesto Principles

The authors of the Agile Manifesto followed up the four values with 12 principles that provide more guidance on the meaning of agility. The principles came into being shortly after the Agile Manifesto itself.[*] The

---

[*] James W. Grenning, closing keynote address, Global Scrum Gathering, London, October 2011

combination of the four Values and 12 Principles describe what it means to be Agile. Here are the principles:

> Our highest priority is to satisfy the customer through early and continuous delivery of valuable software.
>
> Welcome changing requirements, even late in development. Agile processes harness change for the customer's competitive advantage.
>
> Deliver working software frequently, from a couple of weeks to a couple of months, with a preference to the shorter timescale.
>
> Business people and developers must work together daily throughout the project.
>
> Build projects around motivated individuals. Give them the environment and support they need, and trust them to get the job done.
>
> The most efficient and effective method of conveying information to and within a development team is face-to-face conversation.
>
> Working software is the primary measure of progress.
>
> Agile processes promote sustainable development. The sponsors, developers, and users should be able to maintain a constant pace indefinitely.
>
> Continuous attention to technical excellence and good design enhances agility.
>
> Simplicity – the art of maximizing the amount of work not done – is essential.
>
> The best architectures, requirements, and designs emerge from self-organizing teams.
>
> At regular intervals, the team reflects on how to become more effective, then tunes and adjusts its behavior accordingly.

Each of these principles deserves a little individual attention.

> Our highest priority is to satisfy the customer through early and continuous delivery of valuable software.

What is the top priority in most organizations? The walls of many development shops are decorated with posters exhorting people to put the customer first and so forth, but then the organization imposes work rules that make it impossible for anyone to come anywhere close to achieving that goal. How many projects are derailed by early and (seemingly) continuous status meetings? How many organizations' highest priority – demonstrated through their actions – is really control over the people and the details of the project? How many projects are derailed and ultimately destroyed by the overwhelming force of organizational politics?

Behaviors that serve the organization rather than the customer are 100% waste. Keeping intrusive or territorial managers happy provides no demonstrable customer value. Organizations that are serious about agility learn that they have to drop anything that serves only organizational or personal interests and instead focus all of their collective energies on satisfying the customer. The litmus test for any activity, meeting, metric, or anything else that goes on inside of an organization must be: "How does this <insert item here> contribute to satisfying our customers?" Anything that fails this simple test, no matter how entrenched or sacrosanct, should be either modified or abolished outright.

Placing the focus of the organization on making this Agile Manifesto Principle a reality changes the dynamic of software development in fundamental ways. It provides balance and a reality check for existing and proposed procedures, policies, and activities. It also subjects organizations to considerable pain early on as "That's the way we've always done it" or similar answers to questions about the way things are currently done are no longer satisfactory. Adhering to this principle drives far-reaching and dramatic organizational change – for the better.

> Welcome changing requirements, even late in development. Agile processes harness change for the customer's competitive advantage.

This one is tough. How can we welcome late-changing requirements? Remember the Agile Manifesto Value: *Responding to change over following a plan.* This principle adds more depth to that value. How many successful products started out as something else, but ended up becoming the Next Big Thing as a result of a late change of direction? (This is a quiz – do some looking around and see what you come up with. The answers may surprise you.)

Being Agile means having the ability to adapt quickly to changing conditions. Markets change. Competitors introduce new and unexpected products that derail your plans. Global financial markets collapse. People (I absolutely despise the term "consumer") and businesses reduce or even stop spending in certain areas and increase spending in others in response to microeconomic and macroeconomic conditions.

Embrace change as the vehicle that will deliver the decisive competitive advantage. A little later on we'll talk about the mechanics of Agile planning. For now, internalize this Agile Principle and remember, no customer ever paid you for the plan, just the results you were able to deliver.

> Deliver working software frequently, from a couple of weeks to a couple of months, with a preference to the shorter timescale.

One of the secrets to agility is working in small batches – taking small bites of the big project – and delivering those small bites as working increments of value. One of the major sources of waste in traditional, plan-driven development methodologies is the insistence on working in huge batches with large quantities of work in progress. Keep the timelines short, focus on close-in deliverables, minimize work in progress, and you will automatically wring much of the waste out of your development process.

Human beings have a trait called the "motivational horizon." This is the time period over which we mere mortals can focus on a goal and work toward accomplishing it with reasonable efficiency and effectiveness. For most of us, the motivational horizon extends out just six weeks. Six weeks! When was the first deliverable scheduled on your last software project: six months, a year, 18 months out? That's not a delivery schedule that humans can support. So let's come back into the realm of human reality – since, after all, humans are doing the heavy lifting on any development project.

If you went to college in the USA, you probably got a syllabus at the first meeting of every class. If the class requirements involved a term paper or class project, as many of mine did, you probably noticed that the big project that assignment represented was due sometime toward the end of autumn, after the Thanksgiving holiday in the USA, for example. Did you immediately start working on that far-off goal, floating 12 or so weeks in the future? Not so much. Why not? It was too far out, well beyond your motivational horizon. When did you start working on it? Probably right after you returned to campus after a week of home cooking and mom doing your laundry, that is, about a week before the project was due.

We responsible adults scoff at the profligacy of such attitudes – now – but in reality it's simply the human brain working the way it was designed. We focus on what's in front of us rather than spending too much of our finite store of effort and energy on things that are not happening anytime soon. Focusing on short-term goals, with a vision of the larger project in mind, helps us do the right thing (effectiveness) and do the thing right (efficiency).

> Business people and developers must work together daily throughout the project.

It's amazing that anyone ever tried to build a product without continuous collaboration between business and development, but that's been standard operating procedure for decades in the software industry. Infrequent communication at low bandwidths, i.e., through specification documents, prevents business people and developers from even understanding one another, let alone building the kind of dynamic, trust-based relationships that produce great results.

The most common complaint I hear from business people is that development never delivers on time; developers fire back that the business doesn't know what it wants and has completely unreasonable expectations of what can be done by any given date. It's like a marriage in which the partners have high expectations of one another, but refuse to talk to each other face to face and instead rely on text messaging to communicate their expectations and manage the relationship. How likely is that to succeed?

> Build projects around motivated individuals. Give them the environment and support they need, and trust them to get the job done.

Software development – or any complex product development work – is made up of thousands of minute, daily inventions. It is creative work based on knowledge and experience, not routine work based on repetitive procedures and processes. Such work is fundamentally different from the early twentieth-century industrial labor our corporate structures were invented to support. When the work was menial and mind numbing, people often required external motivation to continue with it, hence our vast array of carrots and sticks. That type of work also came close to defining the workers as interchangeable, fungible "resources" that could be plugged in when and where needed.

Such notions are not only outdated but also totally obsolete in the world of complex product development. People are most assuredly not interchangeable or fungible "resources." The work itself is challenging and creative, making carrots and sticks not only out of touch with reality, but blatantly destructive of motivation. If people aren't motivated, find out what has de-motivated them. Corporate work rules, managers, and HR policies are the first places to look. It turns out that the vast majority of people are highly motivated do to good work, so follow this principle and let the great people you went to a lot of trouble to find get on with doing their best work.

> The most efficient and effective method of conveying information to and within a development team is face-to-face conversation.

High-bandwidth communication is key. For human beings, face-to-face conversation is the highest bandwidth communication mode we have available. Anything less is, well, less. The words we use convey only a small fraction of the content in any human interaction. Body position, facial expression, eye movement and contact, gestures, tone of voice – all of these combine with the use of language to convey the full richness of human communication.

When we combine full-bandwidth communication with the interaction of conversation, we greatly reduce the likelihood of misunderstanding or miscommunication. As the bandwidth decreases, however, misunderstanding and miscommunication become increasingly likely. Keep that in mind when deciding whether to co-locate or distribute Team Members. Use technology wisely to approximate face-to-face communication if the real thing is out of reach.

> Working software is the primary measure of progress.

Want to know where your project stands? Look no further than how much working software you have produced and (hopefully) delivered. Nothing else really matters, does it? Tracking percentage of completion against The Plan is meaningless. Customers aren't paying you for The Plan; they want a working product. If you adhere to the first Agile Principle we examined, that one about satisfying the customer through early and continuous delivery of valuable software, you're already aligned with this principle. Just don't lose focus and allow yourself to be distracted by other, so-called "metrics" that detract from following this principle.

> Agile processes promote sustainable development. The sponsors, developers, and users should be able to maintain a constant pace indefinitely.

If you've been around software development for any length of time, you've undoubtedly been through at least one – and probably several – "death march" cycles. In traditional, plan-driven development environments, the hours worked indicator typically runs at a fairly low level at the beginning of a project and then gradually increases until the pre-release barrage hits. Then hours worked jumps dramatically and stays at an unsustainably high level until the product is released. Once the product is released, bugs and all, everyone collapses from exhaustion as the next cycle begins.

According to CareerBliss[*] workers in software and Internet companies are the second **unhappiest** group in the entire US economy, only just slightly less unhappy than miners and agricultural laborers. How is that possible in a dynamic, creative, and generally good-paying field of endeavor? While there are many factors that contribute to such high levels of dissatisfaction, the pattern of excessive, generally uncompensated work hours is clearly a serious problem.

Not only is this work pattern the source of much discontent in the world of software development, it is also inefficient and ineffective. Companies that demand long hours get exactly what they should expect: burned out, unmotivated employees, poorly designed, poorly built products with lots of defects, and dissatisfied customers.

Working at a sustainable pace is not a luxury; it is instead an absolute necessity if we are to satisfy the customer. Henry Ford, who was clearly not a softhearted employer, recognized that overwork was reducing the productivity of his factory workers. So in 1926 he instituted an eight-hour workday, five days per week in place of the previous ten hours per day, six days per week regimen. He got his money's worth as productivity skyrocketed. Really, if Henry Ford could do it, why can't we?

---

[*] Forbes.com, Feb 9, 2012

> **Magician's Secret**
> In case you hadn't noticed, the Agile Manifesto Principles are linked together like threads in a web. Pull one out and the whole thing begins to unravel. As you'll see, the values and principles we're discussing are interdependent, woven into a coherent whole. The same is true of the Scrum practices that support the Agile Values and Principles. You really can't pick and choose what you feel like doing and expect to derive the advertised benefits. It's a single package deal.

> Continuous attention to technical excellence and good design enhances agility.

Recall that being Agile means the ability to adapt quickly to changing conditions. Fellow agilist Dr. Dan Rawsthorne refers to the technical condition of a code base as its "viscosity," a metaphor that fits exactly with this principle.* If the code is sloppy, poorly designed, lacking consistent architecture and design, and unprotected by comprehensive tests, adding new value to it is going to be very, very difficult indeed.

When the Agile Manifesto was first published over a decade ago, many people in the software industry took it as license to engage in what was then not so affectionately called "cowboy coding," ignoring design and architecture and testing and documentation entirely and just cranking out code. Nothing could be further from the intentions of the Manifesto's authors.

Since we are delivering value early and often to satisfy the customer, architecture and design become a part of the value delivery equation rather than separate steps in a sequential process. The architecture and design emerge along with the value, supporting the customer focus that is essential to agility. Comprehensive, automated test coverage allows Agile Teams to do this without fear of damaging existing functionality.

A common misconception is that traditional up-front architecture and design is more thorough than the corresponding Agile variety. In fact, Agile Teams spend more time and effort on emergent architecture and design than is the case in traditional development environments. The reason is simple: as the product emerges the architecture and design must be constantly evaluated and updated to reflect the reality of the product. Refactoring – changing the design (including architecture) without altering the external functionality of

---

* Rawsthorne 2011, p. 121

the code – is neither rework nor waste. It is simply a reflection of the reality of emergent product development. It also means that the architecture and design are always up to date. Obsolete architecture or design inhibits agility as much as any other single factor.

> Simplicity – the art of maximizing the amount of work not done – is essential.

During the last couple of decades, two of the defining characteristics of software have been delivery of features no one wanted and poor quality. Remember hidden menu options and animated paper clips? How about operating systems and software packages delivered to the market with hundreds, thousands, even tens-of-thousands of known defects?

Why even offer the option to hide most of the menu options a software package contains? Here's some insight: in 2002, a massive study by the Standish Group showed that 45% of the features the software industry delivered to the market were never used – never! Another 19% of features were used only rarely. Just 7% of features were always used, along with another 13% that were used often. Hiding most of the menu options was simply a response to the fact that people only really use about 20% of the features software contains.

Imagine what it would be like to build software in a way that delivered the most important, always-used features, complete and working, before applying any serious effort to the rest of the good and less-than-good ideas. That's what Agile is all about. Think of how much code simply wouldn't be written and therefore wouldn't need to be maintained if we adhered to this Agile Principle. Think also in terms of keeping the code itself clean, elegant, and simple. Remember Brian Kernighan's dictum:

"Debugging is twice as hard as writing the code in the first place. Therefore, if you write the code as cleverly as possible, you are, by definition, not smart enough to debug it."

> The best architectures, requirements, and designs emerge from self-organizing teams.

Another interlocking aspect of Agile is its insistence that self-organizing Teams are smarter and more capable of solving any problem than even the most talented individual Team Member. This belief becomes part of the DNA of Teams. Notice also that this principle describes architectures, requirements, and designs as emergent, instead of being built according to some pre-defined master plan.

Self-organizing Teams respect and value the full range of skills and abilities their individual members possess, but draw upon the combined strength of all Team Members to build solutions. A Team Member may have special experience and expertise in architecture or design and as such is an asset to the Team, but is not the person who *dictates* architecture or design to the Team.

> At regular intervals, the team reflects on how to become more effective, then tunes and adjusts its behavior accordingly.

While the Agile Manifesto Principles are interlocking and interdependent, this one is easily the most important single principle to live by. Remember the Plan-Do-Inspect-Adapt cycle we covered earlier? This principle covers the inspect-and-adapt part of that cycle.

Agile Teams are in the business of continuous improvement through inspection and adaptation. Agile Teams review the Plan-Do part of the cycle, fine-tuning and expanding on the things that they did well, while identifying and working to eliminate the things that held them back. It's called Continuous Improvement for a reason – there is always room for improvement!

Teams and organizations often pick off the low-hanging fruit and then lose focus and drop the mechanisms of Inspection and Adaptation. Just don't go there! I believe this principle and the infrastructure that supports it are the single most important thing Agile Teams do. If you do nothing else, keep this principle alive and functioning in your Teams and throughout the organization.

> *Try This: Pocket Principles*
> Working with your Team, distill each of the 12 Agile Manifesto Principles down to a maximum of three words that capture the essence of the Principle for your Team. The words you choose do not have to appear in the Principle. At the end of this exercise, you'll have twelve, two- or three-word expressions of the Agile Manifesto Principles. Next, pick the three most important principles for your Team, right now. Revisit this prioritized subset of the Agile Manifesto Principles every few months to see how things have changed for your Team over time.

> **Quick Quiz**
> Now that we've covered the Agile Manifesto, answer these questions:
>
> *What does it mean to be an Agile organization?*
>
> *Is there such a thing as "The Agile Methodology?"*

> **Game Time: Play the Scrum Fact/Myth Game**
> We've covered a lot of ground, but have yet to say anything specific about Scrum, which makes this the perfect time to play the Scrum Fact/Myth game. On separate sticky notes or index cards, write one statement that you think is a fact or myth about Scrum. Do not indicate on the card whether you think the statement is a fact or a myth! As you work through the rest of this handbook, review your cards and decide whether each item is a fact or a myth. Play this game with your Team if you are learning about Scrum together.

Origins of Scrum

Contrary to popular belief – and misinformed job announcements – Scrum is not an acronym. It is instead a metaphor for an approach to developing complex products that resembles the way a rugby team moves down the field. The metaphor itself is derived from an article in the January-February 1986 edition of the *Harvard Business Review* by Hirotaka Takeuchi and Ikujiro Nonaka titled "The New New Product Development Game." In this article, Takeuchi and Nonaka examined a dozen new products that were conceived, developed, and delivered in time frames that were far shorter than was standard for similar products. None of the products they examined had anything to do with software, which perhaps makes the conversation even more interesting.

Takeuchi and Nonaka identified the common threads in these products and summarized their conclusions as follows:

"The… 'relay race' approach to product development…may conflict with the goals of maximum speed and flexibility. Instead a holistic or 'rugby' approach—where a team tries to go the distance as a unit, passing the ball back and forth—may better serve today's competitive requirements."[*]

The point is that instead of defined development stages with handoffs to other groups occurring only when a stage is completed, a product-development strategy that moves all aspects of the product forward in short bursts is much more effective and efficient. The right thing gets built, the thing gets built right, and all on a time scale much shorter than would be the case in a traditional, staged hand-off environment.

The inventors of Scrum, Jeff Sutherland and Ken Schwaber, drew upon this article and other influences to develop, independently at first, what we now know as the Scrum framework.

Scrum is not the only Agile framework. Some others currently in use include eXtreme Programming (XP), Dynamic Systems Development Method (DSDM), the various Crystal frameworks (Crystal Clear, Crystal Orange, etc., developed by Alistair Cockburn), Feature Driven Development (FDD), Lean Software Development as defined and described so capably by Mary and Tom Poppendeick, and others yet. Most Agile frameworks define the following items in greater or lesser detail:

- Roles and Responsibilities
- Artifacts
- Ceremonies/Events/Activities/Meetings
- Specific Practices

Scrum is far and away the most commonly used Agile framework. The vast majority of technology companies worldwide now claim to be doing something Agile, and in the software and IT realms Scrum is the framework of choice.[†] My assumption is that you are reading this handbook because you now find yourself in one of those companies that wants to use Scrum or something Scrum-like to become Agile.

Ah, what was that? Scrum is not the end in and of itself? Yes, you read that correctly. Scrum is a means to an end, the end being agility. Scrum is a

---

[*] Takeuchi and Nonaka, p. 137
[†] Version One *State of Agile Survey 2011*

wonderful framework for becoming Agile; it provides all the tools you need to begin and sustain the journey. But simply following the rules of Scrum will not make you or anyone else Agile. It is perfectly possible – and I've seen this happen repeatedly – to practice Scrum without becoming Agile. It's not easy and takes a deliberate effort at non-agility, but I'm always amazed at the lengths to which organizations will go to avoid becoming Agile, even while practicing Scrum more-or-less faithfully.

Let's park that discussion for now, but keep it in mind as we examine the Scrum framework and some associated supporting tools and practices borrowed from other frameworks in the rest of this handbook.

> **Magician's Secret**
> Practicing Scrum does not automatically make you, your Team, or your organization Agile! Agility requires conscious effort to translate the values and principles of the Agile Manifesto into reality. Scrum can most definitely help you with that, but you have use Scrum effectively to get there.

Okay, so what is this thing called Scrum anyway? Scrum is a minimalist framework that applies the principles of Empirical Process Control (remember what they were? Hint: there are three of them!) to the development of complex products. As with most other Agile frameworks, Scrum has well-defined roles, events, artifacts, and practices – the rules of the Scrum product development game.

Scrum Roles
- Scrum Master
- Product Owner
- Development Team (Dev Team, Team Member)

Scrum Events
- Sprint
- Sprint Planning
- Daily Scrum
- Sprint Review
- Sprint Retrospective
- Backlog Refinement (I like the name my friend and mentor Jeff McKenna uses for this event: *Story Time*.)

Scrum Artifacts
* Product Backlog
* Sprint Backlog
* Potentially Shippable Product Increment
* Definition of Done
* Product Vision
* Progress charts – information radiators
* Sprint Task Board*

This collection of Roles, Events, and Artifacts are the nuts and bolts of Scrum. They work together in fascinating and powerful ways, helping you, your Team or Teams, and your organization become Agile.

> **Magician's Secret**
> Well, maybe this isn't really a secret, but what I like most about Scrum is that it contains all the moving parts you need to get started, fully formed and ready for use. You really don't have to invent anything to get started with Scrum – just follow the rules and you'll be on your way. Always remember though that Scrum is like training wheels for your racing bicycle. You can stay upright and actually move pretty quickly, with a little practice, with the training wheels on. After riding the bike becomes muscle memory, however, you need to remove the training wheels so that you can go faster. That's for later. For now, practice Scrum to the letter to build muscle memory. Then you can start talking about changes, modifications, improvements, adaptations, etc. **Red Flashing Warning:** If you attempt to change, modify, improve, or adapt Scrum before developing the required muscle memory, a crash is the most likely outcome!!

How Scrum Works

Scrum harnesses the power of Empirical Process Control and the Plan-Do-Inspect-Adapt cycle to generate adaptability and Continuous Improvement by using well-defined roles, events (the Scrum name for Team meetings), and artifacts. The result is two feedback loops: one for the product, another for the Team.

The product feedback loop is constructed from three artifacts: Product Backlog, Sprint Backlog, and Potentially Shippable Product Increment; and four events: Backlog Refinement, Sprint Planning, Daily Scrum, and Sprint

---

* The last three are my additions to the artifacts list, not specifically defined in the *Scrum Guide* but widely used in practice.

Review. We'll go into much more detail on all of the roles, events, and artifacts later, for now we just need the broad outlines to show how the feedback loops work.

The Product Backlog is the ordered list of the ideas for the product. We refine the Product Backlog during Backlog Refinement to break the items at the top of the list down into small, actionable, end-to-end slices of valuable functionality. Those thin end-to-end slices then feed into the Sprint Planning Event, where the Team pulls in as many items as Development Team Members believe they can complete during a one- to four-week time box called a Sprint*. This subset of the Product Backlog that the Development Team pulls into a Sprint is called, not surprisingly, the Sprint Backlog. Every Team has its own, independent Sprint Backlog, even if multiple Teams are working from the same Product Backlog. The Team then uses the Daily Scrum to inspect and adapt as Team Members work collaboratively to deliver the goal for the Sprint, described by the items they agreed to pull into the Sprint.

At the end of the Sprint, the Development Team shows the work completed – and **only** work completed – to stakeholders, customers, sponsors, and anyone else who wants to see what the Team has accomplished. This demonstration of a Potentially Shippable Product Increment, along with some other items, makes up the Sprint Review Event. The Scrum Team, and primarily the Product Owner, collects feedback on the Potentially Shippable Product Increment on display, feedback that then goes right back into the Product Backlog and informs the next product development cycle, providing direction for the next Sprint Planning Event. The Sprint Review Event closes the product feedback loop.

But remember that there is another feedback loop, one for the Team to use for its own improvement. During the course of the Sprint, Development Team Members experience things that work very well, things that work poorly, and things that slow them down or even bring them to a complete stop. Scrum uses an event called the Sprint Retrospective to provide the entire Scrum Team the opportunity to close the teamwork feedback loop so that Team Members can collect data, generate insights, and take specific, measurable actions designed to improve the Team's performance, effectiveness, efficiency, and morale.

---

* The maximum length of a Sprint is 30 calendar days, but most Teams and organizations work in Sprints defined as up to four calendar weeks, with the average being two weeks.

By combining these two feedback loops, Scrum allows Teams and entire organizations to engage in Continuous Improvement in product development and teamwork.

A Cautionary Note

Scrum is built to operate as a complete, coherent whole. Attempts to modify Scrum preemptively or pick and choose bits and pieces that are a convenient fit for current organizational circumstances, traditions, or constraints defeats the purpose of what is, by design, an inherently disruptive process framework. Getting the benefits of an Agile framework like Scrum means you actually have to *use* Scrum. Takeuchi and Nonaka offered a similar conclusion in their groundbreaking article: "These characteristics are like pieces of a jigsaw puzzle. Each element, by itself, does not bring about speed and flexibility. But taken as a whole, the characteristics can produce a powerful new set of dynamics that will make a difference."*

Scrum Values

The nuts and bolts of Scrum consist of those roles, events, and artifacts, along with some other things we'll cover throughout the rest of this handbook. And while it's exceptionally important to play by all of the rules of Scrum, there is also a set of Scrum values that add deeper meaning to the externalities of Scrum. Ken Schwaber and Mike Beedle first elaborated these values in the "Black Book." They are now also contained in the Scrum Guide.† These five values are the very last thing in the Black Book and have long been overlooked, but I believe these simple values are incredibly important to the successful practice of Scrum.

Commitment

Be willing to commit to a goal. Scrum provides people all the authority they need to meet their commitments.

Focus

Do your job. Focus all your efforts and skills on doing the work you've committed to doing. Do one thing at a time – no multi-tasking.

---

* Takeuchi and Nonaka, p. 138
† Schwaber and Beedle 2002, p. 147; *Scrum Guide,* July 2016

Openness
Scrum keeps everything about a project visible to everyone.

Respect
Individuals are shaped by their background and experiences. It is important to respect the different people who comprise a Team.

Courage
Have the courage to commit, to act, to be open, and to expect respect.

To this impressive set of values, I like to add:

Trust
Always be willing to trust and be trusted. Build trust through your actions toward your teammates, customers, and organization.

Having Fun
Too often work becomes drudgery. A conscious focus on building fun into our work and working relationships keeps the environment fresh and enhances effectiveness.

Make It Real
Values are all well and good, but mean nothing if not put into practice every day. With your Team, discuss each Scrum value in turn and, through consensus, complete the following statement for each value:

We believe in <value> therefore we will <do something specific/measureable>

I like to add "Trust" and "Having Fun" once a Team gets the basic values in place. Devise your own values if that fits your Team and the moment. Be sure to post your decisions prominently in your Team Room or other highly visible space. Revisit your value statements periodically to assess how well you are living the values, both individually and collectively. Update your value statements periodically to keep them fresh, real, and alive.

Further Reading

Beck, Kent. *Extreme Programming Explained: Embrace Change.* 2nd ed. Boston: Addison-Wesley, 2005.

Brooks, Frederick P., "No Silver Bullet: Essence and Accidents of Software Engineering,"*Computer*, Vol. 20, No. 4 (April 1987) pp. 10-19.

Cockburn, Alistair. *Agile Software Development.* Boston: Addison-Wesley, 2002.

Hirotaka Takeuchi and Ikujiro Nonaka, "The New New Product Development Game," *Harvard Business Review*, January 1986.

Poppendieck, Mary and Tom Poppendieck. *Implementing Lean Software Development: From Concept to Cash.* Boston: Addison-Wesley, 2007.

Poppendieck, Mary and Tom Poppendieck. *Leading Lean Software Development: Results Are Not The Point.* Boston: Addison-Wesley, 2010.

Poppendieck, Mary and Tom Poppendieck. *Lean Software Development: An Agile Toolkit.* Boston: Addision-Wesley, 2003.

Rawsthorne, Dan and Doug Shimp. *Exploring Scrum: The Fundamentals (People, Product, and Practices).* USA: Self-published, 2011.

Schwaber, Ken and Mike Beedle. *Agile Software Development With Scrum.* Upper Saddle River, NJ: Prentice Hall, 2002.

Schwaber, Ken and Jeff Sutherland. *The Scrum Guide, The Definitive Guide to Scrum: The Rules of the Game.* Scrumguides.org, July 2016.

Sims, Chris and Hillary Louise Johnson. *The Elements of Scrum.* Foster City, CA: Dymaxicon, 2011.

Smith, Jacquelyn. "The Happiest And Unhappiest Industries To Work In," Forbes.com, February 9, 2012 (http://www.forbes.com/sites/jacquelynsmith/2012/02/09/the-happiest-and-unhappiest-industries-to-work-in/)

Sutherland, Jeff. *Jeff Sutherland's Scrum Handbook.* Somerville, MA: Scrum Training Institute Press, 2011.

Chapter 2 Scrum Roles: Scrum Master and Product Owner

"You don't lead by hitting people over the head – that's assault, not leadership."
– Dwight D. Eisenhower

Scrum defines just three roles: Scrum Master, Product Owner, and Development Team. All three roles combine to form a complete Scrum Team. Roles are important because they describe complementary responsibilities and areas of authority and accountability, ensuring an effective separation of concerns between individuals on a Scrum Team and within the larger Agile organization.

> **Magician's Secret**
> The Scrum roles are carefully designed around interlocking – but not overlapping – areas of authority and accountability. More simply, no member of a Scrum Team is held accountable for anything over which he or she has no authority. And that is a beautiful thing indeed!

Scrum Master

Let's start with accountability: the Scrum Master is accountable for the Team's effective use of Scrum. The Scrum Master's "product" is a high-performing Team. The Scrum Master fulfills this accountability by being the facilitator and servant-leader of the Team. This **does not** mean that the Scrum Master tells people what to do every day, or any day for that matter. The Scrum Master has neither authority over nor accountability for the product. This is not a project management or functional management role. Indeed, if the Scrum Master is a project manager or functional manager with reporting relationships within the Team, expect that Team's performance to suffer as a result. Instead, the Scrum Master helps the Team become more effective by building a collaborative Team environment, facilitating communication, ensuring that impediments are removed, and by protecting the Team from external distractions and interference.

Facilitator and Servant-leader

So what does it mean to be a facilitator and servant-leader? A facilitator helps the Team learn how to communicate and work more effectively. A good Scrum Master employs facilitation skills to ensure that the Team makes decisions by consensus, rather than simply capitulating to the loudest voice in the room. The facilitator has no stake in the decision the Team makes, but instead is there to make sure that the Team *makes a decision.* Servant-leadership is a term coined by Robert K. Greenleaf[*] to describe leadership based on service. That seems like an odd combination, service and leadership, but it turns out to be highly effective. In our context, servant-leadership means that the Scrum Master leads the Team by serving the Team's needs. That does not mean the Scrum Master does the Team's work. Instead, the Scrum Master takes on the difficult and demanding task of unleashing the Team's creative and productive energies.

> ***Magician's Secret***
> Every morning as you prepare for the day, look at yourself in mirror and repeat the following statement: "You don't give orders around here." Internalize that directive and you'll be well prepared for your role as Scrum Master.

Servant-leadership also does not mean or even imply that the Scrum Master is passive. Since the Scrum Master is accountable for the Team's effective use of Scrum to become high-performing, the Scrum Master ensures that all Scrum Team Members, including the Product Owner are playing by the rules. That includes, but is not strictly limited to, the following activities:

- Enforcing time boxes to ensure that Scrum Events are effective
- Keeping discussions on track, again to ensure effectiveness of Scrum Events and also the effectiveness of the Team's work
- Reminding Team Members, by asking questions based on observations, to live by their agreed-upon working agreements
- Enforcing the rule of "one conversation at a time" within the Team
- Ensuring that the Product Owner respects the Development Team's authority over estimates and implementation of all work items
- Ensuring that the Development Team respects the Product Owner's authority over the content and order of items in the Product Backlog

---

[*] Greenleaf 1970

- Facilitating communication between the Development Team and the business or rest of the organization
- Updating the Development Team's charts and other artifacts that radiate information
- Steadfastly defending the Development Team from external distractions

Ken Schwaber and Jeff Sutherland define the Scrum Master role more broadly, including organizational coach and change agent in the Scrum Master's purview.* I think that's asking quite a lot of an individual whose primary concern is facilitating the growth of a mature, high-performing Team. My experience and instincts tell me that Scrum Masters should maintain focus on their Teams (one Team per Scrum Master, please!) and leave the difficult and often thankless job of organizational change and coaching to others. That's not to say that a Scrum Master could not or should not morph into an organizational change agent and coach, just that one person shouldn't try to be doing all of that at the same time.

> **Magician's Secret**
> A common statement of Scrum Master responsibility is "removes impediments." Notice that I said above that the Scrum Master ensures "that impediments are removed." The Development Team needs to learn how remove most impediments. At first, the Scrum Master may take a more active role in removing impediments for the Team, but as the Team grows and matures, the Scrum Master needs to make sure that the Team itself is equipped to deal with impediments as they arise rather than always depending on the Scrum Master to handle every problem. Impediment removal is an important aspect of Team maturity, which we'll talk about in the next chapter. Impediment removal is also one way a Scrum Master can effect organizational change while retaining focus on the health and growth of the Team.

Product Owner

In keeping with the theme of authority, accountability, and separation of concerns, the Product Owner is the one and only member of a Scrum Team who is accountable to the business for the *success* of the product. The Product Owner has commensurate *authority* over the product, in particular, the order in which the Team develops and delivers the product's increments of value.

---

* *Scrum Guide*, p. 7

The Product Owner's job is to **maximize the business value of the finished work** the Team produces every Sprint. The Product Owner's decisions regarding the ordering of items to be developed must be unquestioned within the organization. The organization – including members of the Product Owner's Scrum Team – may not override the Product Owner's decisions. The organization may replace, but not override, the Product Owner. Furthermore, the Product Owner must be an individual, not a committee or group. There may not be more than one Product Owner on a Scrum Team and each Product Owner *should* be a member of just one Scrum Team. One Product Owner per Team, one Team per Product Owner is the best, most effective formula in practice today.

Wow, that's a lot of rules defining one role! The reasons for this strict definition of the Product Owner role revolve around the criticality of the functions the Product Owner performs and the truly daunting accountability the Product Owner bears. If the wrong thing gets built – if the delivered product features fail to delight customers or capture business value – look no further than the Product Owner. This isn't about blame; it's about accountability and separation of concerns.

Product Owner As Linchpin

Product Owner is a critical role and a common single point of failure in Scrum adoptions. In my experience, the usual problems with the Product Owner role fall into two categories: 1) not having a Product Owner at all for any of a thousand reasons; and 2) spreading a Product Owner across multiple Teams. The results of the former should be fairly obvious to you – how does the Team know what to build without anyone to decide what is most valuable to deliver now versus what can be delivered later?

The latter issue is more insidious and also more common. An individual can possibly, maybe, sometimes, be successful when serving as Product Owner for two Teams. More than two Teams and things begin to break down very quickly as the Product Owner is simply physically unable to keep the Product Backlog in a ready state for all of the Teams. Even worse, the Product Owner becomes a bottleneck for all of the Teams, affecting the scheduling and duration of Sprint Planning, Backlog Refinement, the Sprint Review, and the Sprint Retrospective. An overworked Product Owner is also unable to review and accept completed work during the Sprint, further complicating the Teams' ability to deliver. Perhaps most damaging of all, an overworked Product Owner is unavailable to answer the Teams' questions during the Sprint, endangering the Teams' collective ability to deliver the right thing each Sprint.

Not The Final Word
These are only basic descriptions of the Scrum Master and Product Owner roles because this is a Team handbook, not a Scrum Master or Product Owner handbook. There are ample opportunities for Scrum Masters and Product Owners to receive training and plenty of books, articles, and blogs devoted to these roles. Refer to the References section at end of this handbook for some reading suggestions. Development Team Members, on the other hand, have always gotten short shrift when it comes to attention. This handbook is dedicated to helping ensure that Development Team Members get their due!

Further Reading
Greenleaf, Robert K. *On Becoming a Servant-Leader.* San Francisco: Jossey-Bass, 1996.

Greenleaf, Robert K. *The Power of Servant-Leadership.* San Francisco: Berrett-Koehler, 1998.

Greenleaf, Robert K. *The Servant as Leader.* Indianapolis: The Robert K. Greenleaf Center for Servant-Leadership, 1970.

Schwaber, Ken and Jeff Sutherland. *The Scrum Guide, The Definitive Guide to Scrum: The Rules of the Game.* Scrumguides.org, July 2016.

Chapter 3 Scrum Roles: The Development Team

"The power of We is stronger than the power of Me."
– *Phil Jackson*

The final Scrum role consists of the members of the Team, called the Development Team. The *Scrum Guide* defines Team Members as "Developers" regardless of specialist knowledge.[*] There are no other roles or titles within a Development Team. This may seem odd or even silly, but it's extremely important. As members of the Development Team role on a Scrum Team, we are all in this together. Hierarchy, status, and other trappings of modern, hierarchical organizational culture are unwelcome intrusions.

> **Try This**
> Ask each Development Team Member to write his or her title on a note card. Collect all the note cards, shuffle them, and have each Team Member pull a card from the deck. Ask each Team Member to describe what **the title** on the card (not the person) contributes to the Team's overall effort and score that contribution on a scale of zero-to-five, with five representing high value, zero representing no value. Write the assigned value on each card. Then ask each Team Member to pass his or her card to someone else and repeat the description and scoring until all Team Members have scored every card. Add up the scores and plot the results on a white board. Which titles are most valuable? Which titles contribute little to the Team? Then ask Team Members to rate the importance of a "developer" – meaning a person whose entire effort is focused on the Team's collective work – and compare to the other titles. Now do you see the point?

We began the discussion of the other Scrum roles with a description of accountability so we'll do the same here: Development Team Members are,

---

[*] *Scrum Guide*, p. 6

collectively as a Team, accountable for delivering a quality product at a sustainable pace.

Is that what you expected? If not, make an opportunity to explore this statement with your teammates.

Development Team Characteristics

Effective Development Teams display a series of characteristics. Some of these items are described in the *Scrum Guide*, others not. Even if you are not using Scrum, these characteristics are broadly applicable to Development Teams in any Agile environment. The entire list is based on experience gained over 30 years of actual practice, so don't view any of these items as optional. Development Teams and – more generally Agile Teams – are:

- Small – three to nine members, **not** including the Scrum Master and Product Owner
- Dedicated full-time to the Team and product
- Self-organizing and self-managing
- Cross-functional
- The sole owners of work item estimates and Sprint commitments
- Accountable for developing a quality product at a sustainable pace
- Responsible for demonstrating a potentially shippable product increment every Sprint to the Product Owner, customers, and stakeholders
- Accountable for Team improvement

Let's look at each of these characteristics in more detail.

Small

Development Teams need to be small, in the range of three to nine members (not including the Scrum Master and Product Owner). Why small? Teams need to keep all internal lines of communication open – whether in use at any given time or not. Since a Team is self-organizing and self-managing, communication is of the utmost importance. The maximum number of lines of communication a Team can sustain is about 36, which just happens to yield a Team of nine members as expressed by the following formula:

$(n^2-n)/2$; where n = number of Development Team members.

The number of concurrent lines of communication required is determined by the number of Team Members, so just solve for n. Scaling up to take on bigger products means adding more fully formed Teams, not adding more people to existing Teams.

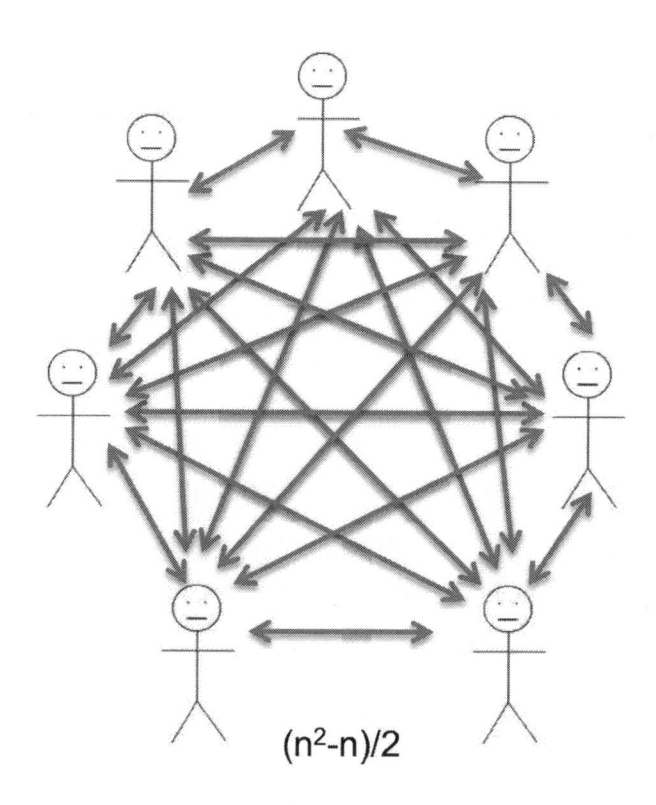

$$(n^2-n)/2$$

Dedicated Full-time to the Team and Product

In contrast to the matrixed, resource-pool organizational model that is so pervasive – and perverse – in our workplaces, Scrum insists that people commit to one Team and focus all of their energies on fulfilling the commitments of the Team. If people are spread across multiple Teams the inevitable result is less effective Team participation at the individual level and correspondingly less effectiveness at the Team level. Since one of the major reasons organizations adopt Scrum is to increase effectiveness, it makes no sense to work against that goal by spreading people across multiple Teams.

The only reasonable exceptions are when individuals meet both of the following criteria:

   a. An individual possesses specialists skills that are in short supply **and**

Chapter 3 Scrum Roles: The Development Team

    b. That skill set is not needed all the time on any one Team

Examples of people who **might** meet these two criteria in your organization are DBAs, technical writers, and perhaps UI/UX specialists – in short, any Subject Matter Expert (SME) who meets the conditions stated above.

So what's the best way to deal with this situation? My recommendation is to bring individuals who possess scarce specialists skills into a Team on Sprint boundaries, meaning the SME attends a Team's Sprint Planning Event and stays with that one Team for the full Sprint, maybe several full Sprints. These temporary Development Team Members are then able to commit fully to the Team's goals and become full-fledged Team Members for as many Sprints as they are needed. When their commitment is over, they can jump to a different Team, repeating the process as needed.

I like to think of temporary Development Team Members as being in orbit around the nucleus of the Team, something akin to electrons orbiting the nucleus of an atom. Electrons can jump easily from one atom to the next when there are open slots for them to occupy. The SME-Development Team Member-electrons remain in orbit around one Team-nucleus until pulled away by a neighboring Team. Jumping back and forth, or even worse, attempting to be in orbit around two or more Teams at any given time results in chaos that damages both the Teams and the temporary Team Member.

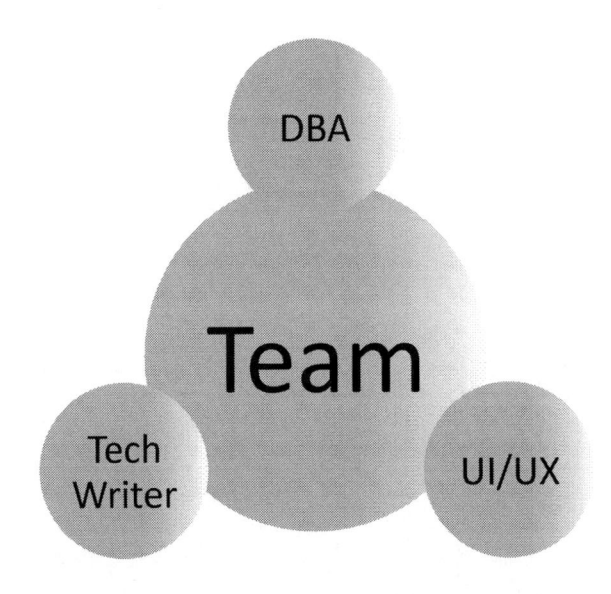

Less optimal is to have a temporary Team Member committed to two Teams simultaneously. This is not a 50-50 split as no one whose attention is being divided has a full 100 percent to give. Subtract at least 20 percent, or more realistically 40 percent, from that temporary Team Member's total capacity for each Team commitment. This is the penalty for the major context switch involved in jumping from Team to Team.

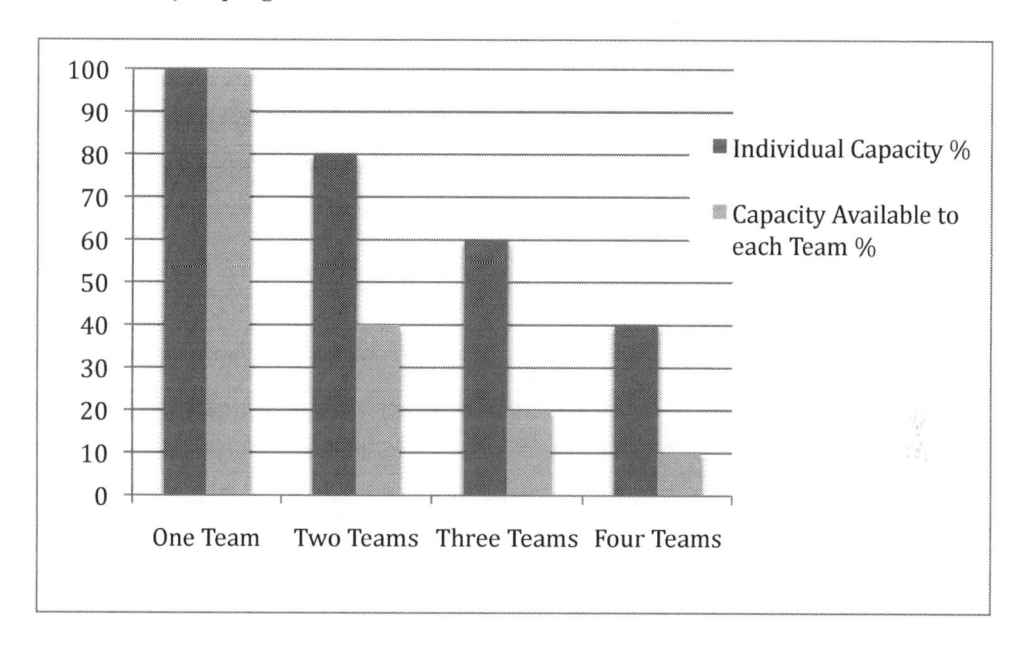

If you are compelled to split people across Teams, limit the damage to no more than two Teams per Sprint – and do still make changes only on Sprint boundaries. You can at least maintain an acceptable level of effectiveness, both for the Teams involved and the individual who has to split his or her commitments, if you follow this model. However, you should work on moving away from splitting people across Teams as quickly as possible to increase effectiveness.

Self-organizing and Self-managing

Development Teams need no external organizational or management control to get their work done. Instead, Teams organize around the work and manage their commitment to the Sprint Goal and delivery on a daily basis. What this means is that the Development Team collectively decides how much work to pull into each Sprint and then decides how to manage delivery of that work every day. Development Team Members self-assign tasks based on what needs to be done on a given day to help the Team meet its Sprint Goal – no one tells

Team Members what to do. Team Members self-assign daily work in collaboration with their teammates. This can be fairly shocking to those schooled in traditional "resource" or project management.

> **Pet Peeve**
> People are not "resources." A resource is a server, workstation, network infrastructure, desk, office space, money, etc. People are human beings, with all the strengths and limitations that lofty status implies. Resources are the tools people use to build great products. The resources themselves don't build anything. Referring to people as "resources" dehumanizes individuals, diminishes their ability to contribute to a Team effort, and demonstrates a deep-seated lack of respect. So make this pact with yourself and your teammates now – "we will never again refer to one another as 'resources.'"

Cross-functional

Development Teams contain all of the skill sets needed to complete the work the business, represented by the Product Owner asks the Team to deliver. That means that the Development Team Members possess individual expertise in a variety of areas, covering the product the Team is delivering from end-to-end.

Agile Teams are not contained within functional silos; they do not deliver one layer in a product. Why not? Remember this Agile Manifesto Principle:

> Our highest priority is to satisfy the customer through early and continuous delivery of valuable software.

Product layers deliver no customer value independently of the other layers that comprise the product. For example, how much customer value does a database deliver – just the database, not the user interface, not the middle tier, not the business layer, just the database? The answer – unless you're in the business of selling databases – is none, zero, zip, zilch.

Since the focus is on delivering business value early and often, Teams must work across functional layers, delivering the product incrementally and iteratively, one slice each Sprint.

Okay, fine, Teams are comprised of a bunch of specialists, right? Well, not so much. Teams must also be small, so there is constant tension between keeping the Team small and being able to deliver complete increments of valuable product. In practice, keeping a Team small is the overriding concern, so we need Development Team Members who are more than narrow specialists. What we really want are "generalizing specialists" – that is, people who are masters of one or more areas and at least moderately able to contribute in more than one other area as well.

This is another aspect of agility that is very hard for traditional management to get a handle on. We hire people for the specialist skills they possess, right? Just scan the job listings organizations large and small post to various job boards. They begin with a specialist title, like "Java Developer" or "System Test Specialist" or "Business Analyst, Mobile Applications" – you get the idea. These job listings then contain a largely impossible list of specialist knowledge, skills, experience, and abilities the "ideal" candidate must possess. When the organization makes a decision on whom to hire, that decision usually results from an evaluation of the specialist skills the candidate appears to possess. So naturally, the organization's management wants to get maximum value and insists that the new specialist drop into a silo with other, similar specialists so that they can all do their high-value, or at least high-cost, specialist work at the highest possible utilization rates.

Now Scrum and other Agile frameworks come along and say that's the wrong way to work, that having people work in specialist silos is not only wasteful, it results in a misplaced focus on specialist work output that in and of itself does not deliver business value. Even worse, the Lean thinkers in the Agile crowd insist that managing people at the specialist level sub-optimizes the entire system of product development, generating massive waste.

All of these things are true. The most effective and efficient way currently known to deliver business value is to build small Teams of generalizing specialists and let the Team Members self-organize and self-manage the Team's work.

So what does this all mean? In practice, being a generalizing specialist is just a fancy way of saying we want good players on our Teams. We want people who can contribute real value to the work the Team is delivering, both in terms of specialist knowledge and as good Team players. What this means is that as the *Team* works daily toward its collective goal, whoever is available takes on the highest-priority task available to be worked on, whether that person is the "specialist" or not. Here's the punch line: ***A cross-functional Team must also have cross-functional Team Members.***

For Teams to self-organize and self-manage their work, they must have the ability, within the Team, to do so efficiently and effectively. Teams that have too many specialist bottlenecks end up engaging in a lot of waiting – waiting on specialist work to be completed, waiting for the end of the Sprint to arrive when no more specialist work is available, or much worse, pulling yet more disconnected specialist work into the Sprint to keep people "busy."

A Team that lacks generalizing specialists, or put another way, a Team of specialists, displays some interesting traits. The usual indicators are people with nothing to do at the start of every Sprint. These people often live in the "tester" silo. The corollary is people with nothing to do at the **end** of every Sprint. These people often live in the "coder" silo. So while the "coders" are sitting back surfing the Internet – or worse, beginning speculative, unplanned work for the next Sprint – the "testers" are trying to complete a Sprint's worth of work in a ridiculously short time frame at the end of the Sprint. There is nothing Agile about this way of working, which some of the people I have trained and coached over the years call "Scrummerfall, Wet Agile, Wagile, or FrAgile," clever terms that I find highly descriptive.

Another indicator of a Team of specialists is a chronic pattern of some Team Members suffering from excessive overwork, while other Team Members are working at a sustainable pace or experience idle time during most Sprints.

Effective Teams avoid both of these troublingly common scenarios (and many others besides) by working deliberately to extend the skills of every Development Team Member. The biggest hurdle is simply the willingness of Team Members to abandon the territoriality or defensiveness they may feel about "their" work and embrace the whole-Team approach. Some people are simply not willing to do this and the Team will have to decide how to handle that situation. Fortunately, most people are perfectly willing to expand beyond their accustomed specialty boundaries to build broader skills that benefit the Team and themselves.

Building cross-functionality on a Team requires conscious effort, but does not involve distraction from the Team's daily work. The tasks are all there, just waiting to be picked up. So build cross-functionality consciously, deliberately, one task at a time. Here's an approach that I have found highly effective. First, as a Team, identify one critical specialist bottleneck. Next, whenever a task in that area is at the top of the stack, have the specialist pair with someone else on the Team. The "apprentice" drives the keyboard while the specialist explains what to do to implement the task, one step at a time in a classic Pair Programming pattern. Repeat until the Team overcomes the current bottleneck, then, in keeping with the Theory of Constraints,* identify the next critical specialist bottleneck and start the pattern over again.

Try a Team Spectrograph†

Cross-functionality is a key characteristic of an Agile Team. But how can you tell if your Team is cross-functional? How can you help your Team become more cross-functional? How can you tell if you're making progress? These are all good questions. Fortunately, there is an answer.

Cross-functionality within a Team doesn't just happen; it has to be deliberately and thoughtfully nurtured. So let's live the principle of Transparency and make it visible! A tool that I have found highly effective is the Team Spectrograph. A spectrograph plots the amplitude of a signal against a segment of the radio-frequency spectrum (my hobbyist background in radio-frequency engineering is showing). We can do the same thing with Team skills, that is, plot the skill levels Development Team Members possess (the amplitude) across the spectrum of skill sets the Team needs to have to deliver its product.

Here's how it works. On a white board or large flip-chart sheet, draw a standard x-y graph. On the x-axis, list the skill sets the Team needs to bring to bear to deliver the work it is being asked to do, each skill representing a tic mark along the x-axis. On the y-axis, draw evenly spaced tic marks from 1 to 10, with zero represented by the baseline of the graph. Then, have each Team Member self-assess his or her skill level on that zero-to-ten scale across all of the skill sets depicted. Have each Team Member use a different color marker and voila! – you have a Team Spectrograph that captures your Team's cross-functionality as of that moment in time. Areas to focus on will be readily apparent by the single peaks shown on the spectrograph, meaning only one Team Member possesses that particular skill, and by lines that converge on zero meaning the Team currently lacks that particular skill.

---

* Goldratt 2004
† I presented this coaching tool in a presentation at the Global Scrum Gathering, Atlanta, GA, May 2012 and again at the Global Scrum Gathering, San Diego, CA, April 2017.

Chapter 3 Scrum Roles: The Development Team

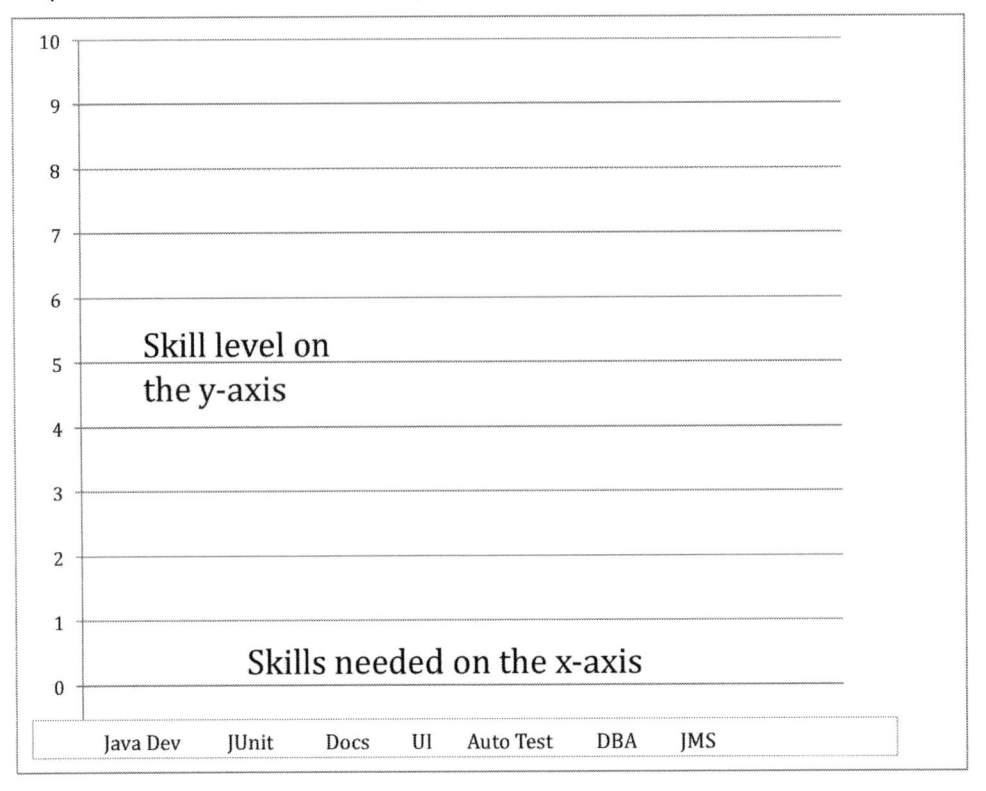

10							
9							
8							
7							
6							
5	Skill level on the y-axis						
4							
3							
2							
1	Skills needed on the x-axis						
0							
	Java Dev	JUnit	Docs	UI	Auto Test	DBA	JMS

Draw the grid....

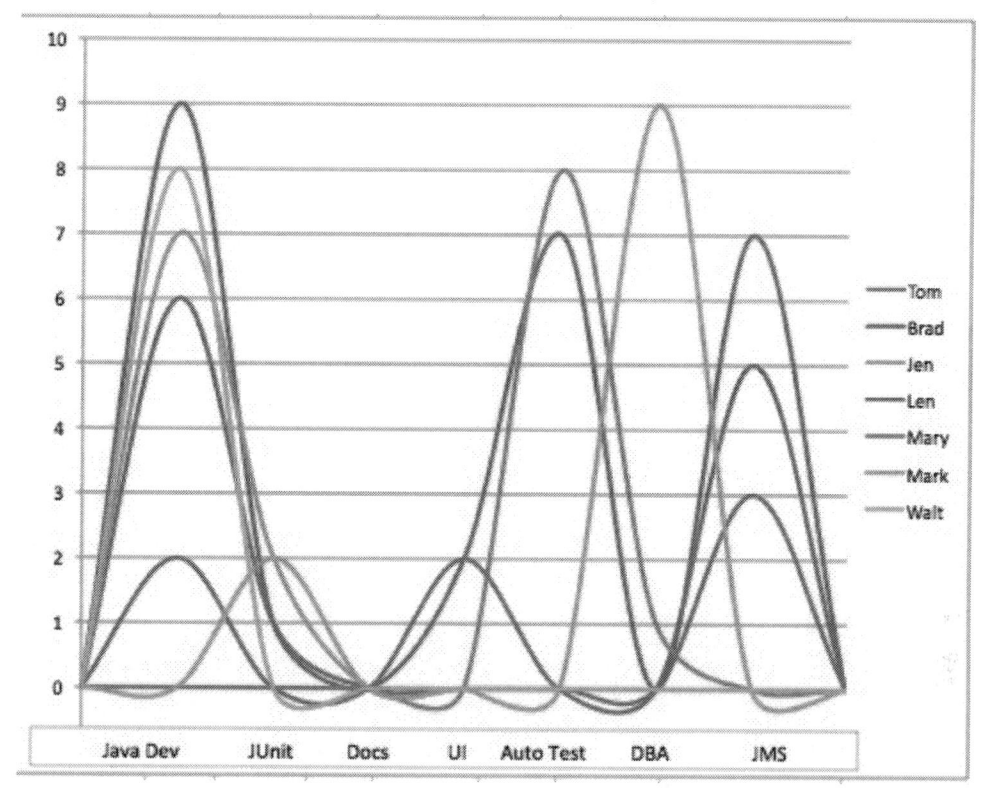

Team Members self-evaluate. This Team lacks the skill set needed to write user or technical documentation, but is otherwise reasonably cross-functional.

Chapter 3 Scrum Roles: The Development Team

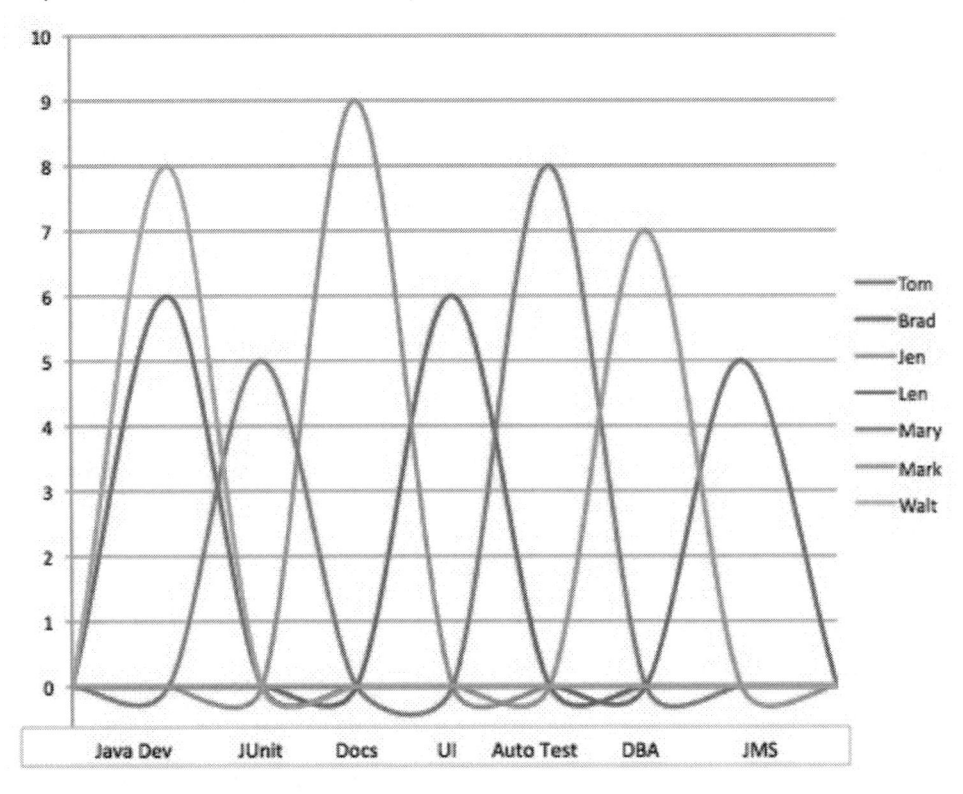

[Chart showing skill levels (0-10) across categories: Java Dev, JUnit, Docs, UI, Auto Test, DBA, JMS for team members Tom, Brad, Jen, Len, Mary, Mark, Walt. Each team member peaks in a single skill area.]

This Team has all necessary skill sets, but Team Members work in skill silos. What if someone goes on vacation or leaves the Team?

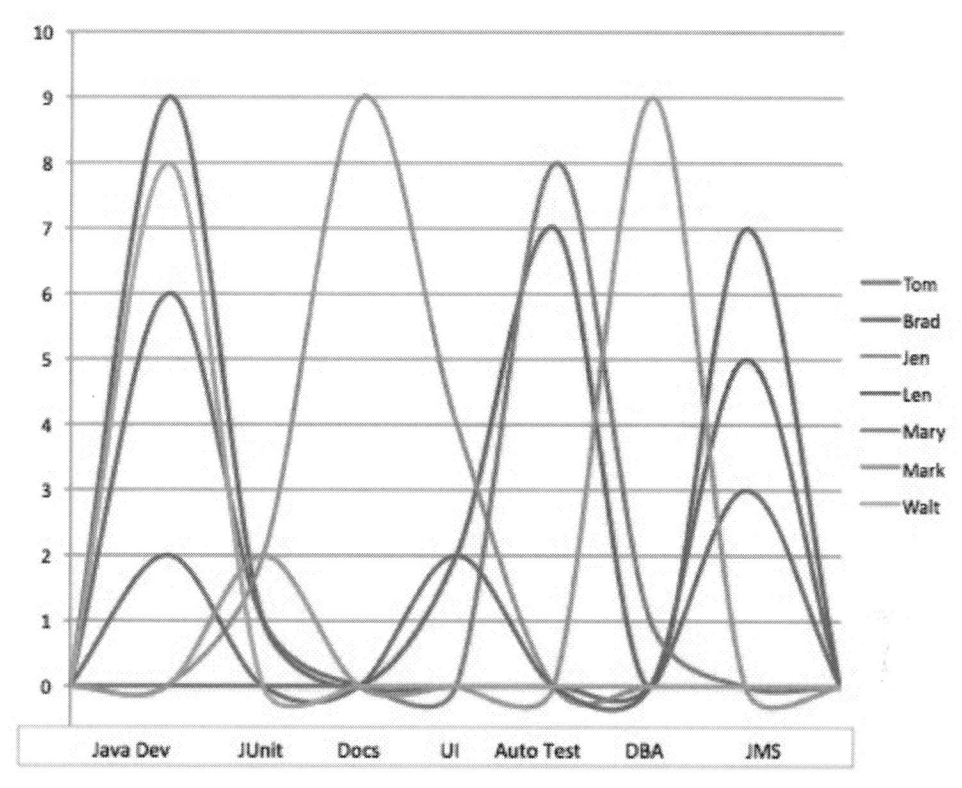

This Team is reasonably well balanced, with all skill areas covered. Only the "Docs" area is completely at risk if that person leaves the Team. The DBA area has minimal backup coverage, but is also a risk.

50   Chapter 3   Scrum Roles: The Development Team

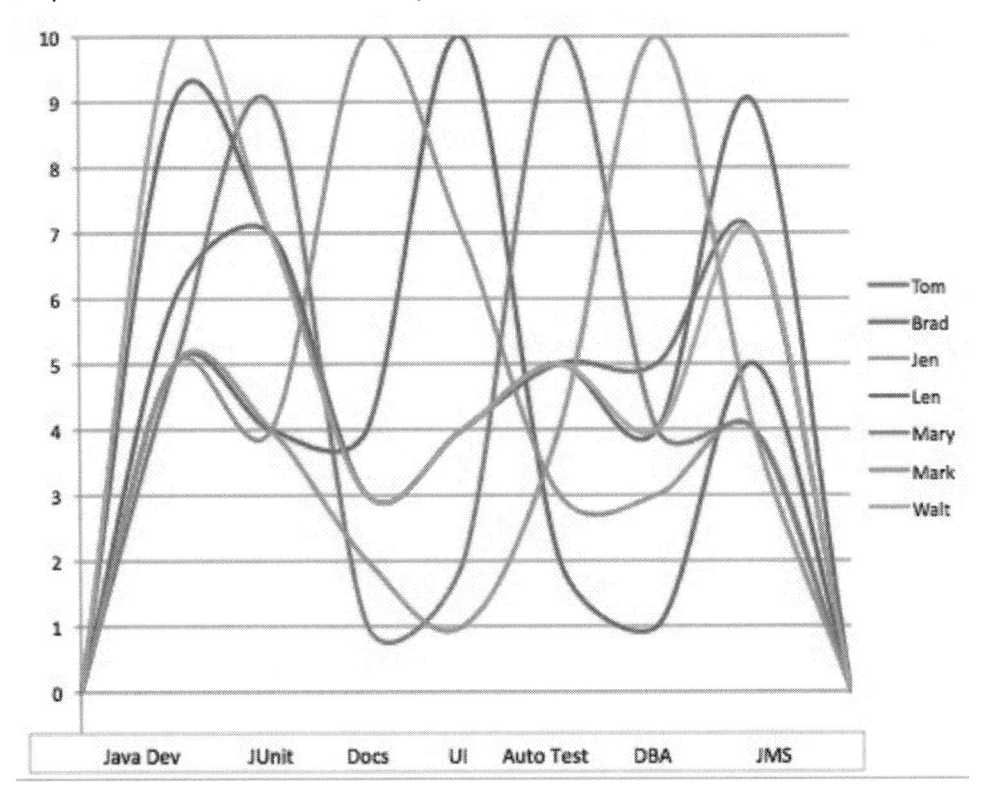

This Team is highly cross-functional and can adapt quickly if a Team Member is sick, goes on vacation, or leaves the Team.

Cross-functional Does Not Mean Interchangeable!

When training or coaching new Teams, I frequently hear something to the effect that "I realize we're all supposed to be interchangeable now...." I also get questions from new Development Team Members about having to give up on continuing to build expertise in specific technical areas. Sometimes people express the latter in the form of a regret.

Wait, stop, hold it right there! Nothing about becoming a Development Team Member demands or even implies interchangeability or the end of building deep, powerful skills in one or two (or more) technical specialties. We're talking about everyone on the Team learning enough about the skills needed to build the product so that the Team can always move forward, regardless of who happens to be on vacation, out sick, busy with a different task, whatever. The idea is to become efficient by reducing handoffs and mitigating the risk inherent in having people with specialist skills that do not spill over into other areas that the Team needs to complete its work every Sprint.

> **Magician's Secret**
> The idea is not to become a jack-of-all-trades, master of none. Rather, think about and work toward becoming a jack of *many* trades, master of *some*.

The Sole Owners of Estimates and Sprint Commitments

This is among the most important aspects of Scrum: the Product Owner has authority over the order of items in the Product Backlog as well as the scope of each item. The Development Team has equivalent authority over the size of Product Backlog Items as well as how many items they pull into each Sprint. Put another way, the Product Owner is responsible for the "what" of the Product Backlog Items: what order (based on business value), what scope. The Development Team is responsible for the "how" of the Product Backlog Items: how big, how many (per Sprint), and also how to implement each item.

The strict boundaries between the Product Owner and Development Team Member responsibilities are vital to ensure that the process that emerges from the application of the Scrum framework upholds the Agile Values and Principles discussed in Chapter 1. The Development Team and Product Owner take on different pieces of the project and product management responsibilities, creating an appropriate and effective balance that rarely exists in non-Agile environments. The Team's authority over the quantity of work pulled into each Sprint is balanced by the Product Owner's authority over the order of work items available to the Team. The Product Owner's authority over the scope of each work item is balanced by the Team's authority over the size estimate and implementation details of each work item.

Accountable for Developing a Quality Product at a Sustainable Pace

Since the Development Team determines how much work to pull into every Sprint, the Team can then also own the quality of the finished product. Think of it this way: The Product Owner is responsible for ensuring that the right thing gets built; the Development Team is responsible for ensuring that the thing gets built right.

However, quality is not the inevitable result of a functioning pull system with a Team working at a sustainable pace. Quality requires deliberate planning, effort, discipline, and constant attention even under the best of circumstances.

In the absence of a pull system and sustainable pace, however, a quality product is virtually impossible to attain.

In order to "build the thing right," the Development Team needs to do several things correctly.

- Pull work only as appropriate to ensure sustainable pace
- Plan for quality outcomes by building an appropriate Definition of Done (see Chapter 4) for all work
- Refactor* the product continuously to ensure that the product always reflects the current design and architecture
- Write tests before writing code and ensure that all existing tests are both up-to-date and automated to run with each build
- Never shortcut quality in design, coding, test coverage, or any other area covered by the Team's Definition of Done

Finally, the Development Team needs to internalize and act upon this Agile Manifesto Principle:

> Continuous attention to technical excellence and good design enhances agility.

All of these factors combine to create a system in which defects and poor-quality design and architecture are either greatly reduced or completely eliminated. Yes, I said that! Defects and quality issues are the result of weakness in *the product-development system,* not the result of individual mistakes or lack of skill. People make mistakes, clearly. But a good product-development system catches those mistakes almost immediately, provides appropriate feedback, and allows the Team to correct mistakes quickly before they become defects or quality issues. We'll talk more about building a product-development system that is inoculated against defects and quality issues a little later.

---

* Fowler 2000

Responsible for Demonstrating a Potentially Shippable Product Increment at the End of Every Sprint to the Product Owner, Customers, and Stakeholders

Since the Development Team builds a potentially shippable product increment every Sprint, it is only fitting that the Team also has both the responsibility and the privilege of showing its work to the Product Owner, customers, and stakeholders. The Team's formal opportunity to show its work is at the Sprint Review, although Teams present completed work items to the Product Owner for approval throughout the course of the Sprint rather than waiting until the Sprint Review. That way at the Sprint Review customers and stakeholders only see completed work that has also been approved by the Product Owner. This is a vast improvement over the original Scrum practices from a couple of decades ago, which combined Product Owner approval and customer and stakeholder feedback on the product into the Sprint Review Event.

Accountable for Team improvement

One of the big payoffs of Scrum or any other Agile approach is the benefit of a continuously improving Team. A Team doesn't just jump into the world fully formed, like an adult Athena popping out of the forehead of Zeus as depicted in Greek mythology. Teams grow more-or-less like the human beings of which they are composed, starting out with limited capabilities and passing through growth stages leading to maturity and prowess.

Team Maturity

An old but powerful framework for Team maturity is the Tuckman Model, named for its inventor, Bruce Tuckman.* The Tuckman Model traces the development of Teams through four stages of maturity, cleverly and intuitively named Forming, Storming, Norming, and Performing.†

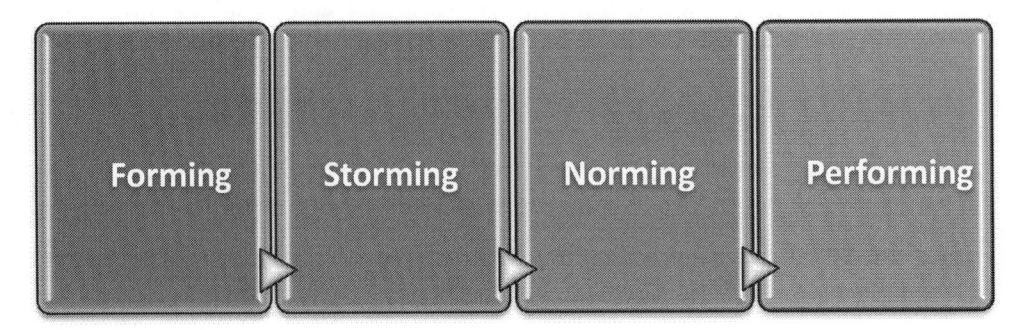

Forming → Storming → Norming → Performing

Forming

When a group of people comes together to form a Team, they invariably face a series of questions and concerns. Here is a partial list:

- Who is on this Team?
- What are the roles? What is *my* role?
- What are we working on?
- How will we do the work?
- What is a Team anyway?

> **Try This**
> That last question is extremely important. So important, in fact, that you need to spend 10 to 20 minutes discussing what it means to be a Team with your new teammates. Brainstorm as a Team and then choose five items to write on note cards that everyone agrees describe the meaning of the word "Team." Then use dot-voting, silent ordering‡, or another whole-Team technique to place the five items in order of importance. Tape the cards to the wall in order and use this list as your initial Team definition.

---

* Tuckman 1965
† Tuckman defined a fifth stage, Adjourning, but since that's something we don't generally want Teams to do, it doesn't figure into this discussion.
‡ Tabaka pp. 196, 205

> **Magician's Secret**
> For me, the one thing that truly defines a Team is *teamwork*. The aggregated efforts of isolated individuals do not constitute teamwork. Rather, teamwork is the result of every member of the Team taking full responsibility for the success of the *entire* Team, sometimes at the expense of individual success, glory, or recognition. Development Team Members ask themselves (often aloud, in front of their teammates): "What can I do today to help my Team achieve our collective goal?" That is the essence of teamwork.

Teams that are Forming need a lot of help – not control or direction, but facilitation and leadership. The Scrum Master (or equivalent if you are not practicing Scrum) is a vital role in helping a group of individuals learn how to start working together as a Team.

Finally, Teams that are Forming generally want to take process shortcuts or simply ditch the process altogether. In an Agile context, this malady often manifests itself through Development Team Members wanting to drop various aspects of the agreed-upon framework. In a Scrum environment, Development Team Members often want to cancel the Daily Scrum – or simply stop attending – claiming that, like Greta Garbo, they just want to be left alone so they can do their work. The same is true of other Events, which Forming Teams often identify as useless, time-consuming, and even a distraction from their work! A committed, patient, even valiant Scrum Master is a Forming Team's best hope for improvement, growth, and maturity.

Storming

The next stage of Team development, Storming, is a vital yet not necessarily very pleasant time for the Team. Teams that are Storming typically encounter the following issues:

- Decisions don't come easily for the Team
- Team Members often vie for position as they attempt to establish themselves in relation to other Team Members
- Difficulties establishing a common understanding of the work, roles, and Team procedures
- The Team needs to be focused on short-term goals to avoid becoming distracted by interpersonal relationships and emotional issues

Teams that are Storming exhibit difficulty engaging in teamwork. Individual work generally takes precedence over the Team's goals and commitments. Development Team Members may seek individual credit by taking on tasks not agreed to as part of the Team's immediate goal and commitment. Team Members may exhibit territoriality – "keep your fingers out of my code!" or a similar statement is not unusual in a Storming Team. Team Members may refuse to take on Tasks that they think are "beneath" their skill level or dignity.

On the opposite end of the spectrum, Development Team Members may refuse to take on any new Task without asking permission of the Scrum Master, Product Owner, other Team Members, or even their managers. On this last point, some Team Members may use manager approval or disapproval to limit the Tasks they work on. I once experienced a situation in which a manager told the "coders" on a Team that they were not to do any testing as they were too expensive to waste their time on a low-value activity!

Some of these issues go beyond the boundaries of the Team, but in general the most effective way to move a Team through Storming is for the Scrum Master (or Agile Coach if you are not practicing Scrum) to keep the Team focused on short-term goals and commitments, with help from the Product Owner as needed. When practicing Scrum there is always a deadline rapidly approaching – the end of the current Sprint. The combination of short Sprints, the insistence that the Team deliver a Potentially Shippable Product Increment every Sprint (meaning the Team actually *finishes* one or more work items every Sprint), and the reality of whole-Team commitment to the Sprint Goal makes Scrum a powerful driver of Team maturity.

Conflict Modes
A Storming Team experiences a higher degree of conflict than is common, or at least acknowledged, in a work group situation. As a result, the way people respond to conflict becomes an important consideration. I recommend spending 20-30 minutes discussing conflict modes with your Team. Always speak only for yourself when answering the following questions:

- Do you seek to avoid conflict most of the time within your Team?
- Is it important that you get your way when discussing alternative approaches to a problem within your Team?
- Do you compromise readily?
- Which is more important to you, ending a disagreement with a teammate or arriving at the best possible solution to a problem?
- Do you stand your ground if you think you're right when discussing alternative approaches to a problem within your Team?

- Are you open to new ideas and solutions regardless of which Team Member suggests them?

A handy tool to use when assessing conflict response on your Team is the Thomas-Kilmann Conflict Mode Instrument (TKI).* This is not the only such tool, but it is quick, easy, and produces results that may help your Team learn how to become more cohesive and mature.

Remember, this is conflict and **not** confrontation we're talking about. Conflict can be harnessed to generate creative, innovative solutions. Confrontation is wholly destructive of Team cohesion and maturity. Work with your Scrum Master to defuse any and all confrontations that may develop within the Team!

> **Try This**
> Spend 20 minutes during your next Retrospective writing or refreshing your Team's working agreements. Here are some example points that might make up working agreement:
>
> *We agree to place Team priorities and interests ahead of individual priorities and interests.*
>
> *We agree to work collaboratively, listening to each other's ideas, thoughts, and opinions without judgment, in order to arrive at the best possible solution to any problem we are confronting.*
>
> *We agree to use Pair Programming to spread knowledge, fill skill gaps, and build teamwork muscle.*
>
> Add specific approaches to the Pair Programming agreement, such as "Whenever Dave is writing stored procedures, he must pair with a teammate." Take Team agreements from nice-sounding abstractions to concrete practices!

---

* For a brief overview of this tool, see Tabaka p. 41

Norming

The Norming phase describes Team that has developed a sense of cohesion and a focus on teamwork. Some characteristics of a Norming Team are:

- Agreement and consensus characterize Team decision-making
- Roles and responsibilities are clear and accepted
- Big decisions are made by Team agreement
- Smaller decisions may be delegated to individuals or "Teamlets" (two or three individuals on the Team)
- Commitment and Team unity are strong
- Team Members may engage in fun and social activities outside of work
- The Team discusses and develops its processes and working style

Notice that nothing in this list says there are no longer any disagreements within the Team. The point is that the individuals have agreed to put the Team's interests and needs ahead of their own interests.

In my experience, one of the most interesting elements of a Norming Team is that Team members take advantage of opportunities to socialize outside of work. Storming Teams rarely engage in anything resembling full Team activities. I've actually heard this statement (or one very much like it) from Development Team Members when the Scrum Master or Product Owner proposes a Team social activity to celebrate a release or other notable achievement: "I see you people enough at work – why would I want to hang out with you after work, too? I'd rather just go home early." This wasn't meant to be hurtful, just a statement of fact. The general assent on the Team made it clear that Team cohesion and maturity were somewhat lacking!

> **Try This**
> Ask each member of your Team to write one word or phrase describing an ideal teammate trait or characteristic on a card or sticky note. Everyone can write out as many cards as come to mind, one trait per card. Then, tape or stick the cards on the wall and, as a Team, group them to find both duplicates and discrete ideas. Ask the Team to select one card in each category to represent that ideal teammate characteristic. Then, ask the Team to put the resulting cards in order of importance to the development of the Team. Pick the top-five teammate traits and discuss why they are important and how to enhance those traits on the Team.

Performing

This is the real payoff for the organization – and almost always one of the main reasons the organization is interested in adopting an Agile framework in the first place. A high-performing Team delivers results faster and at higher quality than is possible under virtually any other circumstances. Some characteristics of a Performing Team are:

* The Team is strategically aware – the Team knows clearly why it is doing what it is doing and can incorporate strategic information into its daily decision making
* The Team has a shared vision
* The Team is focused on over-achieving goals and makes decisions based on common goals and vision
* Disagreements occur but are resolved positively within the Team
* The Team owns its process, structures, and working agreements
* Team members look after each other

On a Performing Team, individuals move seamlessly from one Task to the next, without regard for individual preference. Team Members have been working together long enough, and have gained enough skill in every area needed to deliver the work, that the Team's highest priority is everyone's focus. Remember the Team Spectrograph presented earlier in this chapter? A Performing Team is truly cross-functional across the skill spectrum.

Beyond all of the benefits of cross-functionality, effectiveness, and performance, being a member of a Performing Team is an amazing experience. Individual morale is sky-high as people take more and more control over their work and their shared destiny as a Team. For most of us, being a member of a Performing Team is about as good as it gets in our working lives.

Beware the J-Shaped Curve

So why bother placing all this emphasis on Team maturity? There are major implications for productivity and effectiveness inherent in this discussion. The more mature a Team is, the more productive and effective that Team becomes. The problem with a disruptive Agile framework like Scrum is that it introduces something widely known as the J-shaped curve. Whenever a disruptive change hits a group of people, such as forming Scrum Teams from a set of work groups, performance and effectiveness suffer a noticeable, sometimes serious, degradation. The figure below shows a J-shaped curve indicating relative Team performance overlaid on the Tuckman Team maturity model.

| Forming | Storming | Norming | Performing |

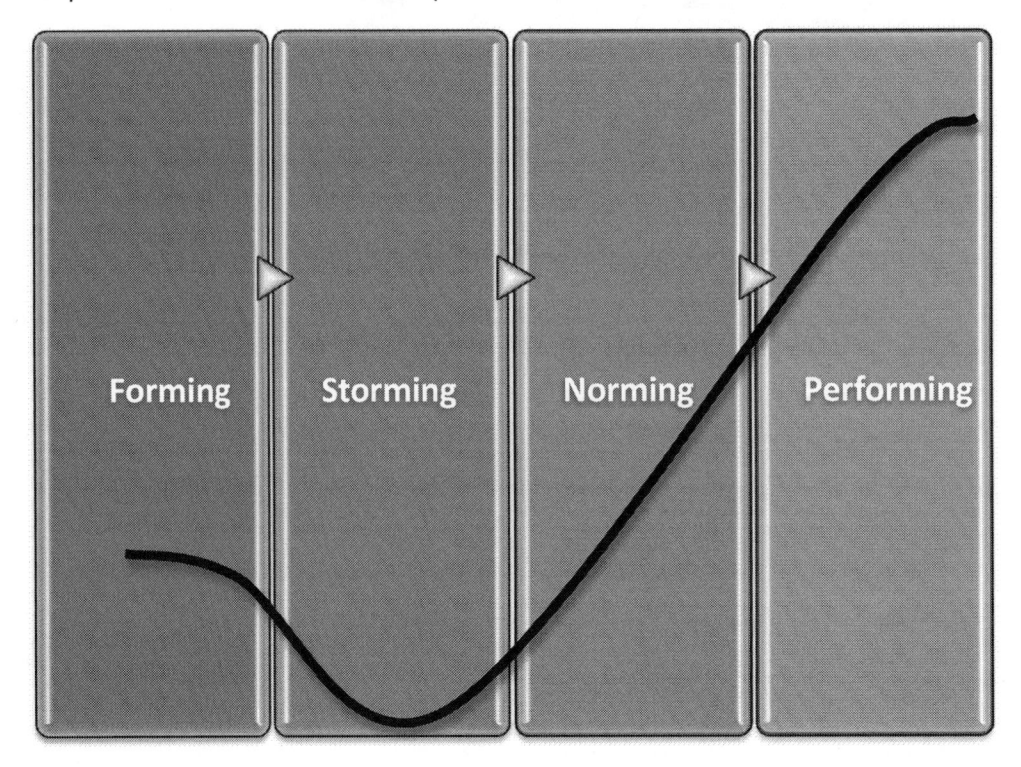

When a Team is Storming, not only is there a decided lack of teamwork, there is also a clear drop in effectiveness and productivity when compared with the work groups from which the individuals on the Team were drawn. Sloshing around at the bottom of the J-shaped curve is no fun for anyone and it is in everyone's interest to get out of Storming as rapidly as possible. An experienced Scrum Master or Agile Coach is absolutely vital to getting out of the trough and onto the shoulder of the upward curve.

> **Magician's Secret**
> Most Teams and organizations that abandon Scrum do so while they are mired at the bottom of the J-shaped curve. Life is so miserable and productivity so poor (comparatively) that it seems like this whole Agile thing was a sham. Going back to the "old ways" would clearly be better, right? The problem is, when your Team or your organization is in this state, you are on the cusp of major improvement. Not only is there nowhere to go but up, the looming upside offers far more than you could ever get by going back to comfortable habits and work styles. My advice is to hang in there, keep working on improving, get help from an experienced external Agile Coach if you need it, and stay focused on the benefits to come.

> **Try This**
> Given what you now know about Team maturity, spend 10 or 15 minutes discussing this topic: How long should a Team stay together?

What If We Never Get Beyond Storming?

Some Teams get stuck in Storming mode, sloshing around in the bottom of the J-shaped curve, and are unable to pull themselves out. That is clearly not a good thing. There can be any number of specific reasons behind the inability of a Team to normalize its internal working relationships. Teams that lack a dedicated Scrum Master may have a very difficult time moving ahead, for example.

Some Teams live in an organizational ecosystem that has not embraced self-organization and self-management. Teams that are burdened with a highly directive, authoritarian organizational environment never have the opportunity to mature, because they remain completely dependent upon outside decision-makers. If a Team doesn't have permission to make decisions, there is no reason to expect that Team to become independent and mature.

Another relatively common problem is a Team being held back by one or more people who just don't want to work on a Team in general or are unable to adapt to working on a particular Team. These are really two different issues, but the solution is the same. In both cases, the Team should do everything possible to integrate everyone into the Team. Failing an internal Team solution, the Team has no choice but to escalate the problem to management for an appropriate solution.

> **Magician's Secret**
> The problem of a non-Team player is both relatively common and difficult. Most people new to Scrum are worried about the Team Member who isn't able or willing to pull his or her weight. In my experience, that's rarely the problem that arises. Much more common is the problem of the Team "hero" disrupting teamwork by dictating technical solutions or simply "fixing" other Team Members' work. It may be difficult to comprehend, but Teams are better, stronger, and more productive without a Team hero. Remember, *teamwork* is the hidden multiplier. Anything that disrupts teamwork is detrimental to the Team's maturity and performance.

A Final Word About Teams and Teamwork

As I mentioned above, building a Performing Team and achieving a high degree of teamwork are two of the main areas that really pay off for organizations adopting Scrum or a similar Agile framework. When you consider for a moment that a high-performing Team is typically at least an order of magnitude more effective and productive than a work group, it becomes apparent that Teams and teamwork are critical to success in any organization.

What is perhaps less apparent – although maybe more so now that you have read this chapter – is that building a Performing Team is very difficult, requiring a huge investment of time, energy, effort, and to some extent money. It is, for example, far more difficult to build and nurture a Performing Team than it is to implement a new technology, say automated testing or continuous integration services, into an organization. Indeed, building effective Teams is clearly among the most difficult aspects of organizational agility. So again, how long should an effective, high-performing Team stay together?

Teams Are Key

Regardless of the Agile framework you chose, the basic elements of building a Team are the same. The important thing to remember is that a Team is not just a group of people working on the same product as isolated individuals. Agile Teams are small, cross-functional, self-organizing, self-managing, and work toward a common goal with a shared vision. A Team engages in *teamwork*, which is the hidden multiplier of productivity. Without a Team, the remaining benefits of adopting any Agile framework are significantly diminished.

Further Reading

Fowler, Martin. *Refactoring: Improving the Design of Existing Code.* Boston: Addison-Wesley, 2000.

Goldratt, Dr. Eliyahu M. and Jeff Cox. *The Goal: A Process of Ongoing Improvement.* 3rd edition. Great Barrington, MA: The North River Press, 2004 (first edition, 1984).

Katzenbach, Jon R. and Douglas K. Smith. *The Wisdom of Teams: Creating the High-Performance Organization.* New York: Harper Collins Publishers, 1993.

Tabaka, Jean. *Collaboration Explained: Facilitation Skills for Software Project Leaders.* Upper Saddle River, NJ: Addison-Wesley, 2006.

Chapter 4 The Product Backlog

"Prediction is very difficult, especially if it's about the future."
– *Niels Bohr*

The Product Backlog is an artifact defined in Scrum, but it describes a more generic concept: *a single-dimensional, ordered list of all the things you've thought of but haven't yet done.* The Product Backlog contains everything needed for the product at any given point in time, including functional and non-functional items, capacity and performance needs, release and deployment items, Team and technical chores – whatever it takes.

Every item on the Product Backlog should *describe something of value to customers or stakeholders.* This is one of the key differences between a Product Backlog and a requirements specification. Another key difference is that a Product Backlog is simply a stack of items, the content and order of which are subject to change as new information and knowledge become available about the product, technology, customers, stakeholders, market conditions, competition, etc.

Adaptive Planning

Since the Product Backlog is just an ordered list or stack of items that you haven't yet done – and are not currently doing – you can change how it is ordered and what it contains quickly and at minimal cost. The Product Backlog expresses "the plan" as you understand it at the moment. Changing the contents or order of items on the Product Backlog is then, by definition, an act of planning. This is the heart of adaptive, Agile planning and the essence of the difference between Agile frameworks like Scrum and XP and heavyweight product development methodologies: the heavyweight methodologies are *plan* driven; Agile is *planning* driven.

Scrum assigns authority over the content and ordering of the items in the Product Backlog to the Product Owner. This makes perfect sense since the Product Owner is the one and only member of a Scrum Team who is accountable for the success of the product. On the other hand, anyone can contribute items to the Product Backlog – customers, stakeholders, sponsors, sales, marketing, Development Team Members – anyone. The Product Owner alone, however, decides whether an item ever goes to the Team to be turned into working product and the order in which items are presented to the Team. It is also the Product Owner's responsibility to keep the Product Backlog up to date so that it shows the true state of the product plan all the time.

The Product Backlog is the living, breathing product plan, always accurate, always complete based on the best information and knowledge available at the moment. This may be quite a shock to those accustomed to plans that are fixed and expensive to change – and therefore don't change.

By way of summary, the Product Backlog is:

- A single-dimensional, ordered list of all the things you've thought of but haven't yet done and are not currently doing
- Includes everything needed for the product: functional, non-functional, etc.
- Contains items that describe something of value to customers or stakeholders
- Ordered by the Product Owner
- Subject to continuous change, both content and ordering, at minimal cost
- Expresses – and radiates – the current state of the product plan

What the Development Team Gets From the Product Backlog

The Product Backlog is incredibly valuable to the Development Team because it answers two critical questions:

1. What do we do next?
2. Is what we're working on valuable?

Let's examine the first question. Deciding what to do next is critical to successful product development. The Product Backlog is such a powerful artifact in part because it answers this question continuously – the thing to do next is the item on the top of the stack. Since there can only ever be one and only one item at the top of a single-dimensional ordered list at a time, the answer to the question "What do we do next?" is neither ambiguous nor imprecise. The item at the top of the Product Backlog changes frequently, both as the Team delivers increments of business value and as our knowledge grows. But the essential point remains true at all times. No one ever has to wonder what's coming up next because the Product Backlog always answers that question.

As for the second question, I can't even begin to count the number of days I spent writing code wondering whether what I was doing was really of any value at all. A common dysfunction in traditional plan-driven environments is that the people doing the work are either not made aware of the value of the work or the work itself is actually of little or no value. A lack of transparency produces the former outcome, while following the plan above all else produces the latter.

One of the most powerful elements of Scrum is the combination of Product Owner and Product Backlog. The Product Owner makes decisions based on maximizing the business value the Development Team produces every Sprint. The Product Backlog reflects that decision-making and in the process answers the question "Is what we're working on valuable?" like this: "We are working on the most valuable thing we could possibly be doing right now." The really cool part of all of this is that the answer never changes – we are always, by definition, working on the most valuable thing we could possibly be doing all day, every day. And that is a beautiful thing indeed.

User Stories

The items in the Product Backlog can be expressed in any way you find effective. Most Agile Teams and organizations have settled on the User Story as the most effective format for expressing the ideas needed to build a product. A User Story is a brief description of product functionality told from the perspective of the customer, stakeholder, or end user.

User Story Template

Here is a wonderful User Story Template:

> As a <user role/persona>,
> I want <goal/functionality>,
> So that <business value>.

User Stories focus the discussion and the work on the customer instead of on the attributes of the product, project, or system under development. This is in sharp contrast with the traditional IEEE-830 requirements format, "The system shall <blah>...." The traditional format is focused entirely on the attributes of the "system," completely ignoring the customer, the intent, and the rationale or business value behind the requirement. Even worse, the traditional requirements format makes it easy to specify implementation details, which is a very bad thing to be doing before actually working on solving the problem the requirement describes.

> **Magician's Secret**
> When you write a User Story, always work with a distinct, well-defined user role or persona. Writing "As a user..." is a vague abstraction that provides no real value. Get to know your real or projected customers, stakeholders, and end users and write effective User Stories that satisfy their needs.

An Example

This is an example of a User Story written following the template I've recommended:

> As Cathy (customer technical support specialist),
> I want to access a customer support record,
> so that I can provide the best possible support
> to each customer.

> **Magician's Secret**
> "Okay great," you're probably thinking at this point. I'm a Development Team Member and you're telling me all about things that the Product Owner has exclusive control over. Why are you wasting my time? Well, you are partly correct. The Product Owner does own, exclusively, the content and ordering of the items in the Product Backlog. You need to know that. You also need to know what the Product Backlog is and what it tells you. But remember that the items that make up the Product Backlog can come from anyone, including and especially Development Team Members. It is therefore important that you know how to write effective User Stories. That said the current discussion does not by any stretch provide exhaustive coverage of User Stories. See the Recommended Reading at the end of this chapter for a deeper dive into User Stories and Product Backlog management.

Whether you adopt this User Story template – or User Stories at all – is immaterial. What's important is to use a template that captures these three vital pieces of information: who it's for, what it is, and why it's valuable or important. The User Story template above fulfills these goals admirably.

Some Useful Terms

Two terms that describe User Stories have emerged from common practice in the Agile community over the years: Epic and Theme.

Epic

User Stories come in all sizes, but there are really two different kinds of User Stories based on size: those stories that will fit within a Sprint and those that are too large to fit within a Sprint. An Epic, or Epic User Story, is simply a User Story that is too large for a Team to pull into and deliver during a Sprint. The size limit of an Epic is relative to each Team and also to the Sprint length. Don't get too hung up on the definition. An Epic is simply a User Story that needs to be broken down into smaller chunks before it is ready for the Team to turn it into working product.

Epics occupy the size range from just a little too large to fit into a Sprint all the way up to truly gigantic proportions, describing the desired functionality for part of a release, an entire release, multiple releases – you get the idea.

> **Question**
> Is the sample User Story on the previous page an Epic?

Theme

A Theme is simply a set of related User Stories. The User Stories that comprise a Theme can be of any size. A Theme may contain small User Stories as well as Epics. The point of a Theme is that it is a container for a coherent set of features that deliver customer value. Themes help the Product Owner see the big picture by placing related User Stories in buckets that the Product Owner can then put in order based on value.

The Three C's of a User Story

A helpful way to think about User Stories is to apply the Three C's as first expressed by longtime agilist and XP coach Ron Jeffries.*

Card

Once upon a time, people wrote User Stories on index cards. Actually, people still do that, although other people use software tools or formatted cards for that purpose. Regardless of whether you use physical cards or a software tool for writing User Stories, keep in mind the metaphor of the card.

A card is **small** – it cannot possibly contain every detail needed to implement the User Story. As such, it forces the User Story to be a terse, compact description of the desired functionality following the User Story template described in the previous section.

A card is also **impermanent**. You can rewrite the User Story, tear it up, break it into two or more smaller, better, or different stories, and move the card up or down the Product Backlog at will – provided you are the Product Owner!

You can also annotate the card with brief notes that help describe the User Story it contains. Again, this is not a requirements specification, just a small piece of card stock on which you can write a few notes resulting from the next C....

Conversation

In case it isn't already clear, a User Story is not a requirements specification. Put another way, a User Story is not a means of communication; it is instead a placeholder for one or more conversations. It is in the conversations – between the Product Owner and customers, Product Owner and Team, Team and customers, etc. – that the richness of communication and detail live.

---

* Jeffries 2001

Confirmation

Finally, we must be able to tell when the User Story is done. The confirmation consists of specific, testable items that define what is in scope for the Story and by extension, what is out of scope for the Story. The confirmation is frequently known as Acceptance Criteria (since the Product Owner "accepts" completed stories) or Conditions of Satisfaction. These terms are synonyms and are equally applicable, so pick the one you like and go with it.

One of the major problems of software development historically is that we have built a bunch of features that no one ever uses. By defining explicitly what is in and what is out of scope for every User Story, the problems of "gold plating" and speculative development are much less likely to get out of control. The Product Owner is responsible for defining the scope of every User Story, making the confirmation element the exclusive purview of that role.

> **Magician's Secret**
> Have you ever heard a coder say something like this? "I know we're going to need <*feature x*> at some point, so I'll just put it in now to save time later." The confirmation portion of every User Story – Acceptance Criteria/Conditions of Satisfaction – particularly when expressed as executable tests, provides the discipline necessary to keep the focus on delivering only what the Product Owner has determined is needed for the Story and nothing more. Additional functionality must be captured in different User Stories. In this way the product moves forward in a deliberate, controlled, disciplined, and very precise manner that heavyweight, large-batch methodologies simply can't match.

Where are the Details?

The User Story template described above is deliberately lacking details, but that doesn't mean the details are unimportant. As you already know, the details live in the Conversation and Confirmation aspects of the User Story. Whenever you have a conversation about a User Story, capture the results and work them into the Confirmation.

"But wait," you say, "isn't Agile about working software over documentation?" Yes, absolutely, but, and this is the key point, working software **over** comprehensive documentation, not exclusive of **any** documentation. When you have a conversation about a Story say, at a whiteboard, take a photo of the whiteboard and add a few notes to provide context. The point is to capture enough information to avoid having to repeat the same conversation over and over. Taking pictures and adding notes is a reminder that you **had** a conversation and what that conversation was about, not documentation intended to take the place of the conversation.

Details as Acceptance Criteria

Great, so now you've had a conversation or two – now what? Let's get back to the Confirmation part of the User Story. Apply the results of the conversations about a User Story to build the Story's Acceptance Criteria/Conditions of Satisfaction. Each Acceptance Criterion* should define a binary, pass/fail condition that you could write as an executable test. Leave out the ambiguity. Define what the Story should look like when it's completed. Oh, and build the Acceptance Criteria using conversation.

> As Cathy (customer technical support specialist),
> I want to access a customer support record,
> so that I can provide the best possible support
> to each customer.
>
> Acceptance Criteria:
> - Pull customer record by last + first name or customer ID
> - Display full customer contact record
> - Open new contact event window
> - Allow Create-Read-Update on all available fields

> **Tip**
> Try using Specification by Example or the Given/When/Then format of Behavior Driven Development (BDD) to write Acceptance Criteria. You can even use an Acceptance Test Driven Development (ATDD) tool such as FitNesse or a BDD-based tool like Cucumber to automate the entire business of writing unambiguous, test-based Acceptance Criteria.

---

* Criterion is the singular form. "Criteria" is the plural.

One final note about Acceptance Criteria: they are the responsibility of the Product Owner. It's not that the Product Owner has to define every one for every Story; it's just that the Product Owner is responsible for the scope of every Story and also has the authority to accept or reject the Team's work on each Story. The Development Team and Product Owner need to collaborate on the Acceptance Criteria for each and every Story to reach agreement on what's in scope, what's out of scope, and how to prove that the Story is finished.

> **Magician's Secret**
> How many Acceptance Criteria should a User Story have? This is an extremely important question! Some agilists insist that each User Story should require just a single acceptance test to prove whether it is finished or not. That implies just one Acceptance Criterion per Story. In my experience, adhering to that rule produces Stories that are often too small. I prefer three as the usual number of Acceptance Criteria for a Story, with a maximum of five. More than five Acceptance Criteria and a Story is either too large or describes related but separable areas of functionality.

Details as Definition of Done

Another aspect of "doneness" for a User Story is the Development Team's Definition of Done. Whereas Acceptance Criteria apply to each Story individually, the Team's Definition of Done applies to all work the Team delivers. We'll talk about Definition of Done a little later so don't worry about it too much right now. Here is a sample of a Team's Definition of Done, which the Team should post in a conspicuous place in the Team Room, just so you get the idea:

> **Team Loki Definition of Done**
> Database schema updated
> New fields added
> Code completed using Test Driven Development
> Functional tests written, automated, and passing
> Regression tests written, automated, and passing
> Integration tests written, automated, and passing
> No failing tests in CI build
> No compiler or build system warnings
> Neighborhood refactoring complete
> UI/UX designed and wired up
> User documentation updated
> User Acceptance Tests (UAT) written and passing
> Product Owner exploratory testing complete
> Code review complete
> Sample dataset updated and populated
> Stress/Load/Performance testing complete
> Deployment scripts updated and tested in staging
> ...

Details as Smaller Stories

Another place where details live is in smaller User Stories sliced off of a larger Story. It's rare that anyone can write a User Story that is the perfect size for a Team to turn into working product right off the bat. Most User Stories go through a process of refinement, a major part of which is breaking the original Story down into bite-size chunks – smaller, actionable Stories.

> **Magician's Secret**
> When first getting started with User Stories, just assume that all of the stories you write are at least an order of magnitude (a factor of 10) too large. Some Product Owners I've worked with wrote stories that were easily 50 times too large for their Teams to deliver during a Sprint. Bias your thinking toward smaller User Stories right out of the gate and you'll be on the right track.

Always think in terms of end-to-end, customer-value when breaking down a Story. Here are a few guidelines to keep in mind:

- Break Stories along operational boundaries, such as CRUD (Create, Read, Update, Delete) – each operation delivers an end-to-end slice of valuable functionality
- Break off non-essential and nice-to-have parts of a Story – always think in terms of the simplest possible solution to the problem the Story describes, deferring corner cases for later – or never
- Break off non-functional items and cross-cutting concerns, such as performance and security
- Break Stories along Acceptance Criteria boundaries

> **Magician's Secret**
> The list of Acceptance Criteria often provides the necessary cue that a Story is too large. If the Story has five or more Acceptance Criteria, I almost always recommend breaking that Story into two or more smaller Stories. The Acceptance Criteria also provide handy slicing boundaries – group together two or three related Acceptance Criteria and write Stories that capture their meaning.

All new Stories that you write when breaking down a Story that was too large go right back onto the Product Backlog for the Product Owner to put in the appropriate order.

Getting to Goldilocks

The Development Team has the final say on whether a Story is too large, too small (it happens!), or just right to be pulled into a Sprint – the Goldilocks Zone for Stories. Active collaboration between the Development Team and Product Owner is vital to ensuring that there is a steady stream of appropriately sized items in the Product Backlog for the Team to work on. And this is where the Product Backlog artifact excels: creating a steady flow of work through the system that is an Agile Team.

INVEST in Your User Stories

A few years ago, Bill Wake came up with this handy acronym to describe six characteristics of good User Stories. I like it because it's easy to remember and helps focus on the power of effective User Stories.*

Independent

Good User Stories can be implemented in any order, meaning they do not have overlapping concepts or dependencies, giving the Product Owner the opportunity to order them by *value*. Interestingly, most dependencies are artifacts of our thinking about the way we break work down. Get in the habit of writing Stories that describe independent vertical slices through the entire product technology stack and most dependencies will disappear.

Sometimes dependencies do actually exist, but they should not cascade down the Product Backlog. Stories that imply architecture, design, or implementation that influences other stories do involve dependencies, but try to limit the effects. A good way to approach this very common situation is to have a conversation that goes something like this: "Stories A, B, C, and D all rely on the same design work, so whichever one we do first will make the other three much smaller. Product Owner, which Story do you want done first?" Easy enough!

Negotiable

The sample conversation above provides a nice segue into the idea that good Stories are *negotiable*. Stories are not detailed contracts. The implementation details of the Story belong to the Development Team, which leaves the Story to capture the essence, the meaning, of the feature as is entirely appropriate. The actual implementation of a Story may change dramatically as the Team builds it out. Again, this is the way it should work, in keeping with the separation of powers between the Product Owner, who owns the "what" and the Development Team, which owns the "how."

Valuable

Stories must provide value to customers or stakeholders, period. Even – perhaps especially – infrastructure, design, and architectural work needs to be associated with an incremental, vertical slice of identifiable, demonstrable customer value.

---

* Wake 2003

This is where the idea that a Story describes a vertical slice of valuable functionality, cutting through all the various layers of the product from top to bottom, comes into play. Unless the product your customers are paying for is a database schema, it is completely inappropriate to write a Story that talks only about developing a database schema. Instead, create as much of the database schema as needed to deliver the specific slice of customer value a Story describes.

Since every Story delivers customer value and since the Product Owner orders the Stories in the Product Backlog by relative value, everyone can rest assured that the Team is *always* working on the most valuable item that they could possibly be working on all the time. By definition, there is nothing more valuable that the Team could be doing right now than the thing they are currently doing.

Estimable

Estimates serve two purposes. First, estimates are the primary planning and forecasting tool for the Product Owner. Second, estimates help the Development Team understand whether or not a Story is the right size to be pulled into a Sprint.

Estimates play another vital role, however. Recall that the Development Team owns the estimates, the sizing of the Stories. We'll talk more about effective estimating techniques a little later (see Chapter 5), but for this discussion the important thing to keep in mind is that estimating is a whole-Team, consensus-driven activity. What this means is that everyone on the Team contributes to the estimates and all estimates are the result of Team consensus. The outcome is that the entire Team understands every Story well enough to provide an estimate. Or not.

> **Magician's Secret**
> If the Development Team cannot provide a consensus estimate for a Story, it is a cue or tripwire indicating that the Team does not understand the Story. If the Team doesn't understand a Story well enough to arrive at a consensus estimate, there is no way the Team understands the Story well enough to implement it!

Small (or Sized Appropriately)

Stories that are implementation-ready are small – small enough to fit comfortably within a Sprint, small enough to be delivered as finished work within a Sprint. Stories that are too large need to be broken down into more granular Stories.

On the other hand, Epics are not small and that may be entirely appropriate if that large Story is looming off in the future somewhere. We'll discuss the sizes of Stories in the Product Backlog in the next section, but for now suffice it to say that Stories that are likely to be implemented in the next couple of Sprints need to be small, while Stories that are further from now are generally – and increasingly – larger.

Testable

Tests answer these vital questions: "How will you know when you're done? How can you prove that you're done?" Remember that Acceptance Criteria define what is in and out of scope for each Story. Writing Acceptance Criteria as tests ensures that the Development Team will be able to answer both of these critical questions about a Story and that the Product Owner and Team can see without any ambiguity whether or not the Story meets its Acceptance Criteria. The acceptance tests are either passing or not passing. There is no intermediate, ambiguous, or partially done state possible and that's a good thing.

The Product Backlog as Iceberg

A handy metaphor for the Product Backlog is to think of it as an iceberg. Let's say you're on a ship – not the Titanic! – and you see an iceberg. What do you see? A small portion of the iceberg is above the surface of the water. You can see every detail, every crevice, scalloped-out spot, and craggy point.

This is like looking at the highly detailed User Stories at the top of the Product Backlog. They are in sharp relief, providing a high-resolution view into the shape of the product. Like an iceberg, these highly detailed User Stories need to be above the waterline. The Development Team is either currently turning them into real product or very likely soon will be. This is the ten percent of the iceberg that is visible above the surface.

Now look at the iceberg just below the surface. You can tell that the iceberg continues well down into the water, but the depth and movement of the water increasingly distort the details. This is like the current release, or maybe more like the next three to six months of work as currently expressed in the Product Backlog. The User Stories at this level are larger, less well defined, and open to interpretation and refinement whenever they rise closer to the surface.

Finally, there is a large part of the iceberg that you simply can't see. You know it's there and that it consists of at least half of the total volume of the iceberg. This is the Product Backlog below the middle layer, usually more than six months into the future. The User Stories in this part of the Product Backlog are large, sometimes very large indeed, and capture big ideas and broad brushstrokes of product concepts.

What happens as the visible portion of the iceberg melts? The part immediately below the surface of the water becomes exposed to the air and is now in sharp relief. As the iceberg slowly melts, it rises, showing what had once been invisible to the observer on the surface.

The Product Backlog is the same way. As the Development Team delivers the highly detailed User Stories at the top, the Stories below progressively come into sharper relief until they too become valuable product.

The process by which items move up the Product Backlog, from large to small, from fuzzy to highly detailed, is called Backlog Refinement.

Backlog Refinement

Just as the sun's energy melts the exposed portion of an iceberg, an Agile Team applies energy to the Product Backlog to refine details and generate a steady flow of User Stories that are the right size and level of detail for the Development Team to consume and deliver as valuable working product. The flow of Backlog Refinement follows these steps:

- **Extract** – Smaller User Stories from Epics. There may be two or more layers of extraction from a high-level Epic. Use only as many layers as makes sense for each individual Epic. Avoid defining process where none is needed
- **Define** – Through conversation, define what the User Story means, what is in scope, what is out of scope, how you'll know when you're done, and how you'll prove that you're done (this should sound familiar!)
- **Refine** – Even well-defined User Stories need to go through a refinement stage to ensure that the Development Team understands the last-minute details and knows how to deliver finished product based on the Story. The User Story is now **ready** (or actionable), meaning the Team can pull the Story into a Sprint and deliver it
- **Plan** – With a set of actionable Stories in hand, the Development Team and Product Owner can collaboratively create a Sprint Plan, the result

of which will be a slice of finished, valuable product – a Potentially Shippable Product Increment
- **Deliver** – The finished product increment, which is the point of all of this after all!

Extract → Define → Refine → Plan → Deliver

Notice that an iceberg doesn't melt all at once; it does so gradually, incrementally. The way the Development Team and Product Owner refine the Product Backlog works in exactly the same way, gradually, incrementally, and Just in Time. Don't plan too far ahead! Think in terms of keeping enough actionable User Stories for about two to three Sprints, but no more than that. Remember, you'll always know more about the product, the market, your customers and stakeholders, and the technology, tomorrow than you do today. When it comes to Backlog Refinement – and Agile planning in general – why do today what you can responsibly put off until tomorrow?

Writing User Stories

As a member of an Agile Team, you will definitely be writing User Stories. There are many effective approaches to writing User Stories. The most basic approach from the Development Team Member's perspective is to write a Story that fills a gap you just discovered, often while breaking down larger Stories or while refining the Stories expected to be planned for a close-to-now future Sprint.

Another common Story writing opportunity occurs when you discover a larger gap in the current set of Stories or discover a new feature area, generally through feedback from customers or stakeholders. In these cases, you need to generate a set of new Stories, usually as quickly as possible. A User Story workshop is perfect for these types of situations. Here's the layout:

- Include Development Team Members, Product Owner, customers, stakeholders, end users, marketing, sales – anyone who has ideas to contribute. The Scrum Master or Agile Coach facilitates
- Everyone gets a stack of cards and a pen or fine-point marker – legibility is important

- Post the User Story template on the wall and review it with everyone before beginning
- The goal is simply to write as many User Stories as possible
- Don't worry about Stories that overlap, duplicate others, or are out of context – just write Stories!
- No prioritization – that's the Product Owner's job after the Stories exist
- Remember, this is brainstorming, so freewheeling discussion and off-the-wall ideas are welcome!
- Afterwards, the Product Owner winnows out the duplicates and begins the process of putting the Stories into a preliminary order

> **Try This**
> Pick a real or imagined product and brainstorm on it as a Team for 30 minutes, the goal being to write as many User Stories as possible in the allotted time. Then, pick an Epic and as a Team break it down into at least five smaller Stories. If you don't have an Epic handy, use our example, shown below.

> As Cathy (customer technical support specialist),
> I want to access a customer support record,
> so that I can provide the best possible support
> to each customer.
>
> Acceptance Criteria:
> - Pull customer record by last + first name or customer ID
> - Display full customer contact record
> - Open new contact event window
> - Allow Create-Read-Update on all available fields

Wrapping Up

This chapter is devoted to one of the primary artifacts of Scrum, the Product Backlog. While defined as a part of the Scrum framework, the concept of the Product Backlog is applicable to any Agile framework or approach. The Product Backlog is simply a single-dimensional, ordered list of all the things you've thought of for the product but have not yet done and are not currently doing. The Product Backlog is the primary tool for adaptive planning, as the Product Owner can change its content and ordering quickly and at minimal cost. Under the rules of Scrum, only the Product Owner may order the items on the Product Backlog, although anyone may contribute ideas.

User Stories make great Product Backlog items because they are brief descriptions of valuable functionality written in ordinary language (not techno-babble or jargon) from the perspective of the customer or stakeholder. User Stories are not in any way the equivalent of requirements specifications; instead they are placeholders for the conversations that tease out the details necessary to turn the idea into working product.

Further Reading

Cohn, Mike. *Agile Estimating and Planning.* Upper Saddle River, NJ: Pearson Education, Inc, 2006.

Cohn, Mike. *User Stories Applied: For Agile Software Development.* Boston: Addison-Wesley, 2004.

Jeffries, Ron *XP Magazine* August 3, 2001.

Wake, Bill. *XP123*, August 17, 2003 (http://xp123.com/articles/invest-in-good-stories-and-smart-tasks/)

Chapter 5 Scrum Events

"To accomplish great things, we must not only act, but also dream; not only plan, but also believe."
– *Anatole France*

When I train or coach Teams new to Scrum, there are inevitably questions:

- Why so many meetings?
- Do I really have to attend every meeting?
- Why can't I just sit in my cubicle, put on my headphones, and do my work instead of spending so much time in meetings?

The answer is simple. Teams use Scrum Events (the Scrum framework term for Team meetings) to plan what to do, collaborate on how to do it, show what they accomplished, prepare what to do next, and learn how to improve as a Team. Every Event serves a specific purpose and, thanks to Scrum's insistence on time boxing, every Event is constructed to be (or become with practice) highly effective.

> **Magician's Secret**
> The time boxes Scrum prescribes are there for a very good reason – to drive Event effectiveness. When everyone knows you only have a certain amount of time to accomplish the goal of an Event, it helps keep the discussion on track and moving forward. The Scrum Master, as facilitator of all Events, keeps time and steers the Team to accomplish the goal within the designated time box. When you hit the end of the time box, just stop! The end of the time box is a tripwire that tells your Team that you need to do something to improve the way you work in the context that particular Event. Extending the Event time simply ignores the tripwire and prevents you from improving your effectiveness.

Scrum defines the following Events, all of which we'll cover in more detail in this chapter:

- Sprint – The container into which all of the other events of Scrum take place and also, of course, the Event that produces the Potentially Shippable Product Increment
- Sprint Planning – The first thing you do at the beginning of every Sprint. The purpose of this Event is to develop a plan for the Sprint
- Daily Scrum/Daily Stand-up – Brief coordination meeting that the Team uses to set its course for each day's work
- Backlog Refinement (Story Time) – The Team must engage in some form of look-ahead planning during every Sprint in order to be efficient and effective. More about the naming and details of this Event later
- Sprint Review – Review the Sprint from the product perspective, describing the Sprint Goal, comparing items planned vs. items completed, and then show the finished work to customers, stakeholders, sponsors, and anyone else who cares to see what the Development Team has accomplished as a means of generating feedback on the product direction. The Sprint Review closes the *product feedback loop*
- Sprint Retrospective – The entire Team reflects on the Sprint, looking in particular for ways to improve teamwork and effectiveness. The Sprint Retrospective closes the *teamwork feedback loop,* representing the Team's opportunity to engage in Continuous Improvement and Team maturation.

The following image shows the relative size and position of the Events during every Sprint:

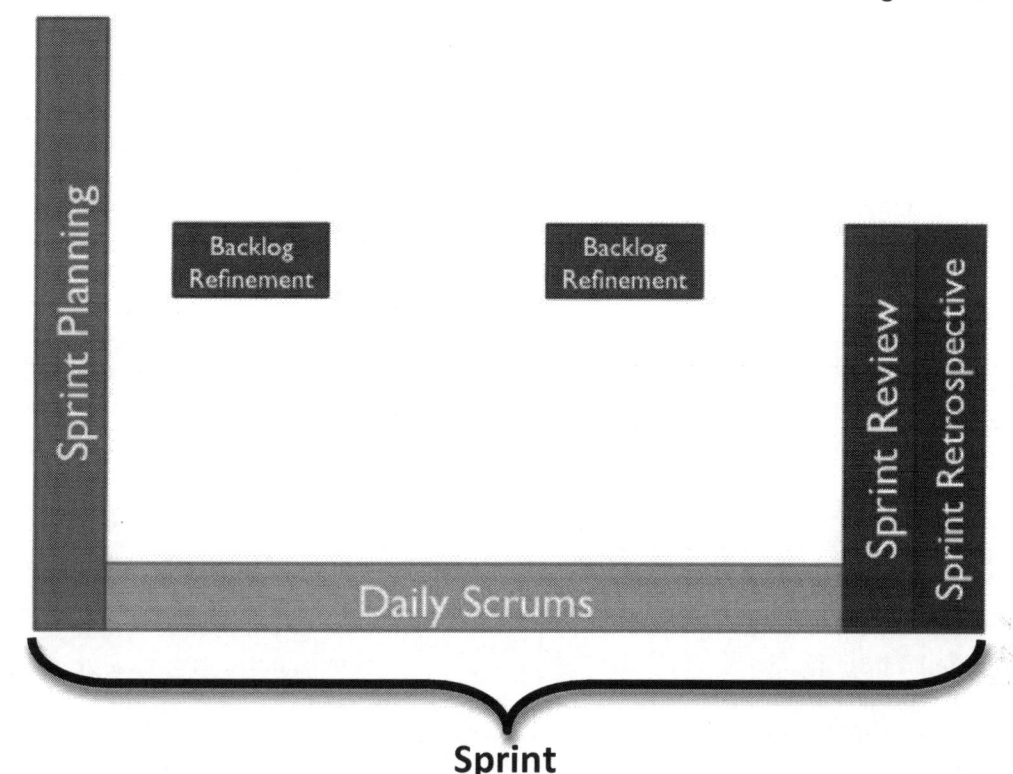

Scrum Master as Facilitator

The Scrum Master facilitates all Scrum Events. That does not mean that the Scrum Master "owns" the Events, nor does it mean that any of these Events are for the benefit of the Scrum Master. The Scrum Master is accountable for the *effectiveness* of the Events, but the Events themselves belong to the Development Team and Product Owner.

> **Magician's Secret**
> If you're a Scrum Master, repeat to yourself the following statement as needed until it becomes muscle memory: "It's not about me. It's all about the Team."

What If We're Not Using Scrum?

Teams and organizations that are not using Scrum can still derive great benefit from a careful exanimation of the Scrum Events, their purposes, and time boxes. You may not be working in Sprints, but you still need to plan as a Team what to do over the near term. A daily coordination and rapid planning/adaptation meeting is equally vital to a Team or organization wanting to derive the benefits of Agile product development. Closing the product and teamwork feedback loops leverages the power of small-batch, rapid-feedback work, which is the foundation of agility – remember Empirical Process Control? And preparing for what's coming up in the near term is absolutely necessary to keep a steady stream of actionable work items flowing to and through the Team.

My advice is to take the spirit of the Scrum Events and apply them to your working rhythms. Use what you learn to improve and change the way you work instead of changing the spirit of the Scrum Events to enable continuation of the status quo. Even better, just unpack Scrum and use its elegant, minimalist roles, events, artifacts, and time boxing to build agility into your Team and organization.

Sprint Planning

The Sprint Planning Event is how a Scrum Team gets set up to work during the Sprint. Nowhere in the Agile Manifesto does it say anything about anarchy or flying by the seat of your pants. As a result, before the Development Team can launch into its Sprint work, the Team needs a detailed plan to use as a guide. As with any Agile plan, a Sprint plan is subject to change as the Team learns more about the work. That does not, however, excuse the Team from engaging in conscientious planning.

The Sprint Planning Event has the following characteristics:

- Parameters
    - The first thing the Team does every Sprint
    - Time boxed at no more than five percent of the Sprint length, which means two hours per week of Sprint length
    - Scrum Master, Product Owner, and full Development Team participate
- Inputs
    - Refined Product Backlog – ordered, estimated, full Acceptance Criteria/Conditions of Satisfaction, well understood, fully actionable. All items meet the INVEST criteria plus any others the Development Team needs to ensure that items are ready for Sprint Planning
    - Velocity – the demonstrated capacity of the Team to deliver finished work during a Sprint, measured in whatever units the Team uses to estimate work items/User Stories (more about this later in this chapter when we look at Backlog Refinement)

- Outputs
    - Sprint Backlog consisting of User Stories the Development Team pulled into the Sprint and the specific Tasks the Team believes are necessary to deliver the selected Stories. This is the Sprint plan, which is subject to change within certain limits discussed the next chapter
    - Sprint Goal – a brief statement that expresses the focus or value proposition of the work to be delivered during the Sprint as represented by the items on the Sprint Backlog
    - Team commitment to deliver the Sprint Goal (**not** the Sprint Backlog!!)

Conducting a Sprint Planning Event is a little more involved, so I've devoted an entire chapter to it. See Chapter 7: Sprint Planning for an in-depth discussion.

Daily Scrum/Daily Stand-up

The Daily Scrum (or Daily Stand-up) is a brief daily meeting for the Development Team to coordinate the day's work. It is most effective when held in the morning, as early as possible. The timing of the Daily Scrum is subject to Development Team agreement, however. It does no good to mandate a time for the Daily Scrum and then have Team Members miss it, or worse, resent it. The Scrum Master is responsible for helping the Team find a workable time and place for the Daily Scrum and also for ensuring that this Event is effective.

The Daily Scrum has the following characteristics:

- Parameters
    - Occurs every work day, same time and place (except Sprint Planning day when it isn't necessary)
    - Time boxed at 15 minutes **maximum**
    - Everyone stands
    - Scrum Master, Product Owner, and full Development Team participate
    - Not for problem solving, but for arranging conversations later, with the appropriate people, to solve problems, issues, and impediments raised
    - Avoids other, unnecessary meetings

- Inputs
    - Everyone is invited, anyone can attend, but...
    - Only the Scrum Team – Scrum Master, Product Owner, Development Team Members – can talk
    - Outsiders may observe, but not speak or otherwise interfere
    - Everyone answers three essential questions (see below)
- Outputs
    - Development Team Members know what everyone on the Team is doing
    - Team Members have one self-assigned, collaboratively agreed Task to work on (but no one has to wait until the Daily Scrum to pick up a new task)
    - No one has more than one open, unblocked Task in progress at any given time
    - Everyone knows the Team's progress toward the Sprint Goal
    - Follow-up conversations are set up
    - All impediments Team Members identified are visible and receive appropriate attention, which may or may not mean attention from the Scrum Master

> **Tip**
> Some Scrum practitioners insist that the Daily Scrum is entirely for the benefit of the Development Team and therefore the Product Owner and Scrum Master should not attend. I am on board with the Daily Scrum being for the benefit of the Development Team, but my experience tells me that only highly mature Teams can function in this context without Scrum Master facilitation. As for the Product Owner, if we're a Team – a Scrum Team that is – why would we deliberately exclude one of our vital teammates from our daily planning event? The best Scrum Teams I've worked with over the years valued participation of all three Scrum roles in the Daily Scrum.

The Three Questions

There is a lot of debate in Agile circles about the "Three Questions" Team Members answer during the Daily Scrum. I have settled on the following formula for Teams I work with:

1. What did I *complete* yesterday?
2. What will I *complete* today?
3. What's preventing me from getting my work done?

I like this formula better than talking about what I "did" yesterday or what I will "do" today because "doing" and "completing" are very different things. When people talk about what they're doing, they tend to get all wrapped up in the implementation details. While the Development Team may find this level of detail appropriate at other times, it is definitely not appropriate for a brief daily coordination and planning meeting. Save the implementation details for design discussions and code reviews. Talk instead about the Task or Tasks you completed yesterday, the Task you are going to take on today (notice the use of the singular "Task"), and what, if anything, is keeping you from being as effective as possible in completing your work.

Another reason to talk about work completed and work to be finished every day is that it forces the Development Team to break work down into Tasks that are no larger than one day each. More than one Team Member may work on a single Task – this is a good thing, think Pair Programming – but every Task takes no more than a day to complete. We'll talk more about Task granularity in Chapter 7 when we cover Sprint Planning, but for now think about the benefits of small, day-or-less sized Tasks in relation to understanding progress toward the Sprint Goal, daily planning flexibility, and Team Member effectiveness, accountability, and morale.

> **Magician's Secret**
> Why stand during the Daily Scrum? This is a very common question, particularly among Forming Teams. So, what's the answer? There are many benefits to standing:
>
> *Standing* reminds the Team to be brief and stick to the purpose of the meeting
>
> *Standing* focuses everyone's attention on the speaker
>
> *Standing* in a circle, effectively shoulder-to-shoulder, demonstrates the physical boundaries of the Team – anyone outside the Team circle is by definition an outsider and may not speak
>
> *Sitting* limits blood flow and actually reduces brain function and IQ

A couple of years ago I was coaching several Teams in an organization when this discussion came up. There were Teams that were sitting and Teams that were standing for their Daily Scrums. With a perfect opportunity in hand, I initiated a small experiment. First, I timed and observed the Daily Scrums of both sets of Teams over the course of a couple of weeks. Then, I asked the sitting Teams to stand and the standing Teams to sit and timed and observed their Daily Scrums again.

The results, although from an admittedly small sample size of about ten Teams total, were startling. The Teams that had been sitting but were now standing cut about 40% off their Daily Scrum time and individual Development Team Members reported a dramatic *increase* in the effectiveness and energy level of the meetings. The Teams that had been standing but were now sitting registered a corresponding 40% increase in Daily Scrum time and individual Development Team Members reported a dramatic *decrease* in the effectiveness and energy level of their Daily Scrums.

So what it boils down to is this: Teams that sit talk about 40% more but actually get less done, while Teams that stand talk about 40% less but actually get more done. So you decide: Why stand during the Daily Scrum?

It's Daily Planning, Not Daily Status Reporting

There is a little status information – the first of the Three Questions is status after all – but that is *not* the focus of the Daily Scrum. The Daily Scrum is also most assuredly not a status meeting for the Scrum Master. Remember, it's all about the Team. It's always all about the Team!

Keep in mind above all else that the Daily Scrum is about making daily adjustments to the Sprint Plan as a means of delivering on the Team's commitment to the Sprint Goal. The Team does this through Development Team Members making individual commitments to the Team – and by the Team collectively holding individual Team Members accountable for those commitments. While Team Members self-assign tasks, no one works on anything without the general consent and agreement of the whole Team. And no one works on anything that doesn't directly contribute to the Team's Sprint Goal.

Impediments

The last of the three questions is about what agilists commonly call impediments. An impediment is anything that is preventing one or more Development Team Members from getting work done in the most effective manner possible. Remember that it is the Scrum Master's responsibility to make sure that impediments *are removed* – it is not the Scrum Master's responsibility *to remove* every impediment!

During the Daily Scrum, the Scrum Master takes note of every impediment the Team raises and ensures that the right people work together to remove those impediments. In most cases, Development Team Members working together can resolve daily impediments. Other impediments, such as infrastructure issues (build or test server down, slow network, dead monitor, etc.) generally need to go to an individual or organizational group beyond the Team's boundaries. It is entirely appropriate that the Scrum Master moves these kinds of impediments to wherever they need to go and follows up as needed until they are resolved. Pushing impediments around the organization would be a serious distraction for the Development Team and it is the Scrum Master's responsibility to ensure that the Team is protected from distractions.

Backlog Refinement/Story Time

You can call this Event whatever you want because it is officially an ongoing activity rather than an Event defined in Scrum.* The name that describes the activity is Backlog Refinement, but my friend and mentor Jeff McKenna calls it Story Time. I like Story Time in part because it's fun and disarming and also because it is equally descriptive. The Team spends time refining User Stories in the Product Backlog, hence Story Time.

I like to set up Backlog Refinement as an actual Event to make sure that it occurs and that the entire Scrum Team participates, just like the other Scrum Events. As usual, the Scrum Master facilitates, ensuring that the Event is effective within the time box, that the discussions are productive and not spinning out of control, and monitoring the Team's energy levels. If the Team begins to droop, and they will because this is hard work, the Scrum Master should suggest a break or even bring the current instance to a close.

The purpose of Backlog Refinement is for the Scrum Team to engage in focused, just-in-time (JIT) look-ahead planning by refining User Stories near the top of the Product Backlog. The rules of Scrum say that a Team can spend as much as ten percent of the total Sprint length refining Stories for future Sprints. That is probably more than generally necessary – consider that ten percent of a two-week Sprint is eight hours – so I generally recommend that the Team spend a couple of hours every week refining the Backlog. Teams that are just getting started almost certainly need to spend more time, in part because the Team is not practiced at Backlog Refinement and also in part

---

* *Scrum Guide*, p. 14.

because the Product Backlog needs more work to get it into good condition to support a steady flow of work.

Refining the Product Backlog means getting User Stories that are likely to be available for the next two to three Sprints ready to be worked on. This can include breaking Epics down into thin, valuable, end-to-end slices of work, filling gaps between existing Stories, refining Acceptance Criteria for existing Stories, high-level exploration of alternative implementation approaches, and certainly estimating Stories. We'll explore estimating techniques shortly.

Backlog Refinement has the following characteristics:

- Parameters
    o Time boxed at no more than ten percent of Sprint length, regardless of the number of instances per Sprint
    o Look-ahead planning for the next two to three of Sprints
    o Product Owner, Scrum Master, and full Development Team participate, as well as any SMEs or stakeholders needed to help answer questions
- Inputs
    o User Stories likely to be worked on during the next two to three of Sprints
    o User Stories that need to be broken down into smaller Stories
    o User Stories that need Acceptance Criteria refinement and/or estimates
- Outputs
    o Detailed, actionable User Stories that meet the Development Team's Definition of Ready
    o Estimates!! (arrived at using a whole-Team estimating technique)
    o Questions for customers/stakeholders

Estimating and Estimates

Agile estimating techniques are very different from traditional estimating. A traditional estimate is typically a calendar overlay that expresses the duration some piece of work will require to be completed. Usually, an expert or manager[*] in whatever area the work involves offers up an estimate of duration based on that individual's experience and expectations. Then, we typically add

---

[*] This formula is derived from early twentieth century Scientific Management as described by Taylor, 1911.

up all the duration estimates and lay out a project plan, perhaps with some buffering to account for the unexpected.

So what's the problem? Well, there are a number of very serious shortcomings, failures, and some outright craziness associated with this approach to estimating:

- Estimates become commitments regardless of buffering, percentages of risk and uncertainty, etc.
- One person's hour of effort, the expert or manager who provided the estimate, does not equate to another person's hour of effort, such as the person who actually ends up doing the work, invalidating the original estimate from the start
- Even if the estimator is the person who will be doing the work, an hour today is not equivalent to an hour days, weeks, or months from now
- Durations cannot be aggregated because of the linear nature of the project estimates – if even one preceding work item is late (takes longer than expected), all following work items are delayed by at least that same amount
- While durations cannot be aggregated, delay/lateness is cumulative
- Optimism bias* makes it impossible for humans to estimate duration because we habitually fail to take into account all the things that could, and usually do, go wrong

Given all that – and this is by no means an exhaustive list – traditional duration estimating simply makes no sense. Humans can't do it, so how about if we use an estimating technique that we can actually put into practice?

Relative Estimates

It turns out that while we humans are exceptionally bad at estimating duration, we are exceptionally good at estimating the relative sizes of things. We don't need to measure the circumference or calculate the volume of a baseball and compare it to the circumference or volume of a golf ball to understand two important things about the two items: The baseball is bigger. Not only that, but it's about three times bigger than the golf ball.

---

* Sharot 2011

Look at the following image:

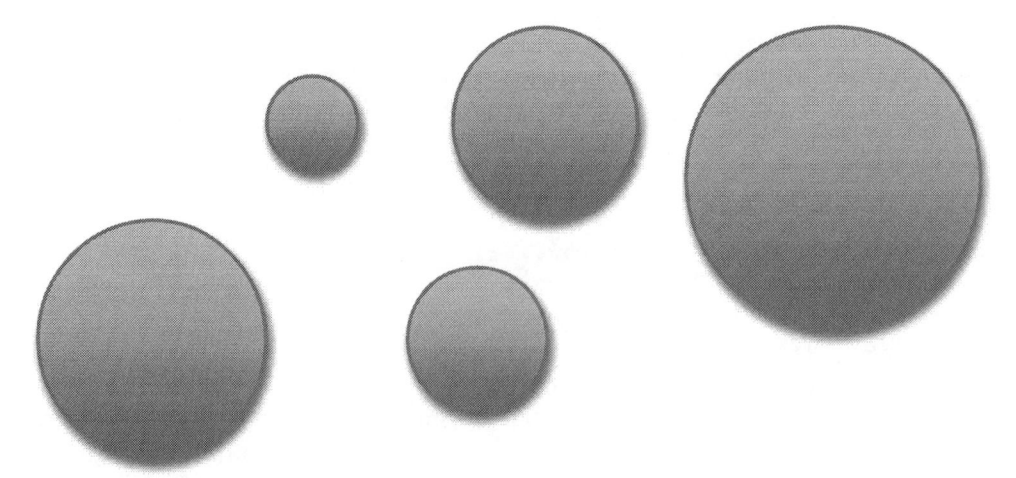

Which ball is the largest? Which one is the smallest? Which ones are in between? If you were to assign a size value of five to the middle-sized ball, what number expressing the relative size difference would you assign to the largest one? How about the smallest one? How about the remaining two? Congratulations! You've just estimated the relative sizes of five similar but different items and as an added bonus assigned numeric values that express those relative size differences.

Relative estimating works because it allows us to answer a question we *can* answer: How big is *this* compared to *that*? We are pre-wired to make such comparisons. On the other hand, we (human beings in general) are fundamentally unable to answer the question: How long will this take?

Relative estimating works as long as the items we are comparing are within an order of magnitude (approximately a ten-to-one ratio) of one another. Once we break out of the order-of-magnitude range, it becomes very difficult to say how much bigger or smaller one item is when compared to another. The bigger item is *a lot* bigger – that's about as much as we can say.

Comparing a baseball and a golf ball is simple because the two are well within an order of magnitude of each other. Now try comparing the golf ball – or the baseball for that matter – to a 75 cm exercise ball. Which one is bigger? That's easy, it's the exercise ball. Ah, but *how much* bigger is it? Hmm, well, definitely a lot but that's as far as we can go because we are attempting to compare two items that, while similar (both are balls) cross the order-of-magnitude boundary.

Now, compare a 75 cm exercise ball with an ordinary beach ball and throw in a 50 cm exercise ball for fun as well. All three are within an order of magnitude so we can make the comparison and assign a numeric value to each ball that expresses its size relative to the other two.

The moral of the story is just this: compare small things to other small things; compare large things to other large things. It's as simple as that!

Story Points

And that's the idea behind Story Points. A Story Point is a numeric value that represents the relative size of a User Story in comparison to other, similarly sized User Stories. Keeping in mind the order-of-magnitude limitation, we can compare small, detailed User Stories to other small, detailed User Stories. We can also compare Epics to other Epics. We just can't compare Epics to small, detailed User Stories, or at least not directly.

Story Points embody the power of relative estimates. Some of the characteristics of Story Points are:

- A measure of the relative size of one User Story compared to other, similarly sized Stories
- Combine implementation effort, complexity, and risk into a single numeric value
- Provide a numeric value that we can use for forecasting and planning
- Clearly separate estimates from commitments!

```
         ┌─────────────────┐
         │  Effort  Complexity │
         │       Risk      │
         └────────┬────────┘
                  ▼
```

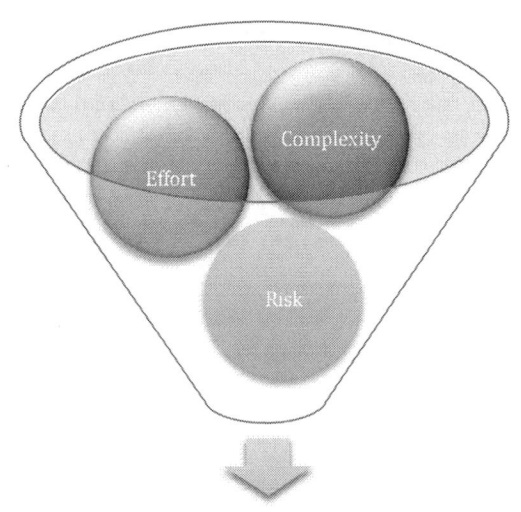

Story Point Estimate

> **Magician's Secret**
> One common objection to relative estimating is that the size of an item depends on who on the Team does the work. My short answer is: "No it doesn't." Since User Stories describe a thin vertical slice through the technology stack, one Development Team Member is very unlikely to be able to do all of the work in every layer of the stack needed to deliver the Story. Since multiple Team Members must combine forces to deliver every Story, the "who works on it" question becomes irrelevant.

> **Magician's Secret**
> Consistency is all that matters in assigning relative estimates to Stories. Just because the Team gets better/faster at delivering Stories does not change the amount of work the Stories describe. A five-point Story is a five-point Story today, tomorrow, next week, next month, next year. Think of it this way, if you have a five-ton pile of gravel to move from your driveway, where the dump truck dropped it, to a border area around your house, does the size of the gravel pile change if you use a front-end loader, a shovel and wheelbarrow, or a tablespoon to move the gravel? Nope. It's still a *five-ton pile of gravel* no matter how you choose to move it.

Approaches to Relative Estimating

There are different ways to get at relative estimates. One technique is not necessarily better than another and you can mix and match as you go, so never feel locked into one estimating technique.

Appropriate relative estimating techniques share some common traits:

* Whole-Development Team activity
* Ensure that all voices on the Team carry equal weight
* Draw out hidden expertise, knowledge, and experience
* Build Team collaboration
* Based on Team consensus, not majority, expert, or loudest-voice rule!
* Focus on understanding the Stories, not on selecting a numeric estimate, as the key value
* Compare the Story under consideration to other, similar work already estimated or completed

The two most popular relative estimating techniques are Planning Poker® and affinity grouping.

Planning Poker®

Planning Poker* is the brainchild of James W. Grenning, one of the authors of the Agile Manifesto. While he no longer uses or even recommends this technique himself, many agilists, myself included, find it extremely useful and appropriate in some Team settings. As the name suggests, Planning Poker is a card game. Learning games bring some fun into the workplace and can contribute significantly to Team growth and maturity.

---

* Planning Poker is a registered trademark of Mountain Goat Software, LLC

The rules of Planning Poker are simple:

1. Each Development Team Member gets a deck of Planning Poker cards; each card has a numeric estimate value printed on it
2. The Product Owner reads a User Story and adds any additional information available, including Acceptance Criteria and any special considerations
3. Development Team Members discuss the Story *briefly* – often the Scrum Master asks the Team to agree on a two- to five-minute time box for the discussions
4. Development Team Members each select a single card representing the relative estimate for the Story under consideration; remember, this is poker – don't show your choice to anyone!
5. Development Team Members show their cards *simultaneously* – the Scrum Master usually calls for the cards, counts down to showing the cards, etc.
6. Development Team Members discuss the outliers, with the high and low estimators initiating the discussion of their estimates
7. After another brief, usually time-boxed discussion, the Team plays another round and repeats the discussion if the estimates didn't converge; only play **up to three rounds** to achieve consensus – playing more rounds will not solve the underlying problem!

> **Tip**
> If this is your first attempt at relative estimating using Planning Poker, pick a Story that your Teammates agree is a "medium" and assign that Story a value of five so that you have a point of comparison. The question of sizing then becomes simpler: is the current Story smaller, larger, or the same size as the "five" Story?

Ponder this question for a moment: Who should play Planning Poker? My answer is quick and very straightforward. *All Development Team Members play.* The Product Owner and Scrum Master *do not play under any circumstances.* I am adamant on this point. The Development Team owns the estimates, period. Any deviation from this rule dilutes the Team's authority and breaks down the carefully balanced boundaries between roles and responsibilities prescribed by Scrum. Product Owners in particular have a strong vested interest in respecting the Development Team's estimates of Stories. The Product Owner's effectiveness depends on making good cost/benefit decisions on a Story-by-Story basis. The Team's estimates provide the vital "cost" element of that equation, helping the Product Owner decide which Stories make business sense and which are too expensive to be justified.

Planning Poker has a number of advantages as an estimating technique:

- Helps avoid anchoring, a phenomenon in which the expert or loudest-voice opinion always wins
- Engages the entire Team, including Development Team Members who wouldn't ordinarily speak up
- Ensures that the Team hears every opinion
- Compels all Team Members to participate in the process of understanding all User Stories the Team is likely to work on
- Helps to ensure that all estimates are based on Team consensus, not on conflict avoidance, capitulation, or cooperation modes
- Builds teamwork and collaboration
- Drives shared vision and understanding of Stories
- It's fun!

> **Tip**
> Why stop at three rounds if the Team is unable to converge on an estimate for a Story? In my experience, three rounds allow the Team every opportunity to achieve a consensus estimate for any and every well-formed, well-understood User Story. If the Team cannot arrive at a consensus estimate after three rounds, playing more rounds is not going to solve the problem.

If the Team cannot converge on a consensus estimate, it is another of those tripwires that tells the Team something important. The most common problem is that the Product Owner simply doesn't understand the Story well enough to answer the Team's questions. A less-common but equally important problem is that the Team lacks the knowledge, experience, or expertise to come to a sufficiently strong shared understanding of the Story to converge on a consensus estimate. (See Spikes later in this chapter for a suggestion on how to overcome this impediment.) If the Team can't even arrive at a consensus estimate for a Story, what are the odds that the Team could pull that Story into a Sprint and deliver it as working product? Slim and none come to mind.

Some agilists recommend going with the largest (pessimistic) estimate if the Team can't converge on a consensus estimate. I really don't like that practice for several reasons. First, re-read the preceding paragraph – the Development Team has to understand a Story to implement it as working product. Second, this policy leads to destructive internal Team dysfunctions including capitulation in the face of the loudest voice in the room, undoing most of the good Planning Poker provides. Play by the rules of the game. It may be a little harder, especially at first, but the benefits will pay for themselves many times over down the road.

Affinity Grouping

Another highly effective Team estimating technique is affinity grouping. The basic idea behind affinity grouping is sorting on a single characteristic by placing similar items together. By extension, the resulting groups of items are then dissimilar and represent categories. In our context, the single sorting characteristic is the relative size of the User Stories being grouped.

Unlike Planning Poker, affinity grouping is not a well-defined game with rules, so you have to make sure your Team is using this technique appropriately. When I coach Teams in the use of affinity grouping, I ask them to follow these steps:

1. Gather the entire Team around a large table or in front of an empty wall or white board
2. The Product Owner holds the stack of Stories needing to be estimated during this session
3. A Development Team Member volunteers to take the Story off the top of the stack, reads the Story to the Team and adds any additional information available, including Acceptance Criteria and any special considerations or notes, and then places the Story card on the table or sticks it to the wall in the physical position that reflects that Story's

size compared to other Stories already placed: underneath an existing Story indicates same size; to the right of an existing Story indicates larger than the existing Story; to the left of an existing Story indicates smaller than the existing Story
    a. If this is the first Story, simply stick it to the wall – position is not important at this point
4. Development Team Members look at the Story placement and decide individually whether they agree or not. Express agreement by leaving the Story in its current position
5. If a Team Member disagrees with the estimate (indicated by the Story's position on the wall or table) he or she grabs the Story, moves it to a different position, *and explains why the move is necessary.* This is critical. Simply moving a Story around the board without explanation defeats the objective which is shared knowledge and understanding
    a. Moving the Story card left (smaller), right (larger), or underneath (same size) in comparison to other Stories on the wall is based on relative size – the only discussion at this point is whether the current Story is larger, smaller, or the same size as another Story in terms of the effort, complexity, and risk of implementation
6. When the card settles into a position, repeat steps three through five for the next Story immediately, with a different Development Team Member pulling the next Story off the stack; if the card does not settle into a position, that is, two or more Team Members continue moving it back and forth, the Product Owner removes the Story from the board and either discusses it later in the session or asks the Team Members why they can't settle on a position for the Story (perhaps both)
7. When all Stories under consideration are in columns of like sizes, draw lines (or use tape) between the columns of Stories and assign numeric values to each column

Affinity grouping has a number of advantages. It's fast and generally easier to get started with than Planning Poker. It's also more physical – based on actually moving the Story cards in relation to each other – making it a great approach for people who think visually. Grouping the Story cards on a wall also gets the entire Team standing and moving, improving energy levels and brain power. Starting with a blank wall or table also immediately breaks the tendency of people to trying to translate relative estimate values – Story Points – into duration. The discussion is focused around the relative sizes of the Stories, not the meaning of the numeric values we may assign to characterize those size differences.

As with Planning Poker, the Product Owner and Scrum Master do not take part in the activity of affinity grouping. The Product Owner provides the Stories and answers questions. The Scrum Master facilitates the session and keeps time. The Team builds the affinity board and assigns the numeric values to the resulting columns. The result of this exercise is a two-dimensional map of the estimated portion of the Product Backlog, sorted by size.

Use an Appropriate Numeric Sequence
Regardless of the relative estimating technique you use, make sure you are using an appropriate numeric sequence for your estimates. There are nearly endless choices, but I like the modified Fibonacci sequence printed on most Planning Poker decks: 1,2,3,5,8,13….

The reason I like this sequence is that it offers a high degree of granularity at the small end, while getting less precise as the estimates increase in size. Bigger Stories are less precise, so getting wrapped around the axle on whether a Story is 12 or 13 Story Points is ineffective and an exercise in false precision.

What about Epics? Some Teams don't estimate Epics. That's fine with me if there is no reason to go there. Most Teams do estimate Epics, however. My recommendation is to separate Epics from actionable User Stories – Stories small enough to be completed during a Sprint – and estimate them using T-shirt sizing: XS, S, M, L, XL, XXL, XXXL…. Assign numeric Story Point values to the T-shirt sizes, such as 20, 40, 100, 200, 350, 500, etc., and you're good to go.

Use affinity grouping for Epics to arrive at the relative sizing, just like with detailed User Stories.

> **Magician's Secret**
>
> *Cap Estimates at eight or even five for Actionable User Stories.* I mentioned in the previous paragraph separating Epics from actionable User Stories and implied that the dividing line should be eight – if the smallest Epic is 13 Story Points, the next smallest number on the modified Fibonacci scale is 8. So that's one reason: to have a clear line of demarcation between Epics and actionable User Stories.
>
> Another, and I think better reason to draw the line at eight or five is to lay down another tripwire that provides your Team with valuable feedback. One of the most common dysfunctions new Teams get trapped into is not breaking Stories down into small enough chunks. Most new Teams end up trying to deliver Stories that are simply far too large to be completed in a Sprint. A part of this problem results from a new, much more comprehensive Definition of Done for Sprint work. The other major part of the problem is that we are simply not accustomed to breaking work down into small, granular bits that can be delivered, complete and working, from end-to-end.

Provided your Team is willing to adjust its estimates based on knowledge gained about fitting Stories into a Sprint, you can use the eight or five tripwire very effectively. Here's the Team agreement: "Any User Story larger than < (eight or five) pick one> is too large to be pulled into a Sprint and must be broken down into two or more smaller Stories."

Another benefit of capping Story Point estimates at five or eight occurs in multi-Team environments. If all Teams agree to the same Story Point cap for actionable Stories, the estimates across those Teams will automatically normalize over time, resulting in Velocity numbers that are in the same band regardless of individual Team differences. Don't carry this too far – and NEVER compare Velocity across Teams – but it can be very helpful for Transparency if the Teams' estimating range is the same.

Spikes

When the Team is unable to come to a consensus estimate of a Story's size, another possible outcome is adding a special kind of story called a Spike to the Product Backlog. A Spike is a Story that describes a small research project that the Development Team needs to conduct in order to be able to estimate and the possibly work on one or more User Stories in the Product Backlog. The Team time boxes a Spike at some number of teammate hours denoting the capacity during a Sprint the Team can afford to devote to the research the Spike describes. The Team Member(s) who take on the Spike during the Sprint are accountable to their Teammates to ensure that they don't exceed the time box without the consent of the entire Team.

The output of a Spike is knowledge to be shared with the entire Team in the form of a presentation of findings, a prototype, a working code snippet, etc., along with a wiki page or other document that captures the results of the research for future reference. Remember, the goal of a Spike is to generate whole-Team knowledge that will make it possible for the Team to estimate and potentially deliver one or more User Stories living in the Product Backlog.

Use Spikes to fill any kind of knowledge gap the Team is experiencing: technical, domain, or otherwise. Just remember that the Product Owner has a say in the matter. Like any Story, a Spike goes into the Product Backlog to be ordered against all other items. If the Team places a time box on a Spike that the Product Owner believes exceeds the value of the dependent User Stories, the Spike is unlikely ever to be a candidate for a Sprint. Better advice is for Development Team Members and their Product Owner to agree on a time box for a Spike that serves the dual needs of Team knowledge and value delivery.

Sprint Review

The Sprint Review is the first of the two Sprint-end Events defined in Scrum. Remember that this Event closes the product feedback loop. To generate product feedback, the Team shows its work completed during the Sprint to customers, stakeholders, end users – anyone with input into the current and future direction of the product. The Product Owner captures the feedback, which then becomes User Stories for the Product Backlog.

The Sprint Review Event has the following characteristics:

- Parameters
    - Time boxed at one hour per week of Sprint length
    - Informal format
    - Full Team participates
    - Two-hour maximum preparation/dry run guideline – just make sure everything works and the Team knows how to show its Potentially Shippable Product Increment
    - Everyone is invited, but customers and stakeholders are the primary audience
- Inputs
    - Increment of potentially shippable product completed during the Sprint
    - Only show accepted Stories – no partially finished work!
    - Sprint Goal compared to accomplishments
    - Sprint Backlog compared to Stories completed
    - Team Member presents
    - Customers and stakeholders invited to try out the new functionality as appropriate
- Outputs
    - Feedback from customers and stakeholders!
    - New User Stories for the Product Backlog
    - Trust generated by meeting commitments

> **Tip**
> Never skip the preparation for the Sprint Review! Make sure you can show all accepted Stories working in whatever environment you have chosen for the purpose, i.e., staging, production mirror, etc. The only thing worse than having to stand up in front of a room of customers, stakeholders, sponsors, executives, and peers and say "we got nothing done" is not to be able to show all the great work you got done because of an environment or other technology failure!

The Sprint Review is not a complicated Event to run. I always recommend that an individual Development Team Member handle the presentation from beginning to end, although other Team Members can certainly add details or answer questions as appropriate. I like it best if the Team decides who will be presenting the Sprint Review this time around at Sprint Planning. How the Team chooses the presenter is up to the Team. You can rotate through the Team Members, ask for volunteers, whatever works. The Scrum Master and Product Owner are ruled out for this job, however. The people who actually did the work should be the ones who show off their accomplishments. Any other arrangement is both inappropriate and a morale killer for the Team.

> **Magician's Secret**
> So why have just one Development Team Member present the entire Sprint Review for the Team? To me, the answer to this question is really important. Having one Team Member present the Sprint Review helps the Team work collaboratively during the Sprint. In addition, the conversation at the Sprint Review stays focused on "our Stories" instead of "my Story" – which often happens when multiple Team Members present at the Sprint Review.

The Product Owner may introduce the presenter and set the stage for the Sprint Review for the customers and stakeholders attending. At that point the Development Team Member presenting takes over. The first part of the Sprint Review is a quick recapitulation of the Sprint: review the Sprint Goal, describe how the Team's accomplishments during the Sprint did – or did not – meet that Goal, and then review the Sprint Backlog, pointing out any changes during the Sprint. The Development Team may have changed the User Stories on the Sprint Backlog – collaboratively with the Product Owner – to achieve the Sprint Goal more effectively. Alternatively, the Team may have completed all of the Stories planned, less than all of the Stories planned, or one or more Stories in addition to all of the Stories planned for the Sprint.

Regardless of what happened, the Team takes collective responsibility for the results of the Sprint. None of this is about negative reinforcement, punishment, blame, or beating up the Team. It's all about being grownups and being accountable for commitments and outcomes. It's also about showing – and showing off – the Development Team's work. It's about generating a powerful sense of Team accomplishment, pride in workmanship, and Team ownership of the product.

The next part of the Sprint Review is to demonstrate the Potentially Shippable Product Increment the Team produced during the Sprint. This is not a comprehensive product review! The Development Team Member-presenter demonstrates the product increment, one Story at a time, allowing or inviting customers to try out the functionality along the way or at the end. The presenter neither shows nor discusses Stories that the Product Owner didn't accept during the Sprint. The presenter already acknowledged anything the Team didn't finish before beginning the demo portion of the Sprint Review, so there's nothing more to say about those Stories – if there were any.

> **Magician's Secret**
> In the early years of Scrum, the Sprint Review was also the point in time when the Team presented the completed Stories to the Product Owner for acceptance. This practice has, thankfully, fallen out of favor. The Team needs to have confidence that everything demonstrated to customers and stakeholders is finished work that the Product Owner has already accepted. The Product Owner simply needs to be available to accept or reject Stories the Team believes to be finished throughout the Sprint. Some Teams like to present Stories to the Product Owner one at a time as they finish them. Other Teams bundle related Stories together to show to the Product Owner. Exactly how the Team and Product Owner collaborate to ensure that acceptance is done before the Sprint Review is up to them.

The Sprint Review ends either when the time box expires or the discussion with those in attendance ends – whichever comes first. The Sprint Review is a great opportunity for the Development Team to interact directly with customers, stakeholders, sponsors, executives, peers on other Teams...you get the idea. Be sure to allow sufficient time for these important interactions to take place!

The new User Stories this Event generates feed the Product Backlog, thereby influencing the product direction and changing the product plan as expressed by – you know the answer – the Product Backlog. Working in small batches, showing your work to customers and stakeholders to generate feedback, and then incorporating that feedback into the product plan dramatically increases the likelihood that the product will succeed. Succeeding by delivering more of what your customers want than your competition is how you win at this game. There's nothing fuzzy headed about any of this: Agile is about winning by being better than your competition. That's about as hard-boiled a business model as you can get.

Sprint Retrospective

The Sprint Retrospective is the last thing the Scrum Team does during the Sprint. It is the Team's formal opportunity to reflect on the Sprint and figure out ways to improve. The Sprint Retrospective Event closes the *teamwork* feedback loop. Since the Team is responsible for getting better at its job, the Team needs to make the most of the opportunity the Sprint Retrospective presents.

The Sprint Retrospective Event has the following characteristics:

- Parameters
    - Time boxed at one hour per week of Sprint length, although may run longer at the Scrum Master's and Team's discretion*
    - Full Team participates – Scrum Master, Product Owner, Development Team Members **only** – no outsiders
    - Scrum Master or external coach facilitates (the latter by Team invitation only)
- Inputs
    - Report on improvement ideas adopted at the previous Retrospective(s)
    - Team input on the course of the Sprint
    - Exercises that drive out Team input
    - Exercises that help the Team generate insights based on the data collected in the previous steps
    - More exercises that drive out specific actions the Team can take to improve
- Outputs
    - Specific items for the Team Improvement Backlog – you do have one of these, right?
    - Specific items for the Organizational Improvement and Impediment Backlogs
    - Team orders the Team Improvement Backlog items and selects the top one or two to work on during the next Sprint
    - Team decides who works on the improvement item(s) and how to determine when they are done – could be the entire Scrum Team, one of the Team roles, or selected Team Members
    - End the Sprint!

---

* This guideline is based on my experience coaching many, many Teams over the years. Other practitioners may have different recommendations. See *Scrum Guide,* p. 12 for example.

I don't intend for this section to be a complete guide to the Sprint Retrospective. The excellent book by Esther Derby and Diana Larsen listed in the *Further Reading* section at the end of this chapter provides a wealth of practical advice for running effective Retrospectives.

There are a few key points I want to make, however. First, the Sprint Retrospective is a closed, Scrum Team-only meeting. I'm emphasizing this point because a major dysfunction occurs when outsiders impose themselves on the Team's Retrospectives. I'm not picking on managers, but typically managers are the biggest offenders in this area. The Team may invite anyone to attend a specific Retrospective or specific part of a Retrospective. If you're a manager and you're not invited, don't take it as a personal insult! Trust the Team to do its job, in this case, making improvements. Ultimately, it is up to your Scrum Master to ensure that uninvited "guests" don't interfere with the serious business of Team improvement.

Secondly, as a Development Team Member always keep in mind that the Retrospective is for you and your teammates. As with all other Team Events, show up on time and be prepared to do your part to help your Team derive the most out of the opportunity for improvement the Retrospective offers. Always speak for yourself only – and be prepared to speak up or participate in whatever exercises your Scrum Master or Agile coach has planned for the Retrospective. Be willing to recommend, accept, and act upon suggestions for improvement. Remember, it's all about the Team.

Next, I am adamant that you never, never, ever skip the Retrospective! If you're too busy to spend a couple of hours with your teammates discovering and implementing ways to be more effective as a Team, I can only say that your Team's priorities are skewed. The best way to reduce your collective Team workload is to get better at delivering what you said, as a Team, you would do during a Sprint. Improvement doesn't just happen magically. It's hard work that requires focused, deliberate attention. If you don't make time and put in the effort required to get better, you simply won't ever get any better.

Some Scrum Teams stop doing Retrospectives after a few months. Sometimes Development Team Members feel that they are too busy to spend the time in the Retrospective – see the previous paragraph for my take on that. More often, in my experience, the Retrospective has gotten stale. The standard "what went well – what didn't go so well – what can we do better?" series of questions runs its course very quickly on most Teams as the low-hanging fruit gets picked and addressed. Use the Derby-Larsen book to infuse the Retrospective with fresh, interesting, and effective exercises and discussions.

If you notice your Team's Retrospectives losing energy or becoming perfunctory, speak up, take action! "But wait," you say, "isn't that the Scrum Master's job?" Well, yes it is, but as a Development Team Member you have both the authority and the obligation to help your Team improve. Anyone can be a Team leader, not just the Scrum Master.

Jean Tabaka used to tell Teams that have dropped the Retrospective (I'm paraphrasing just a bit): "Great! There are no areas in which you can improve as a Team. You've achieved perfection!" That's a wonderful statement because the answer can't help but be "no, we have not achieved perfection." So stick with the Retrospective. One of the first improvements for Teams that have dropped the Retrospective because they found it ineffective is to get better at conducting Retrospectives!

Finally, when the Retrospective comes to a close, go home or go out with your Teammates, but most definitely stop working for the day. The Sprint is over. There is no plan and therefore no work to be done. Bring it to an effective and symbolic close! Come back the next morning, refreshed and ready to plan the next Sprint.

> **Magician's Secret**
> A surprising number of Teams I've coached over the years have adopted the practice of compressing the Sprint Review, Sprint Retrospective, and Sprint Planning for the next Sprint into the same day. It seems like an efficient use of time – spend most or all of one day doing all the big Scrum Events so that there is more time available during the Sprint.
>
> It's a false economy, really – just don't go there. The inevitable result is that the Sprint Retrospective gets squashed between the Sprint Review and Sprint Planning, both of which are "important" product-focused Events. Beyond that serious dysfunction, the Team never has a chance to experience closure at the end of the Sprint. Jamming the three Events together effectively produces continuous Sprints. The negative effects on Team morale and energy are truly insidious.

Plan your Sprint calendar with midweek end/start days – I like starting on Wednesdays and ending on Tuesdays – and plan the Sprint Retrospective as the last thing the Team does on the last day of the Sprint. Close out the finished

Sprint; let it go, leave it behind. Exhale completely. Then come in the next morning refreshed and ready to plan the new Sprint. You'll be amazed at the difference this one simple change makes for your Team.

Wrapping Up

In this chapter we took a quick look at the Events defined in the Scrum framework. We explored the purpose behind the Events as well as the nuts and bolts of conducting each Event. The purpose here is not to provide a complete guide to every possible nuance, but rather to make sure you, the Development Team Member, know what the Events are, how long they can last, and why you're doing them. Each Scrum Event is designed to serve a specific, vital purpose and as such none of the Events constitute waste or overhead. Rather, each Event is designed to produce a specific, measurable output that contributes to the overall effectiveness of the Team. If you're not using Scrum, take what you need from the Events and their time boxes to make your approach as effective as possible.

We also examined relative estimating and two techniques for arriving at whole-Team estimates: Planning Poker and affinity grouping. There is a lot more going on under the hood with relative estimating, so do please dig further into the theory behind Wideband Delphi estimating if you're so inclined.

Further Reading

Derby, Esther and Diana Larsen. *Agile Retrospectives: Making Good Teams Great.* Sebastopol: O'Reilly Media, Inc., 2006.

Sharot, Tali "The Optimism Bias" *Time* Saturday, May 28, 2011 (http://www.time.com/time/health/article/0,8599,2074067,00.html)

Tabaka, Jean. *Collaboration Explained: Facilitation Skills for Software Project Leaders.* Upper Saddle River, NJ: Addison-Wesley, 2006.

Chapter 6 Sprints

"Everything should be made as simple as possible, but no simpler."
– *Albert Einstein*

"Sprint" is the Scrum term that describes a time-boxed period of up to 30 days during which the Team produces a valuable, potentially shippable product increment. Perhaps better put, a Sprint is a time box of between one and four weeks that the Team uses to convert the abstract concepts described by Product Backlog Items (perhaps User Stories) into valuable, working product. Other Agile frameworks use the generic term "iteration" to describe the same thing. Use whichever term you prefer. I use Sprint just to be clear and consistent.

> **Magician's Secret**
> "Sprint" is, in many ways, a very unfortunate term. It implies an unsustainable burst of speed and energy, which is contrary both to the Agile Manifesto Principles and the reality of working in an Agile environment. Product development is a marathon; no one ever would – or could – run a marathon as a series of 100-meter dashes!

Regardless of what you call it, a Sprint is where the rubber meets the road for an Agile Team. In the previous chapter we reviewed all the Events that happen during a Sprint, from Planning through the Retrospective. So great! Your Team has a Sprint Backlog with a Sprint Goal and planned Stories and tasks. Now what do you do?

Delivering a product iteratively and incrementally is very different from traditional, large-batch, stage-based product development. Instead of working toward a distant, large-integration goal, the Team focuses all of its efforts toward delivering a thin slice (increment) of valuable, potentially shippable product at the end of a very short time box (the Sprint). The large product that emerges is composed of multiple iterations of small increments. The point is for each increment – the result of the Team's work during a Sprint – to be a complete, end-to-end, valuable slice of functionality that the Product Owner could potentially release to customers and stakeholders.

The Meaning of "Potentially Shippable"

When we talk about the Development Team building a Potentially Shippable Product Increment every Sprint, what exactly does that mean? The short answer is that the product increment is:

- Finished – Every accepted Story meets all of its Acceptance Criteria and passes all acceptance tests
- Tested – Full unit test coverage is in place and all tests pass
- Integrated – The product increment is integrated into the mainline product codebase and all integration tests pass
- High quality – All code passed Team code reviews and meets current state-of-the-art for engineering practices
- Works! – The product increment does what it is supposed to do end-to-end, meets load and performance needs, and is ready for customer use

Wow, that's a lot of things! "Potentially Shippable" means, really, that the product increment is ready to be deployed to customers in minutes or hours, not days or weeks, should the Product Owner decide to push the big green Release button!

Toward a Definition of Done

The idea of building a product in small increments and delivering each increment as finished work is one of the most disruptive elements of Scrum and other Agile frameworks that include iterative and incremental rhythms. It often produces the appearance of Teams working at a very slow pace compared to the old way of working in functional layers or development stages. The truth is that the Team is doing far more work than previously, taking each Story from concept to a finished, potentially releasable state instead of stopping at "dev done" or "QA ready" or even "QA done," none of which are anywhere near "potentially shippable" in my experience.

This is where the idea of the Definition of Done comes into play. The Definition of Done is a Scrum artifact that describes, in detail, what the word "Done" means in the context of all the work the Development Team delivers. The idea is to build a checklist of items that must be completed in order for the Team to be able to state with confidence that work is finished. The Definition of Done is different than Acceptance Criteria in that it applies to *all* work the Team does. Acceptance Criteria are specific to each Story.

> **Try This**
> Ask your Team to build a Definition of Done by listing out the types of things that are needed in order for the Team to declare work truly finished, that is, *potentially shippable*. Collaborate as a Team by writing items on note cards, one item per card, and then – as usual – stick the note cards on a wall and sort them to find duplicates, gaps, overlaps, etc. When you are done, write out the list on a prominent white board (take a picture!!) or flip-chart sheet and keep it visible in the Team room.

Your Team's Definition of Done may include things like "Unit tests hooked into the automated test framework" or "User documentation complete." What if a Story describes a slice of work that doesn't have a user documentation component? No problem, the purpose of the Definition of Done is to provide a list that the Team can refer to when deciding how to finish work and, equally importantly, when to declare work finished. Stories that do not contain one or more elements covered by the Team's Definition of Done are still just as done.

The Definition of Done is a Team agreement, not an externally imposed standard. Teams are certainly allowed to share their Definition of Done with other Teams and learn from those Teams' Definitions of Done, but no Team should assume that its Definition of Done is universally applicable to all Teams. In an enterprise setting, Teams working on the same product should clearly build a shared Definition of Done, with all Teams having equal ownership. Each Team should post its Definition of Done in a prominent location in the Team room. This is a part of keeping the inner workings of the product and process transparent.

There is a major implication for testing in this business of a Definition of Done. Failing tests may contain some information about quality, but what they really tell you is something much simpler: *You're not done!* Scrum and other Agile frameworks are entirely binary on "doneness" – work either is or is not done. There are no partial states of done, no percentages of completion, just *done* or *not done*. Failing, or even worse, unwritten tests tell you very simply that you're not done.

The Mini-waterfall Trap

Most Teams that are new to Scrum find the transition difficult for various reasons. One of the biggest areas of difficulty is adjusting to a new and very different way of working within each Sprint. Some Teams get hung up on slicing Stories into end-to-end, valuable functionality. Other Teams get stuck because their Stories, while describing end-to-end slices, are just too large to finish during a Sprint.

Even when Teams overcome these and other common difficulties, they often fall into the mini-waterfall trap. Basically, mini-waterfall (or Fast Waterfall, or Scrummerfall, or Wet Agile, or WAgile, or FrAgile – there are many more such terms in use) looks like this during the Sprint:

> Analyze – Design – Code – Merge – Integrate – Test

Team Members work on Stories in the same way they used to work before moving to Scrum, breaking the Sprint up into miniature waterfall stages with large amounts of work in progress (WIP) all the time. Every Story goes through "analysis" before passing to "design." Next is "coding" perhaps. The problem is, just as in standard Waterfall, we trim from the end to meet the deadline, which means "testing" (or "QA" or whatever you call it) falls off the end of the Sprint.

The Mini-waterfall Trap

Another symptom of mini waterfalls is the following Sprint layout I saw recently:

Sprint 04 Milestones:	
04/01	Story Analysis & Design
04/03	Sprint Planning
04/04	Begin Feature Development
04/24	Code Freeze/Ready for QA
04/25	Functional QA Begin
04/28	Sev 1 & 2 QA Defects Fixed EOD
04/29	Sprint Review/Retrospective
04/30	SP04 Release

What does this look like to you?

> **Try This**
> Ask your Team to think about the meaning of dropping some or all of the testing at the end of a Sprint. How does that square with the Team's Definition of Done? If tests are not being written, not being run, or left in a failing state at the end of a Sprint, can the Team really call the associated Stories finished work? What if all Stories planned for the Sprint suffer from one or more of these conditions? Did the Team actually finish *any* work during the Sprint?

Technical Debt

Technical Debt is the accumulation of unfinished and/or substandard quality work over time. In an Agile context, we define unfinished as any work that fails to meet the Team's Definition of Done or any Story's Acceptance Criteria, sometimes both. Some aspects of Technical Debt include:

* Inconsistent architecture and/or design
* Lack of automated unit, regression, and acceptance tests
* Poor/inconsistent code standards
* Code yet to be merged or integrated, including code living in branches other than the mainline
* Mounting manual regression test effort – see test automation above
* Unknown, untested performance
* Bugs – known and unknown
* Adding new functionality breaks existing functionality

> **Try This**
> With your Team, identify areas of Technical Debt in your product, especially those that aren't included in the list above. Collaborate as a Team by writing items on note cards, one item per card, and then stick the note cards on a wall and sort them to find duplicates, gaps, overlaps, etc. Compare the Technical Debt list to your Team's Definition of Done and modify the latter as needed to ensure that you are not accumulating additional Technical Debt.

My friend and colleague Dr. Dan Rawsthorne defines Technical Debt as the viscosity of the code.[*] If working in the code is like moving through air, meaning you can work with little or no resistance, the code is likely very sound and has little or no Technical Debt. If, on the other hand, working in the code is like wading waist deep through mud, you've got a problem.

Technical Debt and the Agile Death Spiral

The problem with Technical Debt is that it accumulates just like credit card debt. As you add more and more to your debt load, it becomes increasingly difficult for you and your Team to function. Just like interest on credit card debt that eventually exceeds your income, if your Team is accruing Technical Debt every Sprint, before long you will find yourself in a death spiral. As the Team's ability to deliver working product declines under the weight of the accumulating Technical Debt, pressure (internal and external to the Team) to

---

[*] Rawsthorne, p. 121

deliver more increases. In response to that pressure, the Team takes even more shortcuts, adding Technical Debt at an ever-faster rate.

The end game happens very quickly. After a few months the accumulated Technical Debt load exceeds the Team's capacity and progress on the product stops altogether. The only way out is to spend as many Sprints as necessary paying down the accumulated Technical Debt, which means *not working on any new features until the debt is paid off.* That's not a formula most organizations can support, so instead the product simply dies as it has become impossible to add any new features to it. There aren't many possible happy endings to this scenario.

The Solution: Focus on Finishing Stories

Tackling Technical Debt requires that the Development Team have a complete Definition of Done and the discipline to adhere to it. This includes discipline from the Product Owner to avoid pushing the Team to work in ways that undercut the Definition of Done. The Team also needs to work in a new way, focusing on finishing Stories rather than working on phases or functional layers that cross Story boundaries. Think of it this way, if the Team finishes everything but the "testing" phase of the ten Stories on the Sprint Backlog, how much work did the Team finish during the Sprint? The answer is nothing, nada, zip, zilch. The Team worked very hard, no doubt, but got nothing done. Working in the mini-Waterfall style essentially makes every Sprint a coin flip. Either the entire Sprint was successful or the entire Sprint was a failure. Oh, and then there's that Technical Debt issue that inevitably builds up as well.

When the Development Team swarms around finishing Stories, every Sprint is extremely likely to be successful because the Team will always have finished work to show at the Sprint Review. This is perhaps a narrow definition of success in the context of a Sprint, but at a very basic level it's a good one. Since the Stories are largely independent of one another, the Team can work down the Sprint Backlog, which is also in priority order, after all, delivering finished Stories one by one throughout the Sprint.

This is the essence of working in small batches. The Sprint Backlog represents a small batch of valuable work. Each Story on the Sprint Backlog represents an even smaller batch of valuable work. Each Task that contributes to the completion of a Story represents an even smaller batch of work, not valuable in and of itself, but contributing to the Story's value. Working in short, rapid cycles within a Sprint, by keeping the Team's focus on delivering finished Stories, makes it possible to keep all work within the framework of the Team's

Definition of Done. When you work this way you'll find that not only are you able to pay down existing Technical Debt, you are also able to avoid adding new Technical Debt.

Approaches to Eliminating Technical Debt

So great, your Team is now focused on swarming around a couple of Stories at a time. Unfortunately, your Team has already created (or inherited) a pretty heavy Technical Debt burden. What do you do? Well, there are really only two things you can do about existing Technical Debt:

1. Stop adding to it, and
2. Start paying it off in increments as large as you can afford

The first one is the easier of the two – not that either one is inherently easy. All you have to do is, as a Team, agree on a rigorous Definition of Done and be disciplined in applying it. Doing so stops the addition of new Technical Debt right away. Your Team will need organizational support to do this as well, but usually casting this approach in terms of quality and customer satisfaction can take you far. And then there's the promise of investing in paying off Technical Debt now so your Team and organization can move faster in the future. If those two arguments fail to convince organizational leadership to take on Technical Debt, well, you just learned something extremely important about your organization!

Okay, so you've stopped adding new Technical Debt, how do you attack the existing debt burden? Unless you can stop all new product development for a few weeks or even months, you'll have to take on the existing Technical Debt on an installment plan. Try allocating ten or twenty percent (or more) of the Team's capacity every Sprint to a special class of Stories that address paying off Technical Debt. If your Sprints are two weeks in length that means every Development Team Member spends one or two days of every Sprint working on paying off Technical Debt. You don't have to set up specific days for Technical Debt repayment, although there's nothing inherently wrong with that approach. Just make sure you have items in every Sprint Backlog that account for Team capacity spent paying off Technical Debt.

Some practices that can help you prevent and pay off Technical Debt include:

- Agile architecture – emergent architecture
- Continuous refactoring (neighborhood refactoring)
- Automated unit tests with code coverage standards

- Test Driven Development/Behavior Driven Development (TDD & BDD)
- Continuous Integration
- Static analysis
- Automated functional tests
- Regression/integration/performance testing, automated and in "live like" test environments
- Automated deployment
- Peer code reviews
- Pair programming
- Build and implement a rigorous Definition of Done!

Again, this is not an exhaustive list, just some ideas to help you get started paying off Technical Debt.

> **Try This**
> Work with your Team to build a list of practices that compliment your Definition of Done in eliminating Technical Debt. Write practices on cards and sort them as you have done numerous times before with other collaborative, whole-Team efforts, and order the list in terms of importance to eliminating the current Technical Debt balance in the product.

Reciprocal Commitments

Sprints are based on the idea of reciprocal commitments. The Development Team commits to focus all of its collective efforts on delivering the Sprint Goal, producing a Potentially Shippable Product Increment as proof. On the other side of the table, the business and Product Owner must also commit to leaving priorities and content of the Sprint Backlog unchanged during every Sprint. The Development Team has no chance of living up to its end of the bargain if the business and Product Owner don't live up to theirs.

> **Try This**
> Determine an appropriate Sprint length for your environment. Meet with your Team, including the Product Owner, stakeholders, and sponsors (if possible) and discuss these questions:
>
> How stable has your Sprint Backlog been in general during the last six months?
>
> How long can the business go without changing priorities – expressed as the order and content of Stories in the Sprint Backlog?
>
> How many times have changing priorities disrupted your Team's Sprints during the last six months?
>
> Is your current Sprint length appropriate to support this rate of change?
>
> Is a lack of organizational focus a contributing factor to instability?

Changes to the Sprint Backlog

If the Stories on the Sprint Backlog cannot remain stable during a Sprint, there are only two options available. The first, and most desirable because it is the least disruptive, is for the Team and Product Owner to negotiate a change to the Sprint Backlog. If the change amounts to swapping a couple of agreed-to Stories for a couple of comparably sized Stories from the Product Backlog *and* the Team hasn't yet started any work on the Stories to be swapped out, well, just make the swap and get on with it.

If the Team *has* started work on one or more of the Stories to be swapped out, things get a little more complicated. First, the Team has to provide the Product Owner with an estimated cost for reverting all work in progress back to a known state – the state before the Team began working on the Stories in question. (The partially finished work has to be reverted to the last known-good state because unfinished work is both waste and Technical Debt.) For example, if two Team Members will have to spend a full day reverting changes and rebuilding the code base, the estimated cost of the change is the fully burdened cost of those two Team Members per day. The reason the Product Owner needs this estimate is to help him or her understand if the benefit of dropping and swapping the Stories in question is worth the cost of doing so. With this information in hand, the Product Owner can then make an informed cost-benefit decision on whether to ask the Team to change to the Sprint

Backlog or simply allow the Team to continue uninterrupted. The new Stories then just go onto the Product Backlog until the next Sprint.

The second and more disruptive way to deal with change to the Sprint Backlog occurs when the necessary changes are so sweeping that they invalidate the Sprint Goal and with it the Team's Sprint Commitment. The only alternative is to cancel the current Sprint Plan. The Product Owner has official authority to cancel a Sprint Plan. However, my view on this is that the Development Team and Product Owner should agree that canceling the Sprint Plan is the only way to move forward. As always, make this a collaborative decision.

The mechanism for canceling a Sprint Plan is both costly and important to follow to the letter. First, the Development Team reverts all unfinished work, including all work in progress. This means all work on Stories that the Product Owner has not yet accepted must be reverted to the last known-good state and the entire codebase rebuilt and the full test suite run, bringing the product to a stable state. Any finished work, including accepted Stories, can stay put because that work meets the Team's Definition of Done and so does not contribute any waste or Technical Debt to the product. Once the product is in a stable, known state, the whole Scrum Team plans a new Sprint for the remaining days on the Sprint calendar. Let's say the Team and Product Owner agree to cancel the current two-week Sprint on Day Five. The Team spends Day Six reverting the codebase and then on Day Seven, the Team spends two hours planning what is in effect a three-day Sprint. In this example, the cost of canceling the Sprint is, at a minimum, the fully burdened cost of the entire Team multiplied by the full day spent reverting the product to a known-good state plus the two hours spent planning the remainder of the Sprint. If any completed Stories have to be thrown away, add the cost of those Stories to the cost of the proposed change.

> **Magician's Secret**
> Why adhere to this costly ritual for canceling and re-planning a Sprint? The idea is to make the cost of change transparent so that the Product Owner, business, and sponsors can make an informed decision. Change during a Sprint is never free and major disruption of a Sprint carries with it a major cost that needs to be visible. The cost of a canceled Sprint Plan, in my experience, is almost always greater than the benefit the business would realize as a result of canceling the Sprint Plan. The punch line is to follow the rules so that the Product Owner can perform a cost-benefit analysis of the proposed change. Usually, given the real numbers involved, it is cheaper to complete the Sprint as planned and simply build the changes into the next Sprint without disrupting the Team's work or rhythms.

Velocity

Velocity is a concept that comes out of working iteratively. Velocity is simply the capacity of the Team to deliver finished work during a fixed time period, such as a Sprint, to put it in Scrum terms. Velocity is expressed in whatever units the Team uses to estimate Stories. If the Team estimates Stories using Story Points, Velocity is the number of Story Points the Team completes during a Sprint. It's really as simple as that.

The Development Team uses Velocity as a guide to how much work to pull into a Sprint. Recent Velocity is usually a very useful indicator for the Team to forecast its capacity. The concept is very simple: Use past performance as a guide to planning the immediate future. For example, if a Team's average Velocity over the last six Sprints is 25 Story Points, all other things being equal the Team is reasonably likely to be able to pull about 25 Story Points' worth of work into the next Sprint.

> **Magician's Secret**
> Be smart about how you use Velocity as a Team planning tool. If the average Velocity of the last three Sprints was 25, but the individual Velocities were 20, 40, and 15, why would you even think you should plan on 25 Story Points' worth of work this Sprint? If your Team's Velocity is fluctuating wildly from Sprint-to-Sprint, you should spend some serious Retrospective time working on figuring out how to be more consistent and predictable as a Team.

Velocity is also the Product Owner's primary forecasting and planning tool. After collecting even a few such data consistent points, the Product Owner has something rare in the product development world: the power to forecast and plan with confidence. With the Team's demonstrated capacity to deliver finished work in hand, the Product Owner can forecast with a high degree of confidence how much Product Backlog the Team can deliver by a given point in the future. Put another way, past performance does indicate future results. The Product Owner's confidence in the forecast is also directly correlated to the quality and consistency of the Velocity data the Team generates. As with every aspect of Agile planning, the Product Owner and the business must recognize that the quality and consistency of the data matter, and even more that the veracity of the forecast declines as the time horizon increases. Nonetheless, forecasting with Velocity is rigorous and defensible as it is based on empirically derived data representing the demonstrated capacity of the Team to deliver finished work.

While Velocity-based forecasting is a Product Owner skill and therefore beyond the scope of this handbook, there are some aspects of Velocity you should be aware of. First, never compare Velocity across Teams! Since each Team's estimating scale is unique, comparisons of Velocity are pointless at best. Indeed, comparing, or worse, measuring Teams based on Velocity is an insidious and destructive practice. It takes nothing for a Team to game its estimates to bump up Velocity, but the cost in cynicism and lost forecasting ability is incalculable. Simply aggregate Velocity across Teams to build a forecast.

Velocity must be an empirically derived data point subject only to collection and analysis, never a performance metric!

> The Velocity Certainty Principle: *Any attempt to influence Velocity invalidates Velocity as a forecasting tool.*

What If You're Not Done?

This is the real world and in the real world stuff happens and not all of it is good. What do you do if you get to the end of a Sprint and you're not done? The thing you *don't* do is extend the Sprint. Sprints begin and end on fixed calendar dates, following a repeating, predictable cadence. If you're not done with everything you planned as a Team to complete during the Sprint, acknowledge the situation and learn from it. The end of the Sprint is another of the many tripwires purposely set to provide feedback and opportunities for learning. If your Team pulled in more work than you could collectively complete during a Sprint, use that feedback to learn how to pull in a more appropriate amount of work next Sprint. Never throw away feedback and learning opportunities; they are your Team's only avenues to improvement.

Another common real-world situation occurs when your Team's Definition of Done does not extend all the way to potentially shippable every Sprint. Recognize that this is a conscious decision to leave some work unfinished until sometime before the next release.

Some Teams and organizations leave work unfinished because they lack the physical infrastructure or simply the people needed to integrate and perform all of the product testing that would be necessary for every Sprint to produce a Potentially Shippable Product Increment. Some examples include:

- Mean Time Between Failure (MTBF) testing
- Stress, performance, load, or usability testing
- Final user acceptance testing (UAT)
- Compliance testing, documentation touchups

Teams and organizations that leave work unfinished end up spending one or more Sprints getting caught up. These so-called release or hardening Sprints add no value and are therefore one hundred percent waste. On the other hand, they may also be the most effective option available to complete work that must be done on the product before releasing it to customers.

My advice is simply this: since release (hardening) Sprints add no value and are then by definition 100 percent waste, minimize the number of Sprints you spend doing this work by moving bits and pieces of it back into the product development Sprints. Put another way, identify elements of your release Sprints that can be mixed into product development Sprints, effectively extending your Definition of Done incrementally. The less risk you load into the end of the release cycle, the more likely you are to succeed in producing a winning product.

Here are some ideas that may help you get started:

- Integrate the entire product every other Sprint (assuming one- or two-week Sprints, every Sprint if you are on a longer Sprint cycle)
- Run the full functional test suite at each integration point
- Run performance, MTBF, and stress tests at every integration point
- Perform usability testing as often as possible, whether the product is integrated or not; test product segments for usability
- Intersperse compliance and documentation work throughout the development Sprints
- Do UAT as early and as often as practical – then push the limits to do it even more often
- Work deliberately toward building continuous integration into your Sprints – it's not just tools and hardware, but an attitude and a commitment within the Team
- Automate, automate, automate. Let the computers do the repetitive work. They're really good at it!

The ultimate goal of all of this is to extend your Definition of Done so that you don't incur the waste of one or more release or hardening Sprints before every release. I have worked with organizations that were able to reduce their release Sprint burden from three months (six Sprints) to one month (two Sprints) over the course of just six months. A large part of that 66% reduction in waste came from Teams adhering to their Definition of Done and simply not adding defects and technical debt into the codebase. The rest resulted from the conscious effort to pull as much pre-release work as possible into the normal product development Sprints. The increase in speed and efficiency in this case had a major impact on customer satisfaction, which had an equivalent impact on the company's bottom line. The drive to eliminate those release Sprints entirely became a major organizational priority from that point forward.

Wrapping Up

Sprints are the heartbeat of an Agile organization and its Teams. In this chapter we looked at what a Sprint is and some common problems and issues that arise, particularly when Teams and organizations are new to the concept of iterative and incremental development and delivery. Attempting to bolt the concept of Sprints onto existing work patterns is a very common dysfunction among organizations and Teams new to Scrum. Using Sprints to build iterative and incremental development muscle almost always requires that organizations and Teams fundamentally change the way they work.

Further Reading

Beck, Kent. *Test Driven Development: By Example.* Boston: Pearson Education, 2003.

Feathers, Michael. *Working Effectively With Legacy Code.* Upper Saddle River, NJ: Prentice Hall, 2005.

Fowler, Martin. *Refactoring: Improving the Design of Existing Code.* Boston: Addison-Wesley, 2000.

Humble, Jez and David Farley. *Continuous Delivery: Reliable Software Releases Through Build, Test, and Deployment Automation.* Upper Saddle River, NJ: Addison-Wesley, 2011.

Martin, Robert C. *Clean Code: A Handbook of Agile Software Craftsmanship.* Upper Saddle River, NJ: Prentice Hall, 2008

Rawsthorne, Dan and Doug Shimp. *Exploring Scrum: The Fundamentals (People, Product, and Practices).* USA: Self-published, 2011.

Chapter 7 Sprint Planning

"Failing to plan is planning to fail."
– *John Wooden*

It's time for a quick review. The Sprint Planning Event is how a Team gets set up to work during the Sprint. Nowhere in the Agile Manifesto does it say anything about anarchy or flying by the seat of your pants. As a result, before a Team can launch into its Sprint work, the Team needs a detailed plan to use as a guide. As with any Agile plan, a Sprint plan is subject to change as the Team learns more about the work.

> **Magician's Secret**
> Why an entire chapter on Sprint Planning? From the Development Team's point of view, Sprint Planning is the most involved of the Scrum Events. Every Team Member is fully engaged in the entire process of planning a Sprint. And while the Product Owner and Scrum Master certainly help out, the Development Team does all of the heavy lifting in Sprint Planning. With that reality in mind, it seems entirely appropriate to cover this vital planning event in detail from the Team's perspective.

When Should You Do Sprint Planning?

Sprint Planning is the first thing you do at the beginning of every new Sprint. When I coach Agile Teams, I really want the Team to hold its Sprint Planning Event as early as possible on the morning of the first day of the Sprint. In most organizations I've worked with, starting Sprint Planning at 9:00 or 9:30 AM works very well. It may be that some Team Members have to arrive a little earlier than usual to accommodate this schedule, but it's only once per Sprint and I've found most Team Members are okay with that. That said, the timing of Sprint Planning, like everything else a Team does, must be set through a consensus decision by the Team.

The other important consideration about Sprint Planning is the day of the week on which you start your Sprints. I like a midweek Sprint begin/end schedule for a variety of reasons, some of which we covered in previous chapters. Just to review, it's absolutely best to close out one Sprint before starting the next one. In practice this means holding the Sprint Review and Retrospective on the last day of the Sprint and then starting up the next morning with Sprint Planning. The reality of closure is extremely important. Since our cycle is Plan-Do-Inspect-Adapt, that means without a plan there is actually nothing to do. And that is a very good thing indeed. At the close of every Sprint there is time, even if just overnight, to exhale, let it go. The power of even that brief but very real break is amazing in terms of Team energy and morale.

Equally important is the way this Sprint cadence helps enforce honesty on the vital point of work that is done and work that is not done. There is no opportunity to finish later. The Sprint is over. Anything the Team didn't finish during the Sprint goes back into the Product Backlog for the Product Owner to evaluate and reorder. The Team can never assume that a Story they didn't finish during one Sprint will automatically carry over to the next Sprint. That's the Product Owner's decision.

With all of that in mind, here's a Sprint calendar I recommend. This is a two-week example, but you get the idea if your Sprint length is different.

Sun	Mon	Tues	Wed	Thurs	Fri	Sat
	1	2 Sprint Review & Retrospective	3 Sprint Planning	4 *Backlog Refinement Development →	5	6
7	8	9 ← Development	10	11 *Backlog Refinement →	12	13
14	15	16 Sprint Review & Retrospective	17 Sprint Planning	18 *Backlog Refinement Development →	19	20
21	22	23 ← Development	24	25 *Backlog Refinement →	26 … (Repeat)	27

> **Magician's Secret**
>
> Why not have Sprints end on Friday and start on Monday? That would provide a nice weekend break between Sprints, enhancing the sense of closure, right? Well, not so much in practice. First of all, most holidays in the USA fall on Mondays. So why build your Sprint calendar to fail a known number of times every year?
>
> Also, in my experience, two major problems result from the Monday start/Friday end Sprint schedule. The first is that Development Team Members are tempted to show work at the Sprint Review that isn't really done. "Oh, we're done with Story x, we just have a few details and some testing to finish up over the weekend." Yikes! Just don't go there.
>
> The second problem that occurs with the Monday start/Friday end Sprint schedule is that Team Members want to get a head start on the next Sprint and start working on it over the intervening weekend. What's wrong with that, you might ask? The problem is that all such work is completely speculative, performed before Sprint Planning and outside of the collaborative Team framework. Such activity can be deadly to Team cohesion and morale and is always wasteful as work inevitably ends up being thrown away after Sprint Planning. Even worse, all such work is effectively "off the books," not accounted for and violating our basic operating principle of Transparency.
>
> Build quality into your Sprint calendar by not allowing these two major dysfunctions to occur. Start with Sprint Planning on Wednesday mornings and end with the Sprint Review and Retrospective on Tuesday afternoons. You'll be glad you did!

What Do You Need to Plan a Sprint?

Again, by way of review, the two main inputs to Sprint Planning are a batch of Ready Stories from the Product Backlog and an indication of the Team's capacity for the Sprint.

The first of these, a batch of Ready Stories, should already be in place if your Team is making effective use of Backlog Refinement. Stories are Ready for Sprint Planning when they are outfitted with complete Acceptance Criteria, the Team has estimated them, which indicates that the Team collectively understands the Stories well enough to consider them candidates for implementation, and the Story size is appropriate for inclusion in a Sprint.

The second input, an indication of the Team's capacity for the Sprint includes Velocity, but also needs to take into consideration anything unusual that affects the Team's capacity, such as vacations, holidays, training classes, etc. Anything that pulls one or more Team Members away from Sprint work for more than a few hours reduces the Team's capacity for that Sprint. Rather than adding up hours, which works no better for Team capacity estimates than it does for work estimates, simply figure out the percentage of Team capacity to deduct from the Team's average Velocity over the last ten Sprints and go with that as a guideline for the Team's capacity. For example, if the Team's average Velocity over the last ten Sprints is 50 Story Points and the loss of capacity looks like about twenty percent, use 40 Story Points as a guide to the amount of work the Team can pull into the Sprint. This isn't rocket surgery, so rough estimates like this are plenty good enough to serve the purpose at hand.

Another word is in order about using Velocity as an input to Sprint Planning. Some Teams disregard Velocity entirely and plan based on their collective "gut" feel for the proposed Stories. Highly experience, mature, stable Teams can do this easily, particularly since these Teams generally break all their Stories down into approximately the same size chunks. All other Teams, however, need to have some clue about their recent capacity to deliver finished work during a Sprint. That clue is Velocity, usually averaged over some number of Sprints with any radical outliers (beyond two standard deviations from the median or mean) tossed out. Velocity history is neither a ceiling nor a floor for the Team's planning; it is simply a reality check on the Team's planning that helps keep optimism bias from distorting what the Team agrees to pull into the Sprint.

The final ingredient for Sprint Planning is the entire Team – Scrum Master, Product Owner, and Development Team Members – assembled to do the planning.

No Surprises

A key element of successful and mostly painless Sprint Planning is conscientious Backlog Refinement. When all Development Team Members have previously seen, discussed, and been able to agree on an estimate for all of the Stories the Product Owner presents at Sprint Planning, the result is an effective and efficient planning event. Okay, so I get it that sometimes new Stories come to light between the most recent Backlog Refinement Event and Sprint Planning, but those occurances should be the exception, not the rule. The fewer surprises the Team has to deal with in Sprint Planning, the faster, smoother, and more successful your Sprint Planning Events will be. Honest.

The Sprint Goal

A part of the purpose of Sprint Planning is to arrive at a consensus Team commitment to a Sprint Goal, which is then represented in the Stories the Team pulls into the Sprint Backlog. Put another way, the Sprint Backlog contains the details of how the Team intends to deliver the Sprint Goal as a Potentially Shippable Product Increment.

> **Magician's Secret**
> In the original formulation of Scrum, the Team's commitment was to delivering the Stories on the Sprint Backlog. This is an area of continuing discussion and change in the Agile community, but I adhere to the current practice that the Sprint Goal is what the Team commits to deliver during the Sprint. In keeping with Agile planning principles, the implementation details are subject to change as the Team generates knowledge through doing work. Scrum is now more closely aligned with the Agile Manifesto in this area.

On the other hand, the Team's commitment to completing the Sprint Backlog Stories can be a useful approach for new Teams. Remember, the quickest route through the painful Forming and Storming phases of Team maturity is to focus the Team's attention on attainable short-term goals. When a Sprint Goal is too high-level or abstract – often the case with Forming or Storming Teams – committing to delivering the planned Stories can be a very useful approach. The caveat here is to make sure the Sprint Backlog represents an attainable, valuable goal. Getting a new Team some quick wins pays long-term dividends.

So what exactly is a Sprint Goal? The Sprint Goal is a brief statement that captures the value that the Team intends to deliver by the end of the Sprint. It's like a vision statement for the Sprint describing the purpose behind all the effort and focus the Team is committing to apply during the Sprint. Here are a few examples:

- Build one-click payment into the Checkout page
- Add trend analysis to the stock performance charting app
- Enhance security by adding browser recognition and the customer-supplied security challenge questions to the login sequence

Notice that these are very brief statements of purpose, not detailed descriptions of everything the Team plans to accomplish during the Sprint. That's the essence of a Sprint Goal – it provides a target to aim for, but does not constrain how the Team hits the target.

The Development Team and Product Owner collaborate on writing the Sprint Goal during Sprint Planning and then the Team commits to delivering a potentially shippable product increment that expresses that goal by the end of the Sprint. The Stories, and even less so the Tasks (more about those later), represent the Team's action plan for achieving the Sprint Goal.

The last thing I want to say about the Sprint Goal is that it helps the Product Owner focus the Sprint on a coherent objective. It's very easy for Product Owners to get caught up in the Stories and lose sight of the objectives those Stories represent. The result is a problem I have encountered repeatedly when coaching Teams: the Product Owner presenting a seemingly random selection of Stories for possible inclusion into a Sprint. If your Product Owner is unable to come up with a unifying theme – a draft Sprint Goal – that describes the intent of the Stories at the top of the Product Backlog, you probably need to work with your Product Owner to get there.

To Commit or Not To Commit?

Scrum has historically called for the Development Team to make a commitment as a part of Sprint Planning. I'm not opposed to the idea of Team commitment, particularly to the Sprint Goal. A formal Team commitment may provide more focus during the Sprint. If so, that's fine, go with a Sprint commitment.

On the other hand, making a commitment every Sprint isn't really necessary to build trust with the organization, if that's the goal. Nor is a Sprint commitment an absolute necessity to getting the Team into a healthy, predictable pattern of delivering finished Stories, which *is* the bedrock of building trust with the organization.

In many cases, it comes down to Team maturity. A new or immature Team may need the added weight of a Sprint commitment to provide the level of focus required to work in a disciplined manner, delivering only what's described by the Stories' Acceptance Criteria, and finishing Stories according to the Team's agreed Definition of Done. Mature, high-performing Teams on the other hand are already focused and disciplined and simply don't need a formal Sprint commitment to stay that way.

My advice is to use part of one or more Retrospectives to evaluate your Team's performance, discipline, and focus Sprint-to-Sprint. If you decide as a Team that you need to enhance focus and discipline, then by all means continue using or reintroduce the concept of the Sprint commitment to your Sprint

Planning. If focus and discipline are strong and Velocity is consistent, then maybe the Sprint commitment has run its course and is no longer needed.

Two Ways to Plan a Sprint

Sprint Planning isn't hugely complex, but it is a lot of work, so I recommend two standard approaches to help give the Event structure. Again, none of this is rocket surgery, so just pick one approach and go with it. You can switch back and forth between approaches as needed to find the way that works best for your Team.

All-in-One Sprint Planning

As the name suggests, this approach to Sprint Planning tackles everything in a single pass. The advantage of this approach is that it keeps the entire Scrum Team together for the entire Sprint Planning Event. New Teams in particular tend to find this planning approach useful because the Product Owner is there to provide immediate answers to questions Team Members have about the Stories.

The time box for this approach to Sprint Planning is two hours per week of Sprint length.

To use this approach, just follow these steps:

- Identify anything unique or disruptive about the Sprint, e.g., vacations, holidays, etc.
- Use this information to estimate the Team's capacity in Story Points; if this is your first Sprint simply skip this step and continue with the remaining steps
- The Product Owner presents the highest-priority Story that is ready for Sprint Planning from the Product Backlog
    - The Product Owner reads the Story, its Acceptance Criteria, and any associated notes to remind the Team of previous conversations about the Story
- The Team discusses the Story and incorporates any new information, reviewing the Story estimate if necessary
- The Team collectively breaks out the Tasks needed to implement the Story, asking the Product Owner questions as appropriate
- The Team may estimate the Tasks (half-day increments are better than hours) or simply try to keep most Tasks similar in size, but a day or less in expected effort

- The Team then answers the question: "Can we add this Story to the Sprint?"
- Repeat these steps for each successive Story until the answer to the question in the previous step is "no"
- The Stories pulled into the Sprint comprise the Sprint Backlog

Finally, the Team and Product Owner review the Sprint Backlog, collaborate on a Sprint Goal, and the Team commits to the Sprint Goal. Team Members then each sign up for a task and get started on the Sprint.

> **Magician's Secret**
> The Sprint Goal and commitment can also happen at the beginning of Sprint Planning, although I find that most new Teams need to see the Spring Backlog they have selected to help them define a Sprint Goal and understand whether they can commit to it.

Two-Part Sprint Planning

This approach to Sprint Planning breaks the Event into two parts (and is also the standard Scrum* format for Sprint Planning): the first produces the Sprint Goal and Team commitment; the second produces the Sprint Backlog. The advantage of this approach is that the Product Owner can leave once the first part is complete, allowing the Development Team to work out the implementation details. I find that this approach to Sprint Planning works well for mature, Performing Teams with deep product domain experience. Teams that are less mature are not as likely to be successful using this approach to Sprint Planning.

First Part

The time box for the First Part of Sprint Planning is one hour per week of Sprint Length.

Follow these steps for the First Part of Sprint Planning:

- Identify anything unique or disruptive about the Sprint, e.g., vacations, holidays, etc.
- Use this information to estimate the Team's capacity in Story Points
- The Product Owner presents Stories that are ready for Sprint Planning from the Product Backlog, covering Acceptance Criteria and any

---

* *Scrum Guide*, p. 9.

associated notes to remind the Team of previous conversations about the Story
- The Product Owner presents about two Sprints' worth of Stories
- The Team discusses the Stories and collaborates with the Product Owner to create a Sprint Goal
- The Team then commits to the Sprint Goal and the Product Owner leaves the meeting, but commits to being accessible to answer questions that the Team may have during the Second Part of Sprint Planning

At the conclusion of the First Part of Sprint Planning, the Team has a pile of Stories – clearly more than they can deliver in a single Sprint – while the Product Owner has Team commitment to the Sprint Goal. There is nothing specific about how the Team will implement the Sprint Goal yet. That's the point of the Second Part of Sprint Planning. The Team has some flexibility to decide how best to implement the Sprint Goal based on the available Stories.

Second Part
The time box for the Second Part of Sprint Planning is one hour per week of Sprint Length.

Follow these steps for the Second Part of Sprint Planning:

- The Development Team reviews each Story *in priority order* and collectively decides how many Stories – and which Stories – to pull into the Sprint, filling up the Sprint Backlog
  - Notice that the Team may choose to include lower-priority Stories while excluding some higher-priority Stories; this is part of the flexibility the Team has to implement the Sprint Goal
- The Team collectively breaks out the Tasks needed to implement each Story on the Sprint Backlog
- The Team may estimate the Tasks (half-day increments are better than hours) or simply try to keep most Tasks similar in size, but a day or less in expected effort
- The Team then invites the Product Owner to review the Sprint Backlog
- Team Members each sign up for a task and get started on the Sprint.

Stories the Team did not choose to include in the Sprint go back to the Product Backlog for possible inclusion in a later Sprint.

Task Packages

Tasks are simply cards, a list, or the electronic equivalents that describe the implementation details needed to deliver a Story. Each Story typically needs a set of Tasks to take it from idea to working product. There is no recommended format for writing Tasks, so do what works for your Team. Tasks usually describe design, coding, testing, documenting, or any other kinds of work needed to deliver a finished Story that meets all of its Acceptance Criteria.

Tasks are the property of the Development Team, but sometimes the Team needs help remembering the categories of Tasks needed to deliver finished Stories. Task Packages are simply those categories, or buckets, into which Tasks commonly fall. Task Packages derive from and support the Team's Definition of Done. If the Task Package list and Definition of Done are prominently displayed in the Team Room, it will be a rare event when the Team misses a necessary Task.

Here is an example of a Task Package list:

- Database
- User Interface
- API
- Coding
- Integration
- Deployment
- Unit Tests
- Acceptance Tests
- Capacity Testing
- Reliability Testing
- Exploratory Testing
- Online Help
- User Documentation

This is not an exhaustive list, just a starting point for your own Task Packages.

> **Try This**
> With your Team, spend ten or fifteen minutes drawing up a list of Task Packages needed to ensure that all work meets your Team's Definition of Done. Have Team Members write task categories on cards and then reconcile the duplicates and extraneous ideas to generate a Task Package list for your Team. Display the list prominently, perhaps next to your Team's Definition of Done!

Managing the Sprint Backlog

During the Sprint the Team self-manages its work every day. What exactly does that mean in practice? To begin with, the work of delivering the Sprint Goal is a collective, collaborative Team effort, **not** the aggregate of the individual efforts of Development Team Members. This means that Team Members work together every day of the Sprint, actively collaborating on Task and Story completion. Pair Programming is a great way for Team Members to build collaborative muscle. When I'm coaching a Team, I always strongly encourage the Team Members to consider adding a Team working agreement that lays out the Team's commitment and approach to Pair Programming.

One of the most important implications of Team self-management plays out in the way work gets done during the Sprint. In a Team-based work environment, whether Scrum or any other Agile framework, it is critical that Team Members self-assign work items throughout each day. What this means in practice is that Team Members sign up for Tasks rather than having a functional manager, project manager, the Product Owner or – worst of all – the Scrum Master assign Tasks to Team Members.

This *does not* mean that individual Team Members can just sign up for the fun or interesting or comfortable Tasks without regard for the needs of the Team. Team Members sign up for Tasks in collaboration with their Teammates. The determining factor behind which Tasks Team Members sign up to do every day is collaborative decision-making about which task or tasks move the Team most effectively toward delivering the Sprint Goal.

Task Boards

The Team's primary Sprint work management tool is the Task Board. When it comes to Task Boards, simpler is better. I recommend that the design of the Task Board reflect accurately the states of work items, whether Stories or Tasks. Remember that there are really only two states for any work item: *not done* and *done*. Two subcategories of *not done* are *planned* and *in progress.* Make your Task Board demonstrate this simplicity and focus on completing work items.

I recommend a Task Board that looks like this:

138 Chapter 7 Sprint Planning

Story	To Do	In Progress	Done	Story Accepted
As a user, I... 8 points	Code the... / Test the... 2 ...e... 1 Code the... / Code the... 2 ...2 Test the... / Test the... 1	Code the... MC 1 Test the... SC 2 Code the... LC 2	Test the... MC 2 Test the... SC 1	
As a user, I... 5 points	Code the... 2 / Test the... 2 Code the... ... Code the... ...	Code the... DC 2	Test the... SC 2	

Notice that the example above contains a column for Stories planned for the Sprint. The Stories are in priority order, determined by the Product Owner, so the Team should work on Stories from top to bottom. This is simply a risk-mitigation strategy ensuring that the Team delivers the highest-value Stories earlier in the Sprint.

The example Task Board also contains a column labeled "To Do" containing the Tasks associated with each Story. Remember that the Development Team owns the Tasks and any Team Member can add, remove, or change Tasks at any time during the Sprint. (The Team collectively decides how exactly to handle Tasks that an individual Team Member has added, removed, or changed.)

The next column moving from left to right is labeled "In Progress" or "Doing" or something that indicates that Team Members are actively working on the Tasks living here. This column is also a subcategory of *not done*. Whenever Team Members decide, individually, as a pair, or as a swarm (see the next section) to work on a Task, they put their name or names on the Task and move it to this column. Tasks the Team is currently working on live in this column until they are *done*, which means that the Task meets the Team's Definition of Done as applicable to the work the Task describes.

When the Team Member(s) working on a Task finish it, they move it to the "Done" column and then decide what to work on next. If more than one Team Member worked on the Task just completed, the Teamlet* may decide to work together on another Task or the individuals may choose Tasks to work on individually, as a pair, or by forming a new Teamlet. The point is that every Team Member is always working on something that helps the Development Team achieve the Sprint Goal.

While a Task lives in the "In Progress" column, the Team Member or Members working on it update its estimated work completed or remaining every day so that the Scrum Master can present the current visual representation of progress to the Team at the Daily Scrum. My recommendation is that Team Members update their Tasks at least 15 minutes before the Daily Scrum so that the Scrum Master has the latest information to present to the Team.

We haven't yet talked at all about what happens to the Stories on the Task Board during the Sprint. My recommended approach is extremely simple: Stories are either planned or finished, nothing in between. When the Development Team finishes all of the Tasks associated with a Story and believes that the Story's Acceptance Criteria are all satisfied, the Team presents the Story to the Product Owner for acceptance. The Product Owner reviews the working product the Team produced based on the Story and either accepts the Story as finished or helps the Team understand why the Story is not done as agreed.

When the Product Owner accepts a Story as finished, the Team moves the Story to the Accepted column. I always recommend that a Team Member who contributed to the Story moves it to the Accepted column during the Daily Scrum or some other time when the Team is gathered around the Task Board. It's a nice little ceremony that helps build the Team's sense of accomplishment and enhances Team morale. *Under no circumstances do I want the Product Owner or Scrum Master moving the Story to the Accepted column.* Think about it for a minute: Who worked on the Story? Who should get props for having delivered the finished Story?

It's very simple for the Team to manage Sprint work using a simple Task Board. Tasks go from To Do to In Progress to Done. Stories move from Planned

---

* A Teamlet is a subset of the Team consisting of two or more individual Team Members. Teamlets commonly form and re-form around Tasks as needed during the Sprint.

(or "Stories" or "Sprint Backlog") to Accepted, reflecting that Stories must meet their Acceptance Criteria in order to be considered done.

> **Magician's Secret**
> Some Teams I've worked with over the years have gotten caught in the trap of multiple stages of "doneness" for Stories and Tasks. Some have added a "Ready for Test" column, explicitly defining – or accommodating – a bifurcation of the Team into "coders" and "testers." Another common complication of the Task Board occurs when the Team decides that "done" has different stages, such as "coding done" and "testing done" and "staging done" and "pre-deployment done" and "ready to deploy." Oftentimes, Teams shorten these stages to something that ends up looking like this: "done-done-done-done-done." Yikes! Great Teams keep it simple, sticking to the *not-done/done* states, and delivering finished, working Stories every Sprint.

Swarming Around Work

A lot of the business of managing work using a Task Board revolves around engaging in teamwork, rather than managing individual work. Most of us are not well trained in teamwork. Think about it: from the earliest days of formal education – for most of us – working with others isn't called *teamwork* it's called *cheating*! Technically inclined people in particular are often not intrinsically disposed to work closely with Teammates, making teamwork a skill most people have to learn.

The best way to learn teamwork is to work as a Team! Use Pair Programming deliberately to build teamwork. Add Pair Programming to your Team's Working Agreement. Here is an example:

> *We agree as a Team to use Pair Programming every day of the Sprint. We further agree that we will switch pairs every four hours <or with every new Task or similar> as a means of building teamwork and spreading knowledge across the Team.*

To me, swarming around work in a Team-based environment means that two or more individual Team Members work together on all or parts of every Task. When we put our heads together on work, we not only come up with better solutions to problems, we also spread knowledge and build teamwork muscle. Working on difficult problems in isolation is far less effective than tackling those problems by collaborating with one or more Teammates.

Some agilists recommend very specific approaches to swarming around work.*
I prefer a flexible, Team-decides approach to swarming based on what makes
the most sense to the Team at the time for a particular Story. Another thing I
insist on when I'm coaching a Team is that the *whole Team* maintains explicit
ownership of all Stories. I never want to hear anyone on the Team say "my
Story." It is always "our Stories" reflecting the whole-Team commitment to the
Sprint Goal that the Stories in the Sprint Backlog represent. In practice this
means that I expect the Team to decide informally which Team Members work
on a particular Story's Tasks rather than breaking the Team into defined
Teamlets with specialties and an implied hierarchy.

Multitasking

I am always amazed at job announcements that say something to this effect:
"Must be skilled at juggling multiple tasks simultaneously," or "Must multitask
effectively." Both of these demands are utterly contrary to the abilities of the
human brain. Numerous studies† in recent years have demonstrated beyond
any doubt that the human brain does not and in fact cannot attend to more
than one task at a time. Any attempt to do so reduces our effectiveness on all
tasks to which we are giving our divided attention. Indeed, "multitasking" is a
misnomer; psychologists have a much more accurately descriptive name for it:
Continuous Partial Attention.

We humans fool ourselves into thinking that we are actually multitasking
when we work on several simple tasks in the same time frame. We can
convince ourselves that we are, in fact, multitasking because the penalty for
context switching between simple tasks is so low. But make no mistake; there
is a context-switching penalty even when moving our attention between the
simplest of tasks. When it comes to more complex tasks, like writing code,
writing tests, building deployment scripts, writing stored procedures, – put
the value-creating work you do here – the context-switch penalty is severe,
costing the average human brain 20 to 30 minutes to recover from the switch.
That time is 100% waste, worse even, because the context switch deletes the
stack of items held in short-term memory that were supporting work on the
previous task. Those items are gone forever. Once you move to a different task,
your brain deletes everything in its five to nine short-term memory slots,
making them available for use on the new task. You can never get those items

---

* For example, see Rawsthorne p. 75 ff.
† See Further Reading at the end of this chapter

back, so that great idea you were just about to formulate is gone forever, like a puff of smoke vanishing in a stiff breeze.

The most effective and efficient way human beings can work is to tackle one task at a time, finishing that one before even thinking about the next one. This is our hard-wired strength: focus and concentration on the task at hand. The Task Board plays to this strength perfectly, keeping the Tasks ready to be worked on, but uncommitted so that each Team Member can focus on their one Task currently in progress. The rest of the Tasks planned for the Sprint as of that moment aren't going anywhere, so there's no need to expend any mental energy on them. Work this way and you will get more done more quickly and more effectively, individually and as a Team, than attempting to multitask. Put simply, multitasking results in the entire Team expending more effort while getting less work done and the work they do finish is of lower quality, by any definition, than work a Team completes while focused on one Task at a time.

A Multitasking Test

With your Team, ask for a couple of volunteers to play a game. Give each player a red marker and a blue marker. Ask each player to pick out a space on a large whiteboard or a flip chart sheet. Each player is going to write the phrase "MULTITASKING IS COUNTERPRODUCTIVE" in blue with the numbers 1-31 in red interleaved between the letters, like this:

M1 U2 L3 T4 I5 T6 A7 S8...

The difference between the two players is that one focuses on a single task while the other multitasks. The single-task player takes the cap off the blue marker, writes the phrase – leaving space for the numbers – then puts the cap back on the blue marker, removes the cap from the red marker, and fills in the numbers following each letter. When finished, the single-task player puts the cap back on the red marker and submits the finished work to the Product Owner (another Team Member or the entire Team) for approval. Acceptance Criteria for the work are that the writing is legible and that all letters are in blue while all numbers are in red, that the letters and numbers are interleaved, and that all spelling and numbering is correct.

The multitasking player does exactly the same work, just one letter and number at a time, working on both tasks simultaneously. There is a context-switch penalty, however, in that the multitasking player must take the cap off the blue marker, write a letter, put the cap back on the blue marker, take the cap off the red marker, write a number, and then put the cap back on the red marker, continuing this pattern until all work is completed. When finished, the multitasking player puts the cap back on the red marker for the last time and submits the finished work to the Product Owner (another Team Member or the entire Team) for approval. Acceptance Criteria for the work are the same as described above for the single-task flow.

Ask both players to take their positions, caps on both markers, and have them start at the same time. Then, as a Team, silently observe what happens. When both players have finished, ask your Team to think about the following questions:

- Who finished first?
- Who worked harder?
- Who had extra capacity to take on more tasks?
- Which work approach produced the higher quality results?

A Heuristic for Task Work

My rule of thumb for Task work – and one I highly recommend Teams adopt as a part of their Team Working Agreement – is as follows: *Every Team Member's name appears on one and only one in-progress, unblocked Task at a time.*

This rule does not preclude multiple Team Members working on the same Task. It *does* preclude any Team Member signing up for or attempting to work on more than one Task at time. And that's the point. Single-item flow is the most effective, most efficient way known to develop a product.

The result of this simple rule is that no one is working on more than one Task at once, meaning no one is attempting to engage in multitasking. Another result of this simple rule is that Tasks not yet in progress are available, by virtue of the fact that they live in the To Do column on the Task Board, for any Team Member to work on, until one or more Team Members sign up for the Task. This simple visual cue helps the Team see what needs to be worked on and also helps drive cross-functional behavior on the Team by making it physically possible for anyone to sign up for any available Task.

Wrapping Up

Sprint Planning is a Big Deal for Agile Teams. If you're not using Scrum you may have a different name for this vital activity, but the purpose remains the same in any iterative, incremental product development environment. It's the "Plan" part of the Plan-Do-Inspect-Adapt cycle on the product side of the equation. There are different approaches to planning a Sprint, but the essentials remain the same regardless of the approach you adopt. Eliminating multi-tasking and focusing instead on single-task flow improves efficiency, effectiveness, and quality. Team working agreements enhance teamwork and overall agility.

Further Reading

BBC News. "Is Multitasking a Myth?" *BBC News Magazine*, August 20, 2010, (http://www.bbc.co.uk/news/magazine-11035055).

Keim, Brandon. "Is Multitasking Bad For Us?" *NOVA ScienceNOW,* October 4, 2012, (http://www.pbs.org/wgbh/nova/body/is-multitasking-bad.html).

Ophir, Eyal et al. 2009. "Cognitive control in media multitaskers." *Proceedings of the National Academy of Sciences,* 106:37, September 15, 2009, (www.pnas.org/content/106/37/15583.short, http://news.stanford.edu/news/2009/august24/multitask-research-study-082409.html)

Rawsthorne, Dan and Doug Shimp. *Exploring Scrum: The Fundamentals (People, Product, and Practices).* USA: Self-published, 2011.

Chapter 8 Making Progress Visible

"When the facts change, I change my mind. What do you do?"
– *John Maynard Keynes*

The first principle of Empirical Process Control is Transparency. Inspection and Adaptation are impossible without Transparency, so this is kind of a Big Deal in Agile. One of the major aspects of Transparency is to broadcast visibility about progress the Team is making in building the product to the entire organization and its stakeholders. Another major aspect of Transparency is to provide the Team with visibility into its progress so that Team Members can collaborate effectively every day.

Traditional Measures of Progress

Traditional measures of progress in software, IT, or other complex knowledge-work environments are based on ideas borrowed from the old world of Defined Process Control manufacturing. The purpose of these measurements was to ensure that economies of scale were properly implemented and to ferret out additional, incremental efficiencies in a mass production setting. Many of the traditional measurements of progress contributed to the cost accounting that mass production is based on.

Knowledge work, software and IT included, is not mass-production based nor is it built on cost-accounted economies of scale, making traditional measures of progress meaningless at best, deceptive and destructive at worst. See if you recognize any of these traditional measures frequently applied to software knowledge work:

- LOSC (Lines of Source Code) per coder per day/week/month
- Lines of code produced per person-hour
- Daily quotas of lines-of-code-produced per coder
- Hours worked per function point
- Utilization per developer measured in hours or percentages

There are many others, but you get the idea. All of these things measure what's called "productivity" in the world of manufacturing. Measuring the productivity of knowledge workers is notoriously difficult, possibly even impossible.* Smart people can easily game any of the standard measures of productivity, but only to the detriment of the product and also their personal morale and professional abilities.

A more appropriate measure of knowledge-worker effectiveness is to focus on outcomes, things like quality, consistent value delivery, customer satisfaction, Net Promoter Score,† product adoption rates, etc.

This is not the context in which to tackle the complicated and highly controversial topic of individual knowledge-worker evaluation. This is a handbook devoted to Teams, so let's keep our focus there. Effective Teams deliver strong outcomes. Effective Teams also know how to handle internal issues that make the Team less effective. As in so many other areas of agility, when in doubt, trust the Team. With that idea firmly in mind, let's look at some approaches to making progress visible.

The Trouble With Burndown Charts

The original Scrum literature insisted that Teams use Burndown charts to track and display progress at the Sprint and Release levels.‡ The main purpose of the Burndown chart was to provide the Development Team with progress visibility to enable effective planning and collaboration. A secondary purpose was to provide the organization with visibility into the Team's progress. Both of those goals are good and need to be supported. Burndown charts are just not, in my view, an effective or even viable way to achieve those goals.

The basis of a traditional Sprint Burndown chart is to plot the aggregate number of Task hours remaining every day. The basis of a Release Burndown chart is to plot the aggregate number of Story Points remaining in the Release Backlog after every Sprint.

---

* For an excellent overview of this topic, see Daniel H. Pink, *Drive*.
† Denning p. 74 ff.
‡ Schwaber 2002, p. 73 ff.; Schwaber 2004, p. 11-12

The Trouble With Burndown Charts

The problem with Burndown charts is that they don't make the right thing visible. The Release Burndown chart shows Story Points remaining in the Release Backlog every Sprint. That's not inherently bad. The problem with the Release Burndown is that it fails to show both changes in the size of the Release Backlog, "scope creep" in traditional terms, and the Team's progress expressed as Velocity. If the Burndown trend line is heading nicely toward zero, then fine. But if not, the information displayed tells you nothing about the problem, which could be stalled Velocity, increasing size of the Release Backlog, or some combination of the two.

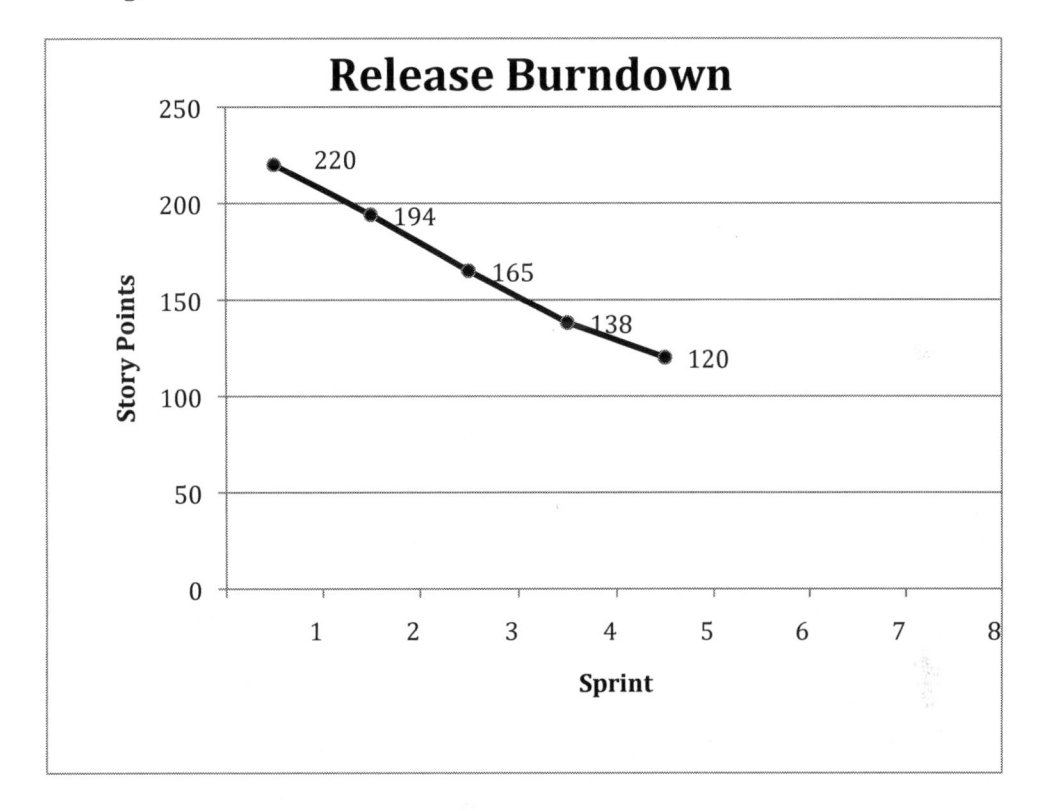

Release Burndown

A line chart plotting Story Points (y-axis, 0 to 250) against Sprint (x-axis, 1 to 8) with data points: 220, 194, 165, 138, 120.

Chapter 8 Making Progress Visible

The Sprint Burndown chart is even more problematic. The Sprint Burndown chart tracks Task hours remaining in the Sprint every day, a measure intended to show progress toward a goal. On the surface, this is a big improvement over tracking person-hours expended on something or another, which serves only the interests of cost accounting.

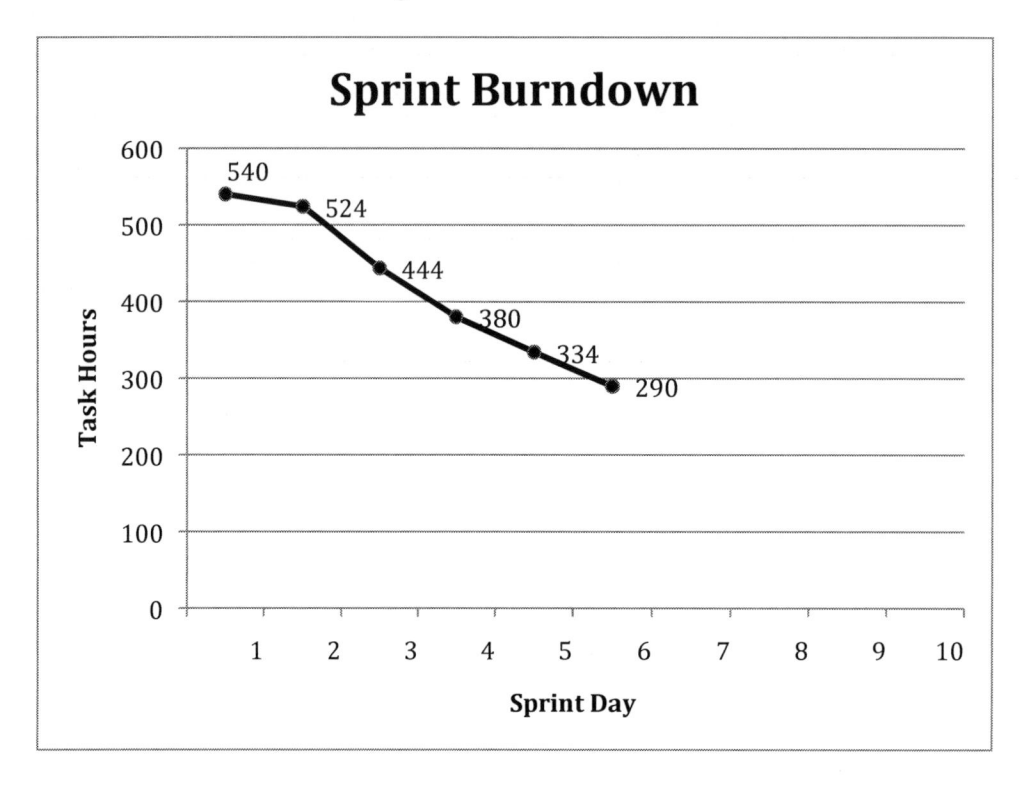

Sprint Burndown

Task Hours vs Sprint Day:
- Day 1: 540
- Day 2: 524
- Day 3: 444
- Day 4: 380
- Day 5: 334
- Day 6: 290

The big problem with tracking and displaying Task hours remaining in a Sprint is that the unit being tracked contains no intrinsic value. Put another way, Tasks are not units of value, Stories are.

Another problem with Task-hour tracking is that it supports an outdated concept of the Team's Sprint commitment. Recall that Scrum originally conceived of the Team's commitment being to a list of Backlog Items (possibly Stories) pulled into the Sprint. Since there is a connection of sorts between Tasks and Stories, it undoubtedly seemed like a good idea to use Task hours remaining to make visible the Team's progress toward completion of the Sprint Backlog Items.

There are several problems with this way of thinking. First, the Tasks belong to the Development Team and are – or should be – constantly subject to change as the Team learns more about the work of the Sprint. The traditional Sprint Burndown is therefore attempting to track a moving target.

Another problem is that tracking Task hours remaining offers no insight into whether the Team is actually likely to complete any Stories in the Sprint, let alone the entire Sprint Backlog. The problem here is that Teams often expend more effort making the Sprint Burndown "look good" rather than focusing on completing Stories. The end result is that the Team completes a lot of Tasks during the Sprint, and has a very pretty Sprint Burndown most days, but doesn't finish many Stories and maybe none at all.

A third problem is that anything to do with tracking hours leads all too quickly and easily back to traditional measures of productivity. Managers, when confronted with a Sprint Burndown that shows the Team as being "behind schedule" for the Sprint, can very easily revert to a mode of pressuring the Team to work more hours to "catch up." Likewise, if the Sprint Burndown shows that the Team is "ahead of schedule" during the Sprint, managers tend to want to pressure the Team to take on more work.

Teams are collectively very smart – that's the point after all – so they very quickly learn how to game the Sprint Burndown to make it always look like the Team is exactly "on schedule" every day of the Sprint. Shifting the Team's focus away from developing the best possible product is always a bad idea. Shifting the Team's focus to how best to game the reporting system is easily the worst possible idea. So let's just not go there.

Build-up Charts

With the modern concept of the Development Team committing to deliver the Sprint Goal instead of a specific set of Stories, burning down Task hours makes no sense at all. In my experience, an effective form of Sprint progress tracking needs to provide visibility into the Team's delivery of value, while at the same time providing the Team with feedback needed to plan daily work.

An effective form of Release progress tracking needs to show not only Stories or Story Points the Team completes every Sprint, but also the location of the Release target, as indicated by the Team-estimated size of the Release Backlog.

Sprint Build-up Chart

A Sprint Build-up chart shows progress in terms of value delivery. The most common form of Sprint Build-up chart plots Story Points completed on the *y*-axis and Sprint days on the *x*-axis. The result often looks like the following example:

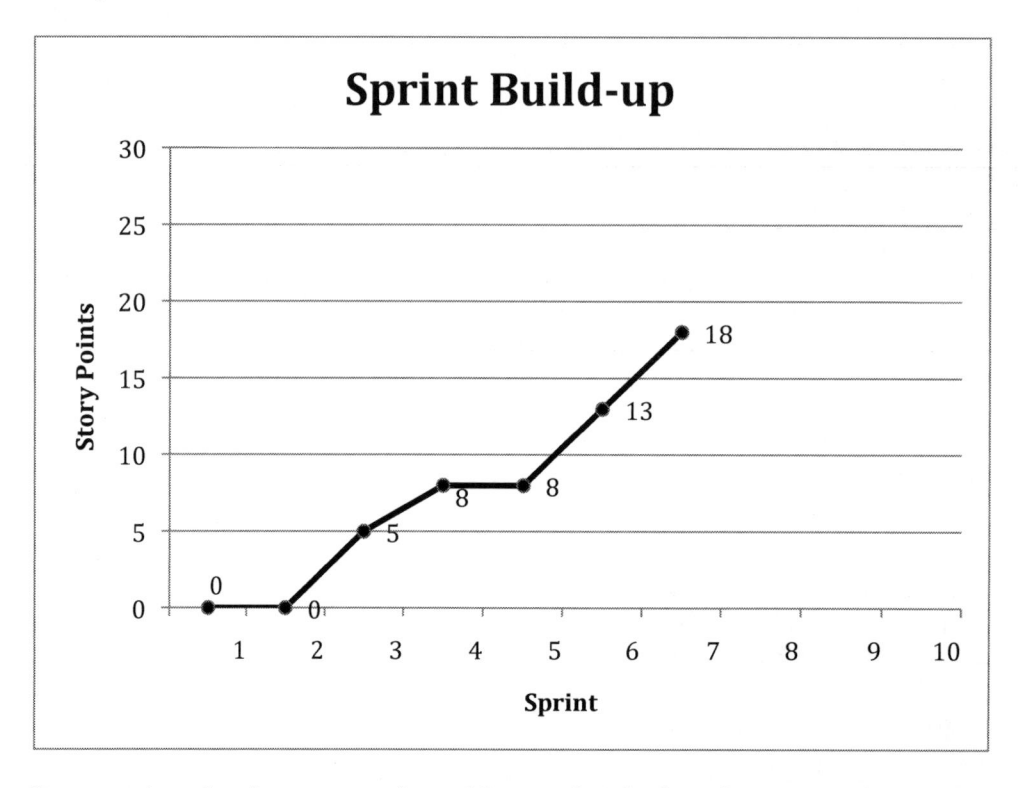

Sprint Build-up

(Chart showing Story Points on y-axis (0–30) vs Sprint on x-axis (1–10) with data points: 1→0, 2→0, 3→5, 4→8, 5→8, 6→13, 7→18)

You can also plot the raw number of Stories finished on the *y*-axis. This works well if your Team's Stories are generally the same size. Plotting Story Points works better if you have a broader range of Story sizes in your Sprints.

A more granular way to construct a Sprint Build-up chart is to plot Acceptance Criteria completed on the *y*-axis. I'm not sure that level of detail is really ever needed or even wanted, but feel free to experiment. Finding what works best for your Team is the key here, not following rules. Experiment with different Sprint Build-up formats, maybe have two going at the same time during a few Sprints so that you can evaluate them against each other and decide as a Team which is most effective. Maintaining more than two Sprint Build-up charts during a Sprint is probably excessive (for your Scrum Master), but having the two data types plotted side-by-side is an effective way for a Team to evaluate which one – maybe both – is effective.

Release Build-up Chart

A Release Build-up chart works on the same principle as a Release Burndown chart, plotting one data point – the Team or Teams aggregate Velocity – every Sprint. The difference is that the trend line goes up from left to right, instead of down, and the top line is the current estimated size of the Release Backlog in Story Points. As the top line moves, indicating changes in planned Release scope, the projected intersection point between the data line and the Release line also moves, providing insight and visibility into the projected Release date. The following example shows how this works:

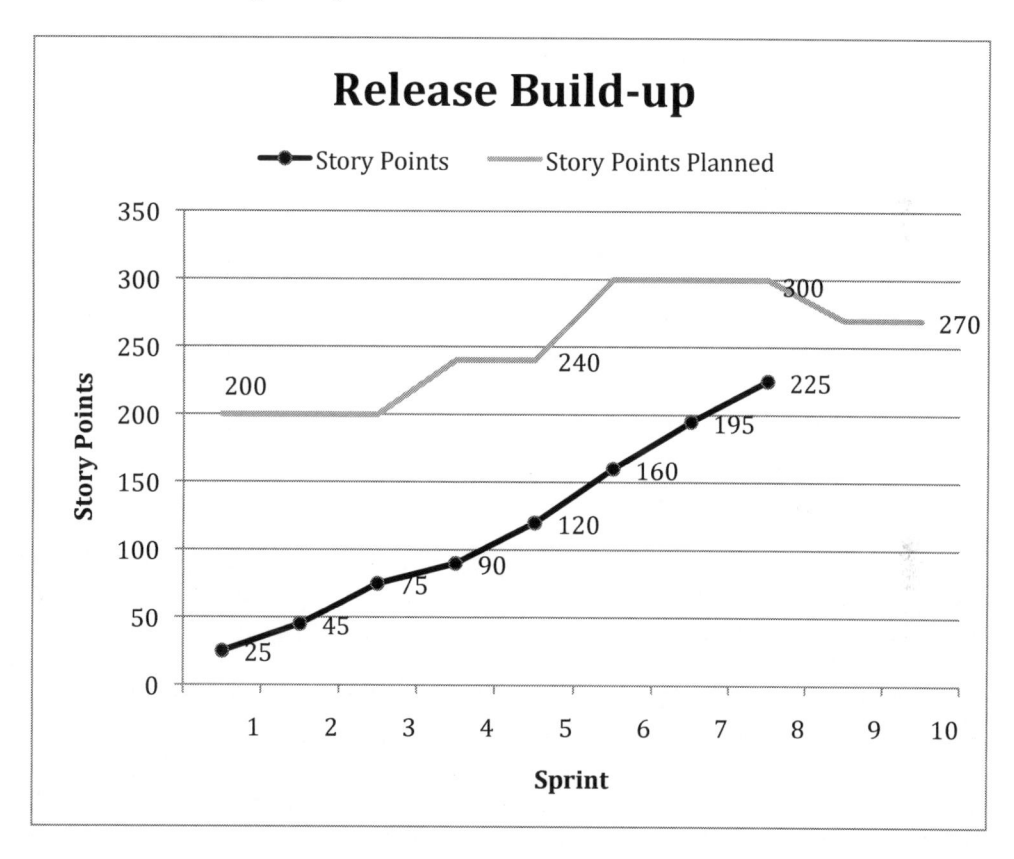

Release Build-up

A chart plots Story Points (y-axis) against Sprint (x-axis, 1–10). The "Story Points" line shows: 25, 45, 75, 90, 120, 160, 195, 225. The "Story Points Planned" line shows: 200, 200, 240, 240, 300, 300, 270, 270.

Organic Transparency

All of the elements of Transparency we have been talking about, going back to the Scrum Events, the Sprint Task Board, the Build-up Charts, and the ultimate artifact, a Potentially Shippable Product Increment every Sprint, are organically generated as a result of using Scrum. In this sense, "organic" means that every Scrum Event and artifact is a part of doing the work, not some artificial, non-value-add activity the Team or organization must pay for in order to generate visibility into the state of product and the process by which the Team is developing the product.

Unlike traditional metrics and reporting, which are time-consuming, wasteful activities, every element of Transparency that emerges from an Agile Team is part and parcel with the delivery of value. The Team uses the Events and artifacts of Scrum, for example, to enable the very work that those events and artifacts make visible to the rest of the organization and beyond. Organic Transparency delivered at no cost – what could be better than that?

Wrapping Up

In this chapter we examined some of the simple ways Agile Teams can and do make their work visible, both internally to the Team and externally to the organization. Agile progress reporting is *organic*, meaning that the Backlogs, Task Board, and all associated graphs and charts are tools the Team uses to organize and manage its work and not an additional chore that adds no value.

Further Reading

Denning, Stephen. *The Leader's Guide to Radical Management: Reinventing the Workplace for the 21st Century.* San Francisco: Jossey-Bass, 2010.

Pink, Daniel H. *Drive: The Surprising Truth About What Motivates Us.* New York: Riverhead Books, 2009.

Rawsthorne, Dan and Doug Shimp. *Exploring Scrum: The Fundamentals (People, Product, and Practices).* USA: Self-published, 2011.

Schwaber, Ken. *Agile Project Management With Scrum.* Redmond, WA: Microsoft Press, 2004.

Schwaber, Ken and Mike Beedle. *Agile Software Development With Scrum.* Upper Saddle River, NJ: Prentice Hall, 2002.

Chapter 9 Collaboration

"The speed of the project is the speed at which ideas move between team members."
– *Alistair Cockburn*

Collaboration is the secret sauce of *teamwork*, which is the characteristic that both distinguishes a Team from a working group and generates the multiplier effects that produce a high-performing Team. But what is collaboration? And how does it work?

> **Try This**
> With your Team, use cards or sticky notes to brainstorm on a definition of collaboration. Organize the individual thoughts into associated groups to arrive at a working definition of collaboration for your Team. Then spend a few minutes brainstorming on specific practices that build and enhance collaboration on your Team. As a Team, order the resulting practices in order of importance and consider adding the top two or three (or more) to your Team working agreement.

A Definition

Collaboration, simply defined, is a group of people working together as equals toward a common goal. The "as equals" part doesn't mean that every member of the Team has equivalent or interchangeable skills, abilities, knowledge, or experience. It simply means that every Team Member has an equal voice in contributing to the Team's decisions and work and an equivalent level of accountability for the Team's collective work.

What drives collaboration? Jean Tabaka offered the best answer I've seen to this crucial question:

> Through shared working, teams create a sense of community and identity for their projects. They are able to collectively converge on a purpose and a driving challenge for the project. In this way,

collaboration becomes a practice that team members apply among the many tools and techniques that define their project.

When teams declare a collaborative imperative in their work, it is their pledge to employ consensus-based decision approaches through participatory decision-making. They apply high-bandwidth information gathering coupled with well-formed and well-articulated priorities. And, they are guided by a leader who fosters participation in defining the project work and who encourages open discussion around the project direction: its organization, its roles, and its deliverables.*

The point of everything we've been talking about to this point is building collaborative, high-performing Teams. High-bandwidth communication, a shared vision of the project and the work needed to turn it into reality, and leadership are the three keys to the kingdom. We've already examined building a shared project vision and Team leadership in some detail. Let's look at high-bandwidth communication now.

High-bandwidth Communication

Human beings communicate over a broad spectrum of auditory and visual bandwidth. We both deploy and read tone of voice, facial expressions, and body language to deliver our message and understand what others are attempting to convey to us. The actual words we use in interpersonal communication are the least important component of what is a complex of visual and auditory cues. So why is it that so many of us think we can rely on the words alone, in printed form no less, disembodied from the delivery context and full bandwidth of communication, to convey complex meaning to others?

---

* Tabaka p. 4

Communication Bandwidth

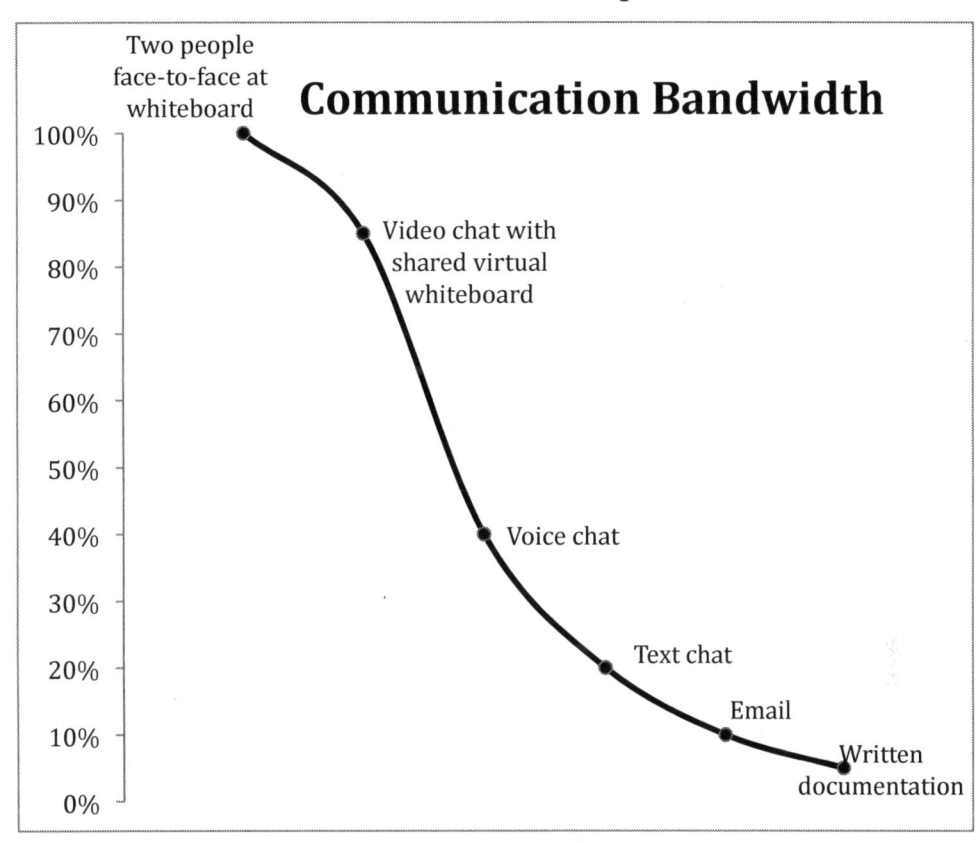

- **Two people face-to-face at whiteboard** — 100%
- **Video chat with shared virtual whiteboard** — ~85%
- **Voice chat** — 40%
- **Text chat** — 20%
- **Email** — 10%
- **Written documentation** — ~5%

Considering that at least 85 percent of the richness – that is, the bandwidth – of human communication lives in the nonverbal region of the communication spectrum, we need to stop fooling ourselves about the effectiveness of using the written word to communicate.

Within a Team the imperative for high-bandwidth communication is even more critical. The ideal, as expressed in the Agile Manifesto Principles is face-to-face communication:

> The most efficient and effective method of conveying information to and within a development team is face-to-face conversation.

The Team Room

The best way to enable high-bandwidth communication on a Development Team is to have all Team Members physically co-located, not just in the same building, but in the same room – the Team Room. The Team Room is where the Team does most, or better yet, all of its work. The best Team Rooms I have seen offer a large central open space surrounded either by floor-to-ceiling walls or at least high cubicle walls to define the Team Room's core area and provide separation between other office space, including other Team Rooms.

The central space in the Team Room can be filled with a large table or several tables pushed together to form the Team's primary workspace. This arrangement works very well when Team Members have desktop computer workstations. The workstations stay put, but the Team Members are free to move around the table as needed to swarm on Stories or Tasks. The central table also works well when Team Members use laptops to do their work. Mobility around the table is definitely not an issue in this case.

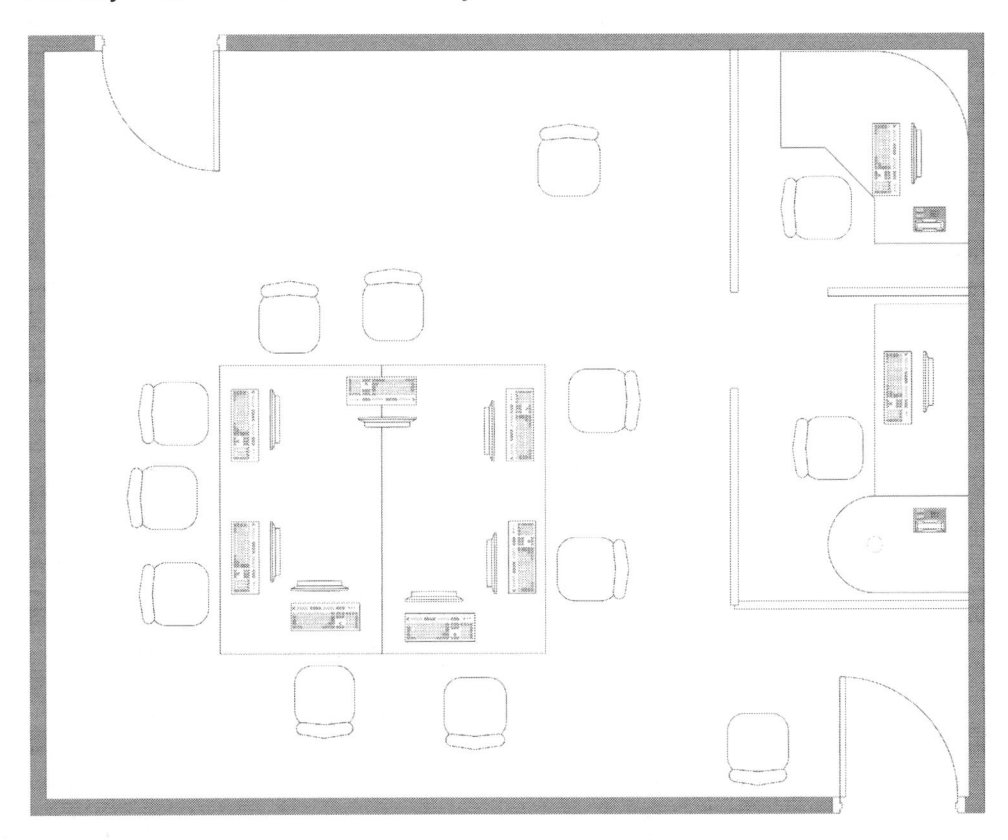

The central space in the Team Room can also be left open, with regular tables or attached cubicle desktops around the perimeter of the room. One highly effective Team Room I worked in used this arrangement. Team Members used laptops for all work and so were highly mobile. On every table the Team had positioned a large monitor with a cable ready to be plugged into a Team Member's laptop. This arrangement supported pair programming and swarming very nicely as it provided a large display for two or more people to view while working. Team Members had no assigned seating in this Team Room. Instead, the Team allowed the work to determine how Team Members distributed themselves around the room.

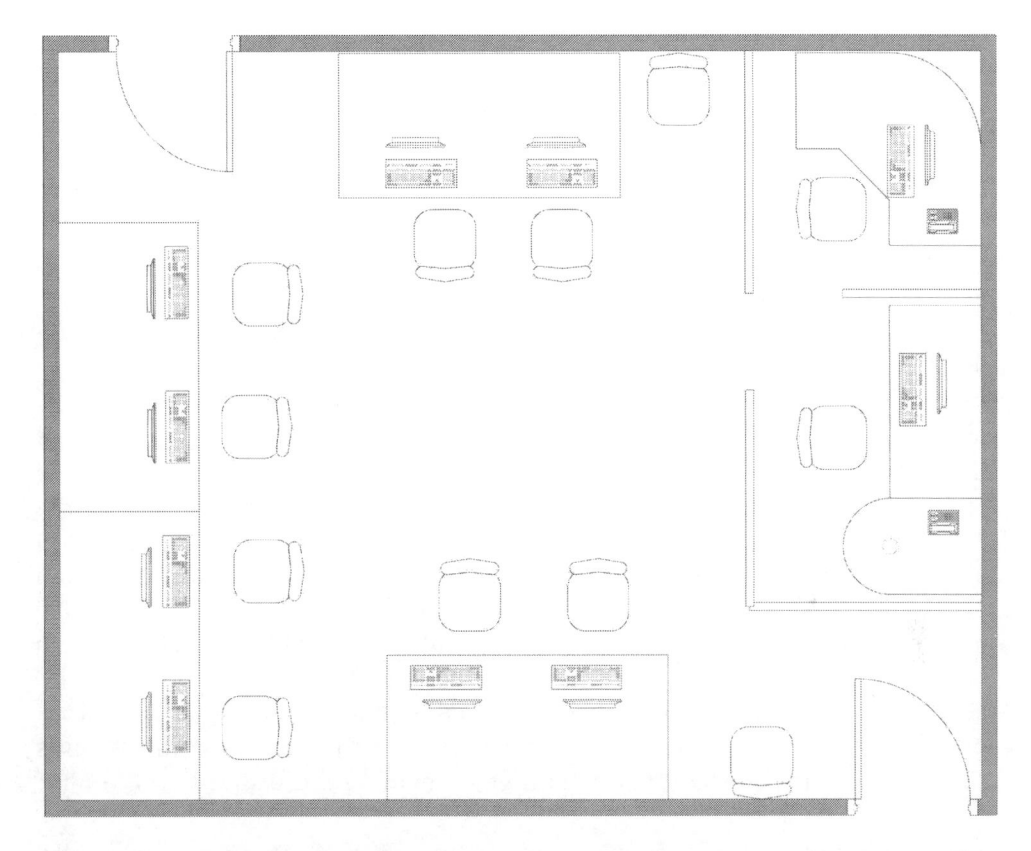

The walls of the Team Room are as important as the main working space. The best Team Rooms have walls that are usable workspace. In a finished room, painting the walls with white-board paint transforms all wall space into effective workspace. Cubical walls can be equipped with integrated white boards to achieve a similar effect. Portable white boards are also highly effective, allowing Team Members to set up a discussion anywhere in the room.

The Team Room walls also accommodate the Sprint Task Board, Sprint Backlog, Sprint Build-up charts, perhaps also the Team's working agreements, impediment and improvement backlogs, and anything else the Team needs to keep visible in order to be effective. White boards are ideal for all of these purposes.

Whether the center of the Team Room is open or used as primary workspace, the Team needs to have space to hold Daily Scrums in the Team Room. When everyone can simply stand up and start the Daily Scrum more or less in place, it eliminates distractions and time wasted walking to a conference room and potentially waiting for the previous occupants to leave, waiting for everyone on the Team to arrive, etc.

Notice that both Team Room layouts depicted above contain a couple of cubicles on one wall. This is a basic "caves and commons" floor plan. The common area is where the Team does most of its work. The caves, the cubicles in this case, provide a physically separated space to which Team Members can retreat for private phone calls or just to get a break from the constant activity of the Team Room.

Dedicated Space

The main point here is that the Team Room is dedicated space reserved for the exclusive use of a single Team. Shared Team Rooms are problematic in that the Teams are constantly in contention over who gets to use the room during which parts of the day. Teams also need to be able to leave the visual element of any conversation – the white board drawings and notes, for example – in place for as long as needed. In a shared room environment, drawings and notes quickly fill up the available space and need to be erased. Taking photos of the white boards is about the only option available to preserve the important information, but doing so removes the discussion from the Team's awareness and instead hides it on someone's phone or computer. Another problem with shared white boards is that the information from one Team is simply noise and distraction for the other Team or Teams using the room.

When two or more Teams share a Team Room, the space is much less effective than dedicated Team space. The Teams sharing a room are also therefore much less effective than they would be if they had separate, dedicated Team Rooms to facilitate their work. In many cases, I have seen Teams simply abandon the shared Team Room because using it is so painful and ineffective.

Communication Modes

Communication within a Team flows on several levels. At its most fundamental, communication between Team Members working together on a problem is direct and focused. In the Team Room, there may be – should be – several such conversations going on simultaneously. It seems contradictory, but healthy, mature Agile Teams are both focused *and* noisy when working. There is little irrelevant information in the room since the entire Team shares a common goal and a common vision for how to achieve it.

Convection Currents

A second-level effect of direct communication between subsets of the Team, sometimes called Teamlets, is a phenomenon called Convection Currents of information. Within the Team Room, there may be three or four separate but related conversations going on simultaneously. The information from these discrete conversations flows around the room in currents of varying strength, depending on relevance to the Team as a whole or to other subsets of the Team.

Team Members tune out the other conversations until a relevant nugget draws conscious attention to the subject under discussion. Often, one Teamlet hits a problem that someone else on the Team has encountered before. When that Convection Current reaches the Team Member or Members who have encountered and possibly solved that problem or a similar one before, their level of attention is drawn to their Teammates' conversation and a new collaboration takes place. The result is rapid flow of information around and through the Team, generating effective and efficient problem solving based on the combined knowledge of the entire Team.

Think of Convection Currents like this: The information flowing around the room from the various conversations swirls above the heads of the Team. Individual Team Members are aware that the information is there, but it's beyond their conscious attention. Only when something in the information swirl grabs the attention of one or more Team Members do they become consciously aware of the subject. Team Members, in effect, come up for air, becoming immersed in the current of information that caught their attention.

> **Magician's Secret**
> In a profession in which most people are accustomed to working in an environment that is either quiet or in which each individual tunes out in some way or another that involves headphones or ear buds, the idea of Convection Currents may seem like a horrible distraction. It does take some getting used to, this business of working in a buzzing Team Room, but the benefits are so compelling that very few people simply refuse to try. If one or more Team Members are finding it difficult to adjust to the Team Room environment, raise the issue at your next Retrospective and ask your Teammates to devise approaches to help everyone adjust to the new environment. The only approaches that aren't on the table when I'm coaching a Team are stopping the conversations entirely or allowing one or more Team Members to opt out of working in the Team Room. We all have to learn how to work as a Team.

Osmotic Communication

Another interesting second-level effect of direct communication within a Team is a phenomenon often called Osmotic Communication or Osmotic Learning. It seems that people learn quite well through a process very similar to osmosis (which is the movement of molecules through a semi-permeable membrane). When information flows around the Team Room, individual Team Members subconsciously absorb key elements of the conversations, learning in the process. Again, this only works when the Team shares a common goal and a common vision for how to achieve it, key factors in keeping the conversation focused on the Team's work.

Drafts

When conversation in the Team Room is focused on the Team's shared goal for the Sprint, good things happen. When any of the conversation in the Team Room strays from that focus, however, the benefits evaporate instantly. Team Members generally learn how to work very effectively in the energetic and noisy Team Room environment, keeping focus on their own work while absorbing the Convection Currents and Osmotic Communication from their Teammates.

Conversation unrelated to the Team's work breaks focus and slows or stops effective work in the Team Room. This unrelated and disruptive conversation is called a Draft. Drafts are, obviously enough, unwelcome in the Team Room. Team Members have full authority to call out their Teammates when the room gets Drafty.

If Drafts become a serious, ongoing problem for the Team, devote some or all of the next Retrospective to devising Team working agreements that solve the problem. The simplest solution is to take responsibility for your own conduct as a member of a Team. If you want to talk about yesterday's game, last night's reality show, or anything else unrelated to the Team's pursuit of the Sprint Goal, simply take it outside the Team Room. It's not that Team Members shouldn't socialize, just not while and where their Teammates are working.

The Importance of Proximity

This extended discussion of high-bandwidth communication has been predicated entirely on close proximity of Team Members. Proximity is the foundation upon which a Team deliberately and energetically builds high-bandwidth communication. The rate of exchange of ideas and the pace of learning within the Team are directly regulated by the bandwidth of communication between Team Members. Face-to-face, in-person communication with the aid of a white board or other apparatus for capturing and expressing ideas facilitates the exchange of ideas and information at very high bandwidth indeed. The multiplier effect of proximity is based on the benefits of Convection Currents and Osmotic Communication. These are simply not available when Teams are not co-located.

This is not an ideal. It is fact.

Dispersed Teams and Collaboration

If your Team is dispersed, as so many are these days, you must face some facts. First, all other things being equal, a co-located Team working in a Team Room has a higher ceiling on the performance curve than an equivalent dispersed Team. The limiting factor is simply the communication bandwidth available to both Teams. The limits on communication bandwidth severely constrain opportunities for collaboration and teamwork on a dispersed Team.

If you find yourself in a dispersed -Team situation, there are a few things you can do to help mitigate the intrinsic disadvantages you've inherited.

Use Technology to Approximate Face-to-face Communication

Every Team Member needs continuous audio and video links to all other Team Members. Use video chat on every desktop or laptop as one option. Even better, install dedicated high-definition audio/visual equipment in the Team workspaces in each location so that the whole Team can achieve something like virtual co-location. Use text messaging to ping Teammates to set up voice and video chats. Don't bother with email for anything other than Team announcements. Email is an extremely low-bandwidth communication medium. It lacks even the immediacy of text messaging. Indeed, email is simply a distraction. The best Teams I've worked with, whether co-located or dispersed, set the expectation that they neither use email within the Team as a serious communication medium nor even check email more than once or twice a day.

What If We're In Different Time Zones?

Distance isn't really the enemy of Team communication, collaboration, and teamwork; time is. With a serious investment in technology, organizations can assemble dispersed Teams that achieve a reasonable facsimile of proximity. In that sense, distance is meaningless as long as our clocks all show the same or similar times.

My take on time-zone dispersion is that if your Team is spread out across more than two time zones, you're in trouble. Let's say you have a simple dispersion pattern in which part of the Team is on the east coast of the USA, while the other part is on the west coast of the USA. That's a three-hour time zone difference. Provided you can get the west-coast contingent to show up by eight AM every morning – a task that is neither easy not particularly likely in my experience – you have at best seven hours of overlap during the day to work with provided the east-coast contingent works until six PM.

That's not bad. You've managed to reduce the total time-zone differential to just one hour. But you're still, even in this ideal dispersed situation, missing out on a minimum of one hour of whole-Team interaction every day. Factor in an hour or so for lunch on both coasts and suddenly you're down to five hours of overlap per day, which is exactly where you started before you asked your west coast Teammates to get to work earlier than anyone else in the region.

If your Team is dispersed across different continents, things become nearly impossible. Time zone differences of five to twelve-and-a-half hours are the norm when Teams are spread across North America, Europe, India, and China. It is unreasonable and distinctly anti-Agile to demand that people in one or more locations work all night in order to accommodate their Teammates on another continent. What to do? Read on....

Build Co-located Teams

Some Teams (and organizations) attempt to deal with the time-zone problem by building complex systems of work handoffs within the Team. Just don't go there – it won't work.

A better solution, or better put, the least-bad option in my experience, is to build distinct teams in each location or in locations that are within two time zones of each other. The new Teams often have issues with functional specialization to overcome – that's usually the reason the people were hired in their respective locations in the first place – but the potential for higher performance is definitely greater than in a widely dispersed Team.

When confronting fundamental realities, you have no choice but to adapt. Organizations have built themselves in a dispersed/distributed fashion generally to support ways of working that are now clearly obsolete – we wouldn't be having this, ahem, conversation at all were it not the case that the current or old ways of working simply aren't effective anymore.

Make the best lemonade you can with the current bag of lemons, but don't just assume that things will always be the way they are now. Organizations must change, first to survive, even more so to thrive. Agile is about change, so once again, we wouldn't be having this conversation if change weren't on the agenda.

Wrapping Up

Collaboration is a major aspect of teamwork. Collaboration and teamwork don't just happen by accident or serendipity – they require deliberate effort and investment, both at the Team and organizational levels. Various communication modes support collaboration, but all are dependent upon real or virtual proximity. Dispersed Teams suffer from a greater or lesser degree of inherently reduced communication bandwidth. Building a collaborative, high-performing dispersed Team is both more difficult and much more costly than building a similar co-located Team. All other things being equal, a co-located Team will always out-perform a dispersed Team simply due to the constraints on communication bandwidth and proximity that the dispersed Team faces.

Further Reading

Cockburn, Alistair. *Agile Software Development.* Boston: Addison-Wesley, 2002.

Tabaka, Jean. *Collaboration Explained: Facilitation Skills for Software Project Leaders.* Upper Saddle River, NJ: Addison-Wesley, 2006.

Chapter 10 Agile Teams in the Enterprise

"Never tell people how to do things. Tell them what to do, and they will surprise you with their ingenuity."
– *George S. Patton, Jr.*

Unless you work for a small company, your Team probably lives in the broader context of the enterprise environment. Agile Teams have to do some things a little differently to accommodate the realities of the enterprise environment. This does not mean compromising key practices or abandoning Agile Values and Principles. It does mean learning how to work with other Teams in parallel on the same product. It also means learning how to thrive within the enterprise ecosystem. These twin concerns are the focus of this chapter.

Scaling Up To Take On Large Projects

Any product that requires the efforts of more than one Team of three to nine people enters the realm of scaling. Traditionally, scaling up to tackle a large project simply means adding more people to the project work group or work groups. Over time, the project development organization tends to become unwieldy and ineffective, the more so as the project encounters delays, as Brooks' Law states so eloquently:

> *Adding manpower to a late software project makes it later.* [*]

Scaling an Agile product (notice the difference – *project* versus *product*) operates under a different and much more practical and effective set of rules. First, never add more people to existing Teams as a way of scaling up for a big product. Remember what happens when you upset a Team's composition? The Team returns to Forming all over again.

---

[*] Brooks 1995, p. 25

To scale up an Agile product, either build one or more new Teams around the product work, or point one or more existing Teams at the product, or some combination of these two approaches. Instead of scaling by adding people, Agile products scale by adding Teams.

This is a beautiful way of scaling because it allows the organization to leverage the considerable horsepower of established, high-performing Teams. Changing the work stream – the Product Backlog from which a Team pulls its work – is far less disruptive than adding new people to a Team. A mature, high-performing Team is going to remain a mature, high-performing Team regardless of the Product Backlog from which it pulls its work.

Okay, maybe that's a little too strong. A Team that suddenly has to pull from a Product Backlog containing Stories that fall outside the business or technical domain of the Team inevitably means that the Team's performance will suffer a drop. Even in this extreme circumstance, however, a mature Team will climb a very steep learning curve much more quickly and decisively than you might expect based on similar experiences with work groups. The Team retains its maturity, its ability to engage in collaborative teamwork, and its collective collaborative and knowledge-generating muscle. Learning a new business domain, tools, programming languages, and whatever else comes with the new work stream is simple in comparison to learning how to be a great Team.

This way of thinking about scaling to take on large products is completely alien to most organizations at this point in the twenty-first century. Get help from an experienced Agile coach, either in print or in person, if your organization is thinking about wrecking its most valuable asset, mature Teams, in a misguided approach to scaling.

Architecture and Design

When working in an enterprise environment, architecture and design require a different approach than in a single-Team ecosystem. The problem is really just this: How to ensure a consistent, flexible, emergent architecture across the entire project? The same is true of design, which needs to be consistent across the Teams working on a product. Imagine – maybe you don't have to imagine! – the chaos engendered when each of the half-dozen Teams working on a product takes a unique approach to design. The result is a serious mess. If you're not there, don't go there!

In my experience, there is no one proven Agile approach to enterprise architecture, regardless of what some practitioners may say or write. An approach I have found successful in several enterprises is to construct a special type of Component Team (see below) whose deliverable is architecture for the other customer-facing feature Teams to consume. This works well when architecture is built iteratively and incrementally, along with the product itself.

The architecture Team works just far enough ahead of the feature Teams to ensure that key architectural elements are in place to support the Teams' work. Every increment of architecture is tied directly to the delivery of tangible business value. Even better, the architecture emerges to serve the development of the product, rather than the other way around, which is the usual case when organizations build all of the architectural elements up front.

Another aspect of the architecture Team that I strongly encourage is that its members disperse to help the feature Teams implement the product based on the most recent increment of architecture. This generally means that architects need to be able to write code. I'm not as stuck on this last point as some other agilists,[*] but I am adamant that the members of the architecture Team communicate directly, in person, with the feature Teams, rather than simply dumping documentation on the Teams.

Design is a different animal entirely. The best way I know to coordinate design across multiple Teams is to use the Scrum of Scrums – and use it properly! – within the project. Flip a few pages ahead for more information on setting up and using the Scrum of Scrums.

Sharing the Product Backlog

A common question in organizations scaling up for a large product revolves around how to provide the various Teams with appropriate work streams. Should every Team have its own dedicated Product Backlog or should all Teams pull work from a consolidated, shared Product Backlog? My quick and usually confusing answer to that question is "yes." My more considered, consultant's answer to that question is "it depends."

Multiple Teams can pull work from a common Product Backlog cleanly and without ever stepping on other Teams' work if you apply a few simple practices. First, each Team must have a dedicated Product Owner to make this work. Second, the Product Owners must work together continuously to refine

---

[*] For example, see Cohn 2010, pp. 143-44

the Product Backlog, ensuring that the Stories are the right size (as determined by the individual Teams), in the right order, and in the right quantity to keep the Teams supplied with Stories to pull into every Sprint.

Each Product Owner represents his or her Team's view into or filter on the Product Backlog. In a sense then, each Team does have its own Product Backlog. The difference is that if one turns off the Team filters, the entire Product Backlog is fully visible and in the appropriate order. Turn on the filter for a particular Team and it appears as if that Team has its own separate Product Backlog, at least at the detailed Story level. Since Epics should – I'll repeat that, Epics *should* – describe features that multiple Teams work on in parallel, the Epics should always be in every Team's view. The granular, refined, detailed Stories flow into the Teams through whatever filtering mechanism makes sense.

If Teams are highly specialized, the filtering is pretty obvious. If Teams are highly specialized, the risks to the success of the project are also pretty obvious. It's much better to have fully cross-functional Teams – or Teams working toward that goal – so that Stories can flow into more than one Team as needed to deliver business value in the most efficient and effective way possible. Cross-functional Teams are also highly effective at preventing inter-Team dependencies from complicating or even derailing the flow of valuable work. Independent Stories flowing into independent cross-functional Teams allows the Product Owners the maximum degree of flexibility in ordering the Product Backlog and delivering the greatest possible business value every Sprint.

Component Teams

A Component Team is a variant on the standard Agile Team model. The difference is in the customer. A standard Agile Team, most of the time at least, delivers product increments to a customer outside of the product development organization. The customer may be inside the larger organization, as in the case of an Agile IT shop, or external to the organization entirely.

A Component Team, on the other hand, serves the product development organization. Its customers are other, customer-facing Teams. Component Teams deliver increments of architecture, infrastructure, or other assets the customer-facing Teams need to deliver business value.

A fine example of a Component Team that I experienced in action was one devoted to building an automated testing framework for about a dozen customer-facing Teams. The Component Team came into being as a result of the organization's recognition that automated testing was vital both to their success with Scrum and to delivering quality, finished increments of customer value every Sprint. With encouragement from yours truly, their Agile Coach, all of the customer-facing Teams adopted "no failing tests" as an item on their Definition of Done.

All testing at that point was manual, which meant that the majority of the test suite, even incomplete as it was at that time, could only be run in the immediate push prior to a release. Even worse, as far as anyone knew the entire test suite had *never* been run on any single release candidate, in part because some tests were dependent on other tests passing and many such tests never passed. No test run had ever been entirely successful – there were always tests failing. Product releases had occurred despite failing tests, as is typical in non-Agile organizations, but this time the integrated code wouldn't even run, so there was no possibility of simply releasing first and bug-fixing later.

Quality problems in the field had been an issue for some time, but only when the latest release candidate wouldn't run did the willpower exist to devote an entire Team to the effort to automate the vast majority of product testing.

Over the course of about 20 two-week Sprints, this Component Team built a complete automated testing framework that could both integrate existing tests and incorporate new tests quickly and easily. The testing framework allowed the customer-facing Teams to run all or part of the test suite as needed with minimal effort. Since the Team built the automated testing framework iteratively and incrementally, they were able to deliver the first usable increment of functionality after just the second Sprint and were then able to gather feedback from their customers – the other Teams – on how to make the next increment better.

When the Component Team finished the major effort needed to construct the automated testing framework, the Team disbanded, distributing its former Team Members to the customer-facing Teams. While it was unfortunate that this mature, high-performing Team disbanded, the benefit in this case justified that outcome. Team Members brought their automated testing expertise to the customer-facing Teams to ensure that the automated testing effort continued without interruption. Enhancements and changes to the automated testing framework then simply became Stories on the Product Backlog that pretty much any Team could pull into a Sprint and deliver.

In this instance, the Component Team delivered a full-featured, fully functioning automated testing framework in about eight months, far less than the three years the organization had originally forecast before moving to Agile. On the product side, the results were truly stunning, with field defects in newly delivered feature areas dropping rapidly to zero. The automated testing framework also helped the Teams pay off Technical Debt much more quickly than anyone had thought possible. Simply running the test suite regularly – and adhering doggedly to the "no failing tests" element of the Definition of Done – made Technical Debt both highly visible and easier to pay down since the code base now had a good immune system to prevent bad things from happening.

The punch line to this story is that Component Teams have a place in an Agile organization. My advice is to use Component Teams sparingly and ensure that their mission and purpose are clearly defined. Component Teams do not directly deliver customer value, but as with the anecdote above their impact can be significant.

Coordinating Sprints and Scrum Events

In a multi-Team environment, it is important that the Sprints and Scrum Events are coordinated. Since each Team needs to know what other Teams are doing, build a structure that provides conduits for information flow. Here are some tips I've learned over the years.

Stagger Daily Scrums

Ask Teams to select Daily Scrum times that do not overlap. Remember, anyone can attend any Team's Daily Scrum, including members of other Teams. Make it possible for Team Members to visit each other's Daily Scrums by not having the Events at the same time to the extent that this is possible and makes sense. If you schedule Daily Scrums with some time in between, as depicted below, Team Members have an opportunity to problem-solve as needed afterwards while still having a chance to attend other Team's Daily Scrums. Others in the organization will also have a better opportunity to move from one Daily Scrum to the next if the Events aren't stacked without time in between.

9:00 AM	9:30 AM	10:00 AM
Team 1 Daily Scrum	Team 2 Daily Scrum	Team 3 Daily Scrum

Synchronize Sprints

I've coached a number of organizations that set up their Sprint calendar so that their Teams' Sprints overlapped. While there are quite a number of plausible-sounding arguments in favor of such a layout, the result has invariably been confusion bordering on chaos.

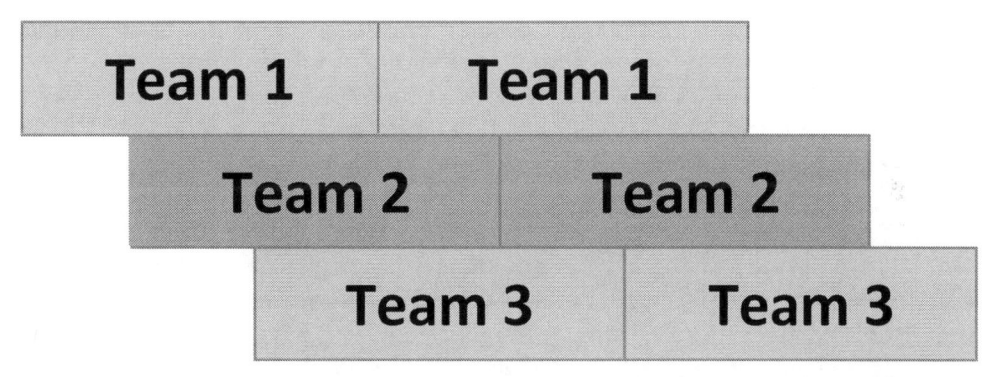

Team 1	Team 1
Team 2	Team 2
Team 3	Team 3

A dramatically better way to work, in my experience, is to synchronize the Sprint calendars of all Teams working on the same product – even all Teams in the organization. This means that all Teams start and end on the same days of the week and that their Sprints are all the same length.

Start	Finish	Start	Finish
Team 1		Team 1	
Team 2		Team 2	
Team 3		Team 3	

Why synchronize the Sprint calendars of all Teams? For Teams working on the same product it's a no-brainer. Since the Teams are pulling work from a consolidated Product Backlog – they are, aren't they? – the Teams all finish their Potentially Shippable Product Increment at essentially the same time, at least on the same day. This allows the Teams to do interesting things, like integrate their product increments and show the whole works to customers and stakeholders in a joint Sprint Review at the end of every Sprint.

Another very healthy benefit of synchronized Sprint calendars is that it helps Teams write Stories that are independent of the work of other Teams. One of the main arguments in favor of staggering the Sprint calendar across multiple Teams is that the output of one Team can then become an input for another Team, somewhere in the middle of the second Team's Sprint. That Team's output then becomes the input for yet another Team and on and on. It sounds good on paper, but in practice the results are disappointing at best and catastrophic at worst as the cascading dependencies cause the same delays, breakdowns, and confusion that dependencies between work groups or Teams always cause.

We can always break down work into independent chunks. Keep repeating that phrase! Even if there are dependencies that really exist, we can reduce their impact by preventing them from driving work in sequence. Split off the dependent parts of a Story, pulling them into a later Sprint after the upstream work is already finished.

> *Magician's Secret*
> You may be one of those highly alert or skeptical readers who noticed that Component Teams, as I described them, live in the world of inter-Team dependencies. They do indeed – collect your gold star! The key is using smart Product Backlog management to ensure that the work of downstream Teams is never brought to a standstill waiting for a deliverable from an upstream Component Team. Simple buffering breaks the direct dependency link between the different Teams. Just allow a Sprint in between the Component Team's deliverable and the downstream Teams' consumption of that deliverable. This simple buffer works in almost every case. The outliers will always demand special attention.

One other objection to synchronized Sprint calendars is that doing so prevents Teams from seeing the work of other Teams, when their work isn't integrated on Sprint boundaries, because the Sprint Reviews are all on the same day. This is a very simple problem to fix. Stagger – perhaps with some overlap – the

Sprint Reviews! Every Team can hold its Sprint Review on the same day, but if the meeting times are staggered Team Members can visit others as time allows. Another approach is the "science fair" Sprint Review. Conduct all the Sprint Reviews at the same time in one large room, allowing people to flow from one Team to the next organically.

The Importance of Continuous Integration

If multiple Teams are working from the same Product Backlog, meaning they are all working on the same product, the only possible approach is to get serious about continuous integration, working in a single source branch, and integrating at the check-in level. Incremental integration – and the related automated test runs – on a check-in basis ensure that the build is never broken for very long and that the fully integrated product can be shown at the Teams' combined Sprint Review without any additional effort or overhead.

Coordinating Work Across Teams

When working in a multi-Team environment, it is extremely important that the Teams coordinate their work. Typical problems Teams need to work out during every Sprint are expected or unanticipated inter-Team dependencies – hey, we don't always get it right! – and resource contention issues.

If two or more Teams need to work in the same area of the code, for example, they need to coordinate so that they avoid the waste and confusion of merging different versions of the same code. Likewise, if two or more Teams need access to limited resources, things like network bandwidth, build server time, test infrastructure, staging machines, anything like that, the Teams need to arrange their use so that they don't wipe each other out.

Scrum of Scrums

The Scrum framework lends itself to a simple mechanism to deal with inter-Team issues. If you're not using Scrum, you need to come up with a similar mechanism and you get to call it whatever you want!

The Scrum of Scrums is simply a meeting between representatives of the Teams that need to coordinate their work during the Sprint. The Scrum of Scrums follows a similar format to the Daily Scrum, but it does not need to occur every day. And unlike the Daily Scrum, the Scrum of Scrums is definitely devoted to problem solving. My recommendation is that Teams set up a regular Scrum of Scrums schedule, same time and place, two or three times a week to start out. The Teams engaged in the Scrum or Scrums can alter the schedule as needed to accommodate their needs. Maybe your Teams need a daily Scrum of Scrums. Maybe you only need one Scrum of Scrums per week. Fine, go with what works – but make sure it's what works! And be prepared to change the schedule based on feedback you collect along the way.

The Scrum of Scrums is straightforward. Here are the parameters I recommend:

- One or two *technical* representatives from each Team show up at the appointed time and place, with their laptops to code solutions collaboratively in real time
    - The roster changes to fit the current technical challenges
- The Teams may invite one Scrum Master to *facilitate*
- This is a problem-solving meeting, *not* time boxed at 15 minutes
    - Set a time box of an hour or two to keep the meeting effective and alter as needed to keep it effective
    - Make sure everyone knows what the current time box is *before* the next meeting!
- Everyone answers three questions on behalf of their respective Teams:
    - What has my Team done since the last Scrum of Scrums that affects other Teams?
    - What will my Team do before the next Scrum of Scrums that may affect other Teams?
    - What impediments are impacting my Team's work that other Teams could help with?
- The output of the Scrum of Scrums is coordinated work, including design decisions that affect all of the Teams represented, and problems solved or solid plans to solve the problems and impediments raised

My recommendation is that the assembled Team representatives run through the questions much like the Daily Scrum, collecting notes for further discussion and problem solving during the remainder of the Scrum of Scrums.

Common Problems With the Scrum of Scrums

The most pervasive – almost universal – problem with the Scrum of Scrums is that it is attended exclusively by Scrum Masters. The assembled Scrum Masters invariably use the meeting for project management. Wait, which Scrum roles have project management responsibilities again? Oh yes, you remember now, it's the Product Owner and Development Team Members. *The Scrum Master has neither direct accountability for nor authority over the project.*

> **Tip**
> Scrum Masters should certainly be meeting regularly, but under a different umbrella, that of a Community of Practice, as described below.

Another common problem with the Scrum of Scrums is that its roster becomes cemented in place and creates an implied or real technical hierarchy within the Teams. Only the architects or technical leads or whatever attend the Scrum of Scrums in this case. This is a serious dysfunction in that it saps the Teams of their problem-solving and innovation muscle. Seriously, do not allow the Scrum of Scrums to take on any hint of hierarchy. Decide as a Team who needs to attend the next Scrum of Scrums for technical reasons, not based on some real or imaginary – and soon to be real – hierarchy. The Scrum of Scrums is by the Teams, of the Teams, and for the Teams. Do everything possible to keep it that way.

Scaling the Scrum of Scrums

In very large enterprises, it can be necessary scale up even the Scrum of Scrums. Fortunately this is a very simple matter of rolling up to the next level as needed. So you can end up with a Scrum of Scrum of Scrums, a Scrum of Scrum of Scrum of Scrums.... Well, you can probably come up with a more elegant naming convention, but this awkwardness captures the essence of scaling.

The next level above the Scrum of Scrums draws one or two representatives from each Scrum of Scrums. Repeat as required to roll up technical coordination and problem solving in your organization.

What About The Product Owner?

Scaling the Product Owner is the subject of some controversy in the Agile community, probably because Scrum itself has nothing to say on the subject. Every Team needs – must have – a dedicated Product Owner. Every product must have an individual Product Owner who is accountable for the business success of the product. So how can that work in a multi-Team environment where several Teams are working on the same product, pulling from the same Product Backlog, in parallel?

Good question – and in my opinion the source of much of the confusion and controversy on this subject.

The solution that I have experienced the most success with in practice is to create a hierarchy of Product Owners something like that depicted below:*

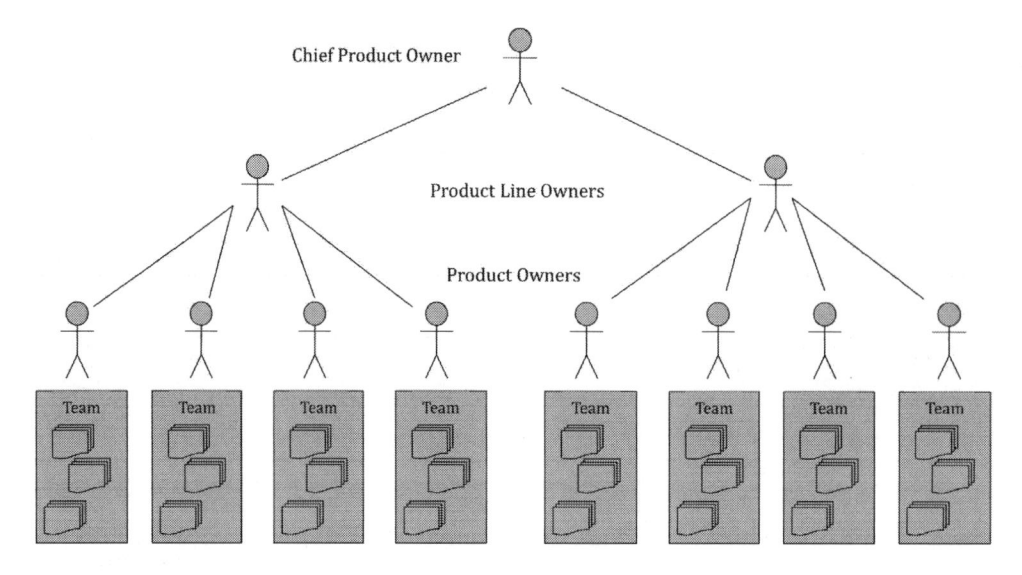

Yes, I did indeed use the word "hierarchy" to describe scaling the Product Owner role. The hierarchy is not necessarily one of organizational rank or reporting structure. It is, however, a decision tree. The reasons behind the need for a hierarchical Product Owner decision tree are not difficult to comprehend.

Each Team-level Product Owner wants the maximum amount of his or her Stories delivered. This focused approach serves the product and the Team well when appropriately balanced. The problem is that the Product Owners working together on a product are so immersed in the day-to-day details that they cannot possibly have the higher-level view needed to make product-level decisions of priority, feature sets, and other big-picture aspects of the product that affect the Product Backlog.

For this we need someone who does not have Team-level responsibilities, a Product Line Owner in the diagram above. The Product Line Owner has the authority to change the order of Epics in the Product Backlog, for example. The Product Line Owner has the appropriate vision, and authority, to break deadlocks between Team-level Product Owners. Product Line Owners engage

---

* Adapted from Cohn 2010, p. 327 ff.

at the strategic level within the product or product line, while the Team-level Product Owners are all over the tactical side of Story and feature delivery.

Enterprises that have more than one product or product line also need someone to take the portfolio view. In the Product Owner hierarchy depicted above, that person is the Chief Product Owner. The Chief Product Owner is typically a high-level executive with the authority and budget to direct the appropriate prioritization and energy into the product lines and products that make up the enterprise portfolio. The Chief Product Owner also has the appropriate vision and authority to break deadlocks between Product Line Owners.

Interestingly, in many organizations with which I have been involved as an Agile coach, the Chief Product Owner is also the person most responsible for removing the big organizational impediments that inevitably arise. I think this makes perfect sense. The Chief Product Owner is the one person accountable for the success of the enterprise portfolio and therefore the one person who has both the authority and the motivation to ensure that the really big organizational impediments don't negatively impact the success of the enterprise portfolio.

Communities of Practice

Communities of Practice are neither new nor directly related to Agile.[*] A Community of Practice is simply self-organizing group of people who share a common interest in a particular domain. A Community of Practice contains three elements: the Domain, the Community, and the Practice.

Communities of Practice work to develop and spread knowledge across organizational boundaries. They do this by developing deep expertise in the domain area around which the community has self-organized. Communities of Practice are, to hammer home the point one last time, self-organizing and self-directing. They require only support and encouragement from the organization to form, sustain, and grow.

Communities of Practice are a great fit for Agile organizations in which self-organization and breaking down silo barriers have become if not the norm at least accepted practices.

---

[*] Wenger 1998

In my coaching life, I have worked to help Communities of Practice form by providing awareness and encouragement. The Community has to form through self-organization, however. Any attempt to force Communities of Practice on people is doomed to fail.

Communities of Practice can form around technological domains, role-based domains, anything. Some examples that I have seen work in organizations include Communities of Practice for Java programming, automated testing, ERP systems, and, best of all Scrum Masters and Product Owners.

Communities of Practice need to meet up to be effective at learning and spreading knowledge, of course. All meetings, as well as membership, are open to the general organizational public. A Community of Practice is neither a secret society nor the keeper of some fancy set of keys to the kingdom. The point is for membership to *spread* knowledge and expertise in the domain, not to guard knowledge and expertise like some Medieval Guild.

A Community really needs just a place to meet, a little cover from management for the time spent meeting, and maybe a small budget for books, pizzas, coffee and tea, snacks, things like that. More established Communities of Practice might lobby for more funding so that members may attend and present sessions at domain-relevant conferences or other learning events.

Among the most successful and powerful Communities of Practice in my coaching experience are those established by and for Scrum Masters. Learning the art and practice of Scrum Mastering requires deep experience and sharing of knowledge with others facing the same kinds of challenges. Simply put, a Scrum Master Community of Practice is a powerful tool for building and expanding this expertise in an Agile organization. Prospective Scrum Masters and those who are simply curious about this new, oddly named role in the company can learn a great deal from those of their peers who are hip-deep in the day-to-day concerns of the job.

If your organization doesn't currently have Communities of Practice, try creating one in your area of interest, whatever it might be. You might just be surprised at the response and results you can achieve with the power of self-organization.

Wrapping Up

Scaling Scrum (or any other Team-based Agile framework) to an enterprise level involves some unique challenges. The key thing to keep in mind is that the basic unit in any discussion of scaling up is the Scrum Team itself, not the number of individuals in the development or IT departments. Coordinating work between Teams and building an effective Product Owner organization are two of the biggest challenges on the road to enterprise agility. But don't overlook the importance of architecture and design in the enterprise setting. Leverage the power of self-organization through the Scrum of Scrums and Communities of Practice to build a truly effective, truly Agile organization.

Further Reading

Brooks, Frederick P., Jr. *The Mythical Man Month: Essays on Software Engineering.* 2nd ed. Boston: Addison-Wesley, 1995.

Cohn, Mike. *Succeeding with Agile: Software Development Using Scrum.* Upper Saddle River, NJ: Addison-Wesley, 2010.

Larman, Craig and Bas Vodde. *Large-Scale Scrum: More With LeSS.* Upper Saddle River, NJ: Addison-Wesley, 2017.

Pichler, Roman. *Agile Product Management With Scrum: Creating Products that Customers Love.* Upper Saddle River, NJ: Addison-Wesley, 2010.

Schwaber, Ken. *Agile Project Management With Scrum.* Redmond, WA: Microsoft Press, 2004.

Schwaber, Ken. *The Enterprise and Scrum.* Redmond, WA: Microsoft Press, 2007.

Wenger, Etienne. *Communities of Practice: Learning, Meaning, and Identity.* New York: Cambridge University Press, 1998.

Chapter 11 Implementing Scrum

"If you can't explain it simply, you don't understand it well enough."
– *Albert Einstein*

The next step is to take everything you've learned to this point and put it into practice. Implementing Scrum is non-trivial, but also not impossible given an appropriate approach and an organizational environment willing to explore and embrace change. Always remember that the point is not to "do Scrum" in some perfect fashion. The point is to use Scrum to achieve agility as a business, to be successful as a business, and to create a workplace that people are eager, excited even, to come to every day.

So if the point is not to "do Scrum" perfectly – whatever that even means – then why all the focus on following the Scrum framework completely and conscientiously? It boils down to this: Scrum is fully formed right out of the box. It is ready to use without modification. Scrum contains all of the moving parts needed to begin (or continue) your Agile journey. You don't have to invent anything to get started with Scrum, but you do have to implement all of the moving parts as intended if you are to be successful with Scrum. From a Team perspective, there are some specific steps necessary to get the ball rolling. This chapter is devoted to those steps, drawn from my experience helping hundreds of Teams get started with Scrum.

Scrum is Disruptive – So Find a Sponsor

Scrum is disruptive by design. It is not intended to accommodate existing work practices or organizational structures. It introduces a radically different way of building products and as a result brings with it the promise – and the pain – of effective organizational change. The structures currently in place in your organization were built to support, or at least accommodate, a very different way of working. Those organizational structures are not appropriate for Scrum and will, every time, either limit your success with Scrum or prevent you from using Scrum at all.

Given all of that, an organizational sponsor is a necessity. The ideal Scrum sponsor is someone with sufficient organizational authority to support the implementation of Scrum and also the ability to sell the necessary changes to those whose work, roles, and authority Scrum will inevitably challenge. Another critical qualification for Scrum sponsor is a thorough understanding of Scrum theory and practice, preferably gained through experience. A sponsor who can relate Scrum success stories from direct experience brings a high degree of credibility to the table. If that experienced sponsor does not exist in your organization, second best is a sponsor who is knowledgeable about Scrum in the abstract and passionate about using Scrum to improve products and the organization as a whole.

The implication here is that your Scrum sponsor needs to be someone who occupies a box in the corporate org chart above the functional specializations and silos that divide most organizations. Even better would be a person whose purview extends across product implementation and into the business itself. It's not enough to get just the technology side of the organization on board; Scrum demands daily interaction with the business as well, so we must have the business on board in order to be successful. Remember the Product Owner role? The Product Owner is accountable to the business so we need the business on board if we are going to succeed.

Whoever your sponsor is, make sure that person is in it for the long haul. Getting Scrum up and running in your organization, and keeping it running, demands long-term thinking and vision. More than once I have experienced Scrum crashing back to earth when the sponsor either loses interest or leaves the organization.

Train Everyone Involved

Training is essential for everyone involved in the effort to get going with Scrum. Hopefully this is obvious, but I am always shocked at the reluctance to provide competent Scrum training to everyone whom the rollout of even a single Scrum Team will affect. This, of course, begins with role-specific training for the Scrum Master, Product Owner, and Development Team Members. In addition, the stakeholders within the organization who are impacted by the introduction of Scrum need to be provided with more than the usual one-hour Agile overview session. I recommend that organizational stakeholders – which if your product is internally consumed also includes customers – receive the training most appropriate to their role in the organization, either Scrum Master or Product Owner role training.

Why train everyone and not just the Scrum Team members? That's an easy one. Everyone has to understand both the rules of the game and the expectations placed on them in making this move to Scrum.

Managers have to understand that they are not there to give orders or to "help" the Team by telling people how to do their jobs. Instead, managers become the first line of defense against organizational impediments and the organizational gravity those impediments create. Managers also have to understand that the Development Team is a self-managing entity that needs space to work without redirection or distraction. Finally, managers have to understand that they do not have the authority to bypass the Scrum structures – Product Backlog, Product Owner, and Development Team authority – that determine what the Team works on and how the Team does its work. Again, managers need to take part in standard role-based training, probably Scrum Master training since the role of management is most directly tied to impediment removal.

Stakeholders need to realize that the old fire-and-forget, contract-driven ways of working no longer apply. The stakeholders' full participation and indeed partnership with the entire Scrum Team is necessary if the Team is to build a product that meets their needs, either as direct customers/end users of the product or as business stakeholders.

Choose a Product

This may seem like an obvious prerequisite, but there are some things going on with the decision about choosing a product that deserve some attention. First off, the product you choose should be important and valuable to the organization in clearly tangible ways. Although tempting, it does no good to choose a trivial, non-valuable product as a way to reduce the risk of introducing a disruptive framework like Scrum. The Team developing the product has to know that the product is both valuable and of vital importance to the organization. Anything less is a waste of the Team's time and effort and will be detrimental to the Team's effectiveness and morale.

We're talking about a single Scrum Team here, so the product does have to be of the appropriate size, at least in its initial form, for that one Scrum Team to deliver. That does not mean the product has to be tiny. Our objective is to build a powerful, productive Scrum Team, an outcome that produces surprising results from a very small number of people.

The balance between appropriate size and value/importance makes the choice of product potentially difficult, but also offers an opportunity for the organization to deliver a product that might otherwise not get the attention it deserves.

Assemble Your Team – Product Owner, Scrum Master, Development Team Members

Once you have chosen a product to build, assemble your Scrum Team. The first step in this critical activity is to find a Product Owner for the product. The individual you choose to be Product Owner *must* be passionate about the product. The Product Owner *must* also be an expert in the business domain the product serves. Finally, the Product Owner *must* be an excellent communicator who can work directly with customers and stakeholders – and the Development Team – to ensure that the Team's work generates the maximum possible business value. For other qualifications the Product Owner must possess, refer to Chapter 2.

Product Owner Hits The Ground Running

The Product Owner then needs to work with stakeholders to create a Product Vision that captures and communicates the essential elements of the product, in particular who is the product for, why is it valuable both to customers and the organization, what will success look like, and how will we know when we've achieved success. There are a variety of product visioning techniques in wide use, including an Elevator Pitch, Product Box, Trade Show Flyer, Trade Journal Article, and Product Roadmap. Use as many of these techniques as needed to build a coherent, viable Product Vision.

Scrum Master Self-selects

Next, identify a Scrum Master to serve the Team. The best person to serve as Scrum Master is the person who both understands the role – through training and experience or at the very least through training – *and wants to take on the role of Scrum Master.* So many organizations have foundered in their first attempt at Scrum simply because they ignore this advice and arbitrarily appoint Scrum Masters from their existing pool of functional managers, project managers, technical leads, etc. Being a Scrum Master is often difficult and sometimes thankless, making it absolutely vital that the person playing this role is intrinsically motivated to be successful at it.

My advice is, *after training,* ask for volunteers to take on the role of Scrum Master. Evaluate the volunteers and choose the individual most likely to succeed in leading the Scrum rollout in the organization. As with any role selection there is an element of risk here, but don't agonize over it. Pick a highly motivated individual who is passionate about enabling Teams and teamwork and call it good.

Finally, make sure the organization has made room for successful Scrum Master practice by designating this role as exclusive, meaning Scrum Masters are Scrum Masters only – there is no "day job" in addition to being a Scrum Master. Failure to do so is another fatal flaw in many Scrum implementations I have experienced.

Development Team Self-selects Too

The final step is, obviously, to assemble the Development Team to build the product. This is also a bit tricky so here's what I recommend. Have the Product Owner introduce the product by sharing the Product Vision with a likely set of people from the implementation part of the organization. It's clearly best if everyone in the room has already been trained in Scrum, though that may be difficult to achieve at this stage. Make sure that the majority of potential Development Team Members have been trained in Scrum at the very least.

After the Product Owner presents the Product Vision and the assembled prospective Development Team Members have had a chance to ask questions and discuss the Product Vision, ask the assembled group to discover and map out the technology and the skill sets needed to deliver the product, end-to-end. Use the Team Spectrograph described in Chapter 3 to facilitate this activity.

Now that the technology and skill sets are clear and visible, ask for volunteers to fill the various slots identified and become Development Team Members. Some people will invariably choose not to become involved at this point, which is fine. Make sure that the major skill sets are represented on the Team that results and that the Team is small, no more than seven Development Team Members. Another crash point when getting started with Scrum is to create Teams that are too large and unwieldy to be successful. Some people may be disappointed at not being able to join this first Scrum Team. Put them on a waitlist for the next Scrum Team. You may also find that there are one or two Team slots unfilled. Repeat this activity with a smaller, more skill-focused set of candidates to fill the remaining Development Team slots.

The same organizational caveats that apply to defining the Scrum Master role apply to the Development Team. All Team Members are dedicated to their team and to the product – no exceptions, no separate "day job" and no outside-of-the-Team commitments for anyone. I know I keep hammering this point home, but it is critical to your success with Scrum. I've seen far too many Scrum Teams collapse as a result of Development Team Members being matrixed across other products/projects or Teams.

Team Working Agreement

Before going any further, get all the Development Team Members together to build and commit to a Team Working Agreement. The Scrum Master facilitates the generation of ideas, discussions, and the commitment ceremony. I really like using the five Scrum Values plus a couple of others (as described on pages 27-28) as the basis for building a Team Working Agreement. The Product Owner is optional in this activity, though being present as an observer at least isn't a bad idea unless the Team feels constrained with the Product Owner there. Remember, it may take some time to build trust depending on your starting point.

Expect to engage in at least two one-hour sessions building your initial Team Working Agreement. Allow a day or two in between sessions to allow the first set of commitments to soak in to with Team members before refining and adding more. And make sure commitment to each actionable value statement is explicit.

Try This

Use the Fist of Five technique to measure and register commitment to each proposed value statement. In response to any suggestion up for the Team's consideration – such as "Can we commit to implementing <*value statement x*>?" – the response is one of the following number of fingers held aloft for all to see by each Team Member:

Five Fingers: Enthusiastic support and commitment

Four Fingers: Solid support and commitment

Three Fingers: No personal preference but *full commitment to implement the decision of the Team*

Two Fingers: Veto – we need to discuss and refine to get to at least three fingers. If the objection cannot be overcome, the item is dropped from consideration.

One Finger: Index finger please! An emphatic veto. See the rule for Two Fingers to address the objection.

You now have a fully formed, although not yet functioning, Scrum Team composed of intrinsically motivated individuals, ready to get going. So let's get going!

Do As Little As Necessary to Get Started...And Then Get Started!

Hooray – you have assembled a Scrum Team! Now, let's get to work. And by get to work I mean let's do as little preparatory work as possible before starting to develop the product. That *does not mean* just dive in without thought or preparation. It also *does not mean* spending weeks or months doing that initial thought and preparation. Find the balance point between not enough and just enough and then get started, because knowledge comes from experience. Before generating knowledge, it's all just assumptions and speculation.

Refine The Product Vision

The first step is for the Product Owner to present the Product Vision to the Development Team, discussing customer and stakeholder goals and how the product will meet their needs. This should be a freewheeling discussion that potentially leads to refinement of the Product Vision, not a presentation of a directive from management. The Scrum Master should facilitate this activity to encourage both questions and feedback on the Product Vision from the Team. Coaching the Product Owner in advance to be prepared for questions and feedback would be a great approach!

Expect to spend an hour or two reviewing and refining the Product Vision with the Team. Keep this a low-ceremony activity, no managers, just the full Scrum Team. Snacks are always a good idea as well. Incorporate any agreed upon changes into the Product Vision and then move on.

Generate and Refine The Initial Product Backlog

Now that the Product Vision is shared, refined, and owned by the entire Scrum Team, start breaking the Vision into smaller chunks by holding a Team User Story writing workshop. A good approach is to think about the customer-user journey through the product, end-to-end, and then generate Epics covering that journey. Stay high-level here. The details will emerge over time. Next, ask the Product Owner to choose an Epic that contains valuable functionality to deliver to customers and stakeholders first. This Epic is the source of the first Potentially Shippable Product Increment, which will be the outcome of the Team's first Sprint.

Dive into that first Epic, breaking out smaller Stories that follow the thin, vertical slice, INVEST-based approach. Extract 20-30 Stories from that first Epic, add Acceptance Criteria, think about high-level architecture and design elements that might be needed to implement the Stories. Keep the thinking at this point very high-level, as in "We think we'll need to integrate with our CRM system to extract customer data, probably use an MVC-style architecture for the application layer, and persist data in a cloud-based service that we already use for other, somewhat similar products the company has already built."

Once the Team has written the initial set of 20-30 Stories and given some thought to architecture and design approaches, refine the Stories further, collaborating with the Product Owner to understand the customer/business value of each Story and solidifying the Acceptance Criteria to the extent that the Team is comfortable with the scope of each Story and the testing approaches likely to satisfy the "T" in INVEST. It's also time to estimate the Stories using a relative, comparative estimating technique like affinity grouping. Bring all Stories to the point where they meet the INVEST criteria, but don't go any further than that.

Expect to spend between a couple of days and a week building and refining the Product Backlog. The Team may spend some of that time doing exploratory coding to answer questions and discover feasible approaches and maybe mock up a prototype or two to help generate some clarity. No actual deliverable work happens yet! Just don't go there.

Now that the Team has 20-30 Stories refined and, in the Team's estimation, ready to be planned and delivered, you're done preparing. Don't do any more.

Do you feel like you know everything about the product? No? Good! You should feel a little on edge, clear in the realization that you really don't know very much at all about the end result. That edginess, that uncomfortable uncertainty reflects reality accurately. The best – and only – way to achieve more clarity and confidence is to start working, plan a Sprint, deliver a small but fully functional slice of the product, and review the results with customers and stakeholders. The fog will clear, incrementally, iteratively, as you build the product and incorporate feedback from customers and stakeholders in to each Sprint Plan.

Plan The First Sprint and Get Started!

Refer to **Chapter 7 Sprint Planning** to review what you need to generate an effective Sprint Plan. Assemble your Scrum Team, decide what to do, and then get going. Deciding what to do is the critical aspect of that very first Sprint. An effective Sprint Goal is the most important driver of success right out of the gate. Evaluate these two example Sprint Goals for their effectiveness in helping you get off to a great start:

> *Example Sprint Goal 1:* Analyze the Stories and do the design for the first phase of the project. Begin working on the database schema.

> *Example Sprint Goal 2:* Deliver basic customer preferences functionality along with a bare-bones UI to allow users to provide feedback on the preferences categories and the overall direction of the product.

And now consider a couple of questions. Which of these Sprint Goals would result in a Potentially Shippable Product Increment at the end of the Sprint? Which of these Sprint Goals would be most effective in generating meaningful stakeholder feedback at the Sprint Review?

The point of every Sprint is to produce some increment of value that could, potentially, be delivered to customers. And yes, that includes the outcome of the very first Sprint. Always think in terms of delivering an increment of the product that is tangible and valuable every Sprint. *This is especially vital for the first Sprint.* You (should) want to engage with your stakeholders immediately and there is no better way than to show them a small, fully functional, valuable, and Potentially Shippable Product Increment at the end of the first Sprint.

Waiting to deliver anything tangible and valuable until two or more Sprints down the road sets a poor precedent for the Scrum Team, the organization, and most importantly for stakeholders – nothing has changed, it's just the same old big-batch, long development cycle game we've been playing all along. Don't go there, please! Start strong and keep it going Sprint after Sprint.

Insulate the Team From Organizational Politics

Organizational politics can crush a Scrum Team before it can even get started. The competing interests of various functional managers, mid-level managers, and executives can, and all too frequently do, prevent a Scrum adoption from ever getting off the ground.

Chapter 11 Implementing Scrum

The Scrum Master role is charged with defending the Team's effectiveness in part by providing a buffer between the Team and the destructive force of organizational politics. Most organizations are optimized at least implicitly to prevent changes to managerial prestige and authority so expect some degree of tension when introducing a disruptive framework like Scrum. The critical aspect here is to use your executive sponsor as a shield so that you can be successful within the existing organizational context.

Beyond having executive sponsorship, Scrum Masters need to set the stage for their Team's success by having conversations with people across the management spectrum in the organization, helping set the expectations for the Team's success and equally the expectations of the changing and perhaps even completely new role of management in the organization. In Agile organizations, managers do not act as taskmasters, instead they work to improve the effectiveness of Teams by removing impediments and providing whatever support the Teams need to improve.

Some of the conversations Scrum Masters have with managers can be difficult, depending on the organizational context and the personality, motivations, and concerns of the individual manager. I recently had the following (paraphrased) conversation with a Scrum Master at a large company:

Me: "Managers have to understand their changing role in the Agile organization and it is the Scrum Master's job to provide coaching and support to help both the organization and the Team be effective. The first hurdle is to make it clear to managers that they cannot interfere with the Team's work."

Scrum Master: "How can I have that conversation with a manager? They constantly interfere with people on my team."

Me: "Help the managers understand the cost of the disruption they are causing in terms of lost focus, value, and effectiveness. Every wasted minute of the Team's time has a cost. You can and should make that cost visible."

Scrum Master: "I can't do that! Managers at my company always tell everyone what to do and are constantly redirecting people."

Me: "Remember that Transparency is one of our basic operating principles."

Scrum Master: "I would get fired if I did what you're saying."

My unspoken response was – *wow, just wow.* That's a company that is not long for the world. Living in fear of managers produces a toxic work environment in which people are not allowed even to care about customer outcomes. Companies that operate based on fear of reprisal will neither produce great products nor will they retain anyone who wants purpose and fulfillment in their work. And that is clearly a losing proposition.

Build a Fault-Tolerant Environment

The first Scrum Team will be the primary agent of discovering product and organizational dysfunctions and the Development Team will be the primary engine of unearthing all of those dysfunctions. As a result, the organizational environment must be fault tolerant. This is another major Scrum Master coaching opportunity. Make sure everyone involved or even concerned with the Scrum rollout is aware that one of the major benefits of Scrum is providing transparency into everything that is both right and wrong with the product and the organization. So first off it's not all bad news. Some things are likely to go very, very well. Nurture those things, wherever you find them!

On the other hand, deficiencies in the product development organization and the larger company will be both visible and generally intolerably painful. I like to look at such things as opportunities for improvement rather than negatives. The more problems, impediments, and dysfunctions that rise to the surface as a result of launching your first Scrum Team, the more opportunities the organization has to improve. Just between us, most organizations have gigantic opportunities for improvement that go unrecognized because they are hidden under layers of bureaucracy and obfuscation. So my advice is to take hold of the improvement opportunities Scrum presents and run with them. As with any improvement approach, the problem must undergo root-cause analysis and then the relevant part or parts of the organization must devise specific, actionable, measurable improvement ideas. Oh, and then someone must commit to implementing the improvement ideas.

All of this sounds good enough, but there is a dark side to be aware of. In some, perhaps most, organizations using Scrum to become Agile, there is an inherent negative bias against problems, impediments, and dysfunctions. Some people feel threatened when a problem is identified in "their" area. Some people blame Scrum for causing the problems and demand either changes to Scrum (to hide the problems) or dropping Scrum altogether. Even worse, some people blame the Development Team Members for finding problems, impediments, and dysfunctions that extend beyond the boundaries of the Scrum Team. Other people get discouraged when confronted with the sheer weight of the mess in front of them. My advice is simply this: Don't give in to despair, look at each problem as an opportunity, devise a solution, and run an experiment to see if the proposed solution is effective. Either way, repeat these steps until the impediment or problem is fixed or loses importance in the face of other issues. Oh, and if your organization doesn't value improvement, Scrum is probably not going to be effective.

At its best, Scrum is an impediment-surfacing machine. Expect plenty of opportunities for improvement and celebrate your success whenever improvement occurs.

Make It Real!

An aspect of any Scrum implementation that I cannot emphasize enough is to make it real for yourself and your teammates. That means following the Scrum framework conscientiously and completely. I've seen plenty of attempted Scrum adoptions fail almost immediately as a result of not actually doing Scrum. When Scrum is just the process flavor of the month, when there is a lack of organizational commitment to implementing Scrum fully, people quickly become cynical and lose interest. If the Development Team doesn't have the authority to own how much work they pull and how they implement that work every Sprint, forget it. Smart people – and Teams are composed of smart people – see through BS pretty much instantly. Just don't go there. Make it real. Earn the trust of your Team, the business, customers, stakeholders, and executives by really doing Scrum.

The combination of Team authority to make decisions and the focus on customer-based business outcomes generates a powerful dynamic that captures and holds the attention of everyone involved. Cutting corners with Scrum or, even worse, changing Scrum to make it fit more comfortably with the existing organizational environment, eliminates the possibility of generating that powerful dynamic and the compelling outcomes it produces. So I'll say it again – make it real.

Go Big Or Go Home?

Some people are cautious by nature and are strongly inclined to try to implement Scrum a little at a time, as a means of mitigating the risk of a disruptive change causing chaos. It is a tempting thought. Scrum itself is designed to control risk – business risk, technical risk, social risk, and cost and schedule risk. The problem is you can't control those areas of risk with an incomplete form of Scrum. You need the whole Scrum package before you can generate the knowledge and feedback necessary to control risk.

Set yourself up for success. Adopt Scrum and use it as the primary tool to control risk. There is clearly a leap of faith involved in implementing Scrum with even a single Team. The good news is that Scrum has a huge amount of experience and knowledge backing it up. You aren't alone, nor are you the first to experience the uncertainty of jumping into Scrum. So take the leap, do it right, and set up yourself, your Team, and your organization for success.

Now, Do It Again

Okay, you've spun up your first Scrum Team, learned how to work in a cross-functional environment, resolved some impediments, generated business value using the feedback built into Scrum, and celebrated your success. Great! Now, do it again. And again. And Again. Repeat that initial success until the entire organization is built around Scrum and Agile Values and Principles.

The books cited in the Further Reading section below contain some ideas for replicating your initial Scrum Team's success. I'm not a big fan of breaking up a successful Team for any reason. I much prefer that first Team to serve as Subject Matter Experts in Scrum for the rest of the organization while continuing to build on their success.

Wrapping Up

Getting going with Scrum in your organization can be challenging and exasperating, exciting and at least mildly terrifying all at once. The rewards of building a powerful, adaptable Scrum Team go far beyond building a great product. Give yourself, your Team, and your organization the chance to have that experience. Find a sponsor, choose a product, build your Team, cultivate the organizational environment, and enjoy the ride!

Further Reading

Cohn, Mike. *Succeeding with Agile: Software Development Using Scrum.* Upper Saddle River, NJ: Addison-Wesley, 2010.

Larman, Craig and Bas Vodde. *Large-Scale Scrum: More With LeSS.* Upper Saddle River, NJ: Addison-Wesley, 2017.

Epilogue: Never Stop

We've come a long way together from the beginning of this book. I hope you have found it a valuable use of your time and that you continue to discover value in these pages. Whether you are just getting started on an Agile Team or are months or years into your Team experience, there is a long, challenging, and rewarding road ahead of you. Your journey as a Development Team Member is always in progress, never at an end. There are always obstacles to overcome, improvements to implement, skills to build or enhance, products to develop and deliver.

Whether you work in a small company or a large enterprise, there is always something to work on to get better at what you do as a member of a Team; always something you can do to make your Team better, stronger, and more capable. Building Agile muscle memory by practicing Scrum is one thing, but that goal is not the end point. Agility brings with it the strength and momentum to engage in Continuous Improvement, which is by its very nature an ongoing process, not an event.

Use the power of self-organization to make your Team and organization great. Are you building cross-functional skills deliberately, purposefully on your Team? If not, why not? Are you using Communities of Practice to enhance and spread skills horizontally across your organization? Again, if not, why not? Have you expressed appreciation for the efforts or one or more Teammates in the last few days? And on and on it goes.

Above all else, keep your chin up; keep working toward building truly effective teamwork on your Team regardless of the potholes, tiger traps, and other obstacles that lie in and along the path to building a great Team. Today's disaster is an opportunity to learn, to grow, to become stronger as a Team player and as a whole Team tomorrow. Sometimes you just have to engage your sense of humor and move on. Other times you need to apply powerful analytical techniques, many of which we have covered in this book, to build an understanding of what happened and to generate insights into how to move forward.

Whatever you do, never stop improving! Yes it's hard work. No it's not always fun. No one, including yours truly, promised that the road to becoming a great Agile Team would be smooth, easy, quick, or an exercise in never-ending fun. The promise is in the rewards, both personal and professional, of being a part of something bigger than yourself, of making a vital contribution to the formation and continuing growth of a powerful, confident Team.

When you move on – and in the technology world as it is you most assuredly will at some point – take what you've learned about Teams and teamwork with you so that you can play a vital role in building yet another great Team. If you move out of daily delivery and into management, take what you've learned and become a leader instead of a boss. Maybe your next move will be into the realm of Agile training, coaching, and mentoring. If so, as an experienced Development Team Member you possess powerful qualifications to help others build their own Agile Teams.

A Team is an amazing thing to be a part of. A Team is a uniquely human construct that defies the laws of (at least Newtonian) physics by being a whole that is much, much greater than the sum of its parts. Use what you've learned here and, more importantly, what you learn every day working as a Development Team Member, to help your Team be better today than it was yesterday, better tomorrow than it is today.

References

This section lists all books, articles, and other source materials cited or referred to in this book. This is a good start on an Agile bibliography for those interested in building out a Team library.

BBC News. "Is Multitasking a Myth?" *BBC News Magazine*, August 20, 2010, (http://www.bbc.co.uk/news/magazine-11035055).

Beck, Kent. *Extreme Programming Explained: Embrace Change.* 2nd ed. Boston: Addison-Wesley, 2005.

_____. *Test Driven Development: By Example.* Boston: Pearson Education, 2003.

Brooks, Frederick P., Jr. *The Mythical Man Month: Essays on Software Engineering.* 2nd ed. Boston: Addison-Wesley, 1995.

_____. "No Silver Bullet: Essence and Accidents of Software Engineering," *Computer*, Vol. 20, No. 4 (April 1987) pp. 10-19.

Cockburn, Alistair. *Agile Software Development.* Boston: Addison-Wesley, 2002.

Cohn, Mike. *Agile Estimating and Planning.* Upper Saddle River, NJ: Pearson Education, Inc, 2006.

_____. *Succeeding with Agile: Software Development Using Scrum.* Upper Saddle River, NJ: Addison-Wesley, 2010.

_____. *User Stories Applied: For Agile Software Development.* Boston: Addison-Wesley, 2004.

Denning, Stephen. *The Leader's Guide to Radical Management: Reinventing the Workplace for the 21st Century.* San Francisco: Jossey-Bass, 2010.

References

Derby, Esther and Diana Larsen. *Agile Retrospectives: Making Good Teams Great.* Sebastopol: O'Reilly Media, Inc., 2006.

Feathers, Michael. *Working Effectively With Legacy Code.* Upper Saddle River, NJ: Prentice Hall, 2005.

Fowler, Martin. *Refactoring: Improving the Design of Existing Code.* Boston: Addison-Wesley, 2000.

Goldratt, Dr. Eliyahu M. and Jeff Cox. *The Goal: A Process of Ongoing Improvement.* 3rd edition. Great Barrington, MA: The North River Press, 2004 (first edition, 1984).

Greenleaf, Robert K. *On Becoming a Servant-Leader.* San Francisco: Jossey-Bass, 1996.

_____. *The Servant as Leader.* Indianapolis: The Robert K. Greenleaf Center for Servant-Leadership, 1970.

_____. *The Power of Servant-Leadership.* San Francisco: Berrett-Koehler, 1998.

Humble, Jez and David Farley. *Continuous Delivery: Reliable Software Releases Through Build, Test, and Deployment Automation.* Upper Saddle River, NJ: Addison-Wesley, 2011.

Jeffries, Ron *XP Magazine* August 3, 2001.

Katzenbach, Jon R. and Douglas K. Smith. *The Wisdom of Teams: Creating the High-Performance Organization.* New York: Harper Collins Publishers, 1993.

Keim, Brandon. "Is Multitasking Bad For Us?" *NOVA ScienceNOW,* October 4, 2012, (http://www.pbs.org/wgbh/nova/body/is-multitasking-bad.html).

Larman, Craig and Bas Vodde. *Large-Scale Scrum: More With LeSS.* Upper Saddle River, NJ: Addison-Wesley, 2017.

_____. *Scaling Lean & Agile Development: Thinking and Organizational Tools for Large-Scale Scrum.* Upper Saddle River, NJ: Addison-Wesley, 2009.

Martin, Robert C. *Clean Code: A Handbook of Agile Software Craftsmanship.* Upper Saddle River, NJ: Prentice Hall, 2008

Ophir, Eyal et al. 2009. "Cognitive Control in Media Multitaskers." *Proceedings of the National Academy of Sciences,* 106:37, September 15, 2009, (www.pnas.org/content/106/37/15583.short, http://news.stanford.edu/news/2009/august24/multitask-research-study-082409.html)

Pichler, Roman. *Agile Product Management With Scrum: Creating Products that Customers Love.* Upper Saddle River, NJ: Addison-Wesley, 2010.

Pink, Daniel H. *Drive: The Surprising Truth About What Motivates Us.* New York: Riverhead Books, 2009.

Poppendieck, Mary and Tom Poppendieck. *Implementing Lean Software Development: From Concept to Cash.* Boston: Addison-Wesley, 2007.

_____. *Leading Lean Software Development: Results Are Not The Point.* Boston: Addison-Wesley, 2010.

_____. *Lean Software Development: An Agile Toolkit.* Boston: Addision-Wesley, 2003.

Rawsthorne, Dan and Doug Shimp. *Exploring Scrum: The Fundamentals (People, Product, and Practices).* USA: Self-published, 2011.

Royce, Dr. Winston W. "Managing The Development of Large Software Systems," *Proceedings,* IEEE WESCON (August 1970), pp. 1-9.

Schwaber, Ken. *Agile Project Management With Scrum.* Redmond, WA: Microsoft Press, 2004.

Schwaber, Ken and Mike Beedle. *Agile Software Development With Scrum.* Upper Saddle River, NJ: Prentice Hall, 2002.

Schwaber, Ken. *The Enterprise and Scrum.* Redmond, WA: Microsoft Press, 2007.

Schwaber, Ken and Jeff Sutherland. *The Scrum Guide, The Definitive Guide to Scrum: The Rules of the Game.* Scrumguides.org, July 2016.

Sharot, Tali "The Optimism Bias" *Time* Saturday, May 28, 2011 (http://www.time.com/time/health/article/0,8599,2074067,00.html)

Shewhart, Walter. *Statistical Method from the Viewpoint of Quality Control.* New York: Dover, originally published 1939, reprint edition 1986.

Sims, Chris and Hillary Louise Johnson. *The Elements of Scrum.* Foster City, CA: Dymaxicon, 2011.

Smith, Jacquelyn. "The Happiest And Unhappiest Industries To Work In," Forbes.com, February 9, 2012 (http://www.forbes.com/sites/jacquelynsmith/2012/02/09/the-happiest-and-unhappiest-industries-to-work-in/)

Stacey, Ralph D. *Strategic Management and Organizational Dynamics: The Challenge of Complexity*, 2002.

Tabaka, Jean. *Collaboration Explained: Facilitation Skills for Software Project Leaders.* Upper Saddle River, NJ: Addison-Wesley, 2006.

Takeuchi, Hirotaka and Ikujiro Nonaka. "The New New Product Development Game," *Harvard Business Review*, January 1986.

Taylor, Frederick Winslow, *The Principles of Scientific Management.* New York & London: Harper, 1911, reprint edition, 1934.

Tuckman, Bruce W. "Developmental Sequence in Small Groups." *Psychological Bulletin*, Vol. 63 No. 6, 1965.

Version One State of Agile Survey 2011 (http://www.versionone.com/state_of_Agile_development_survey/11/)

Wake, Bill. *XP123*, August 17, 2003 (http://xp123.com/articles/invest-in-good-stories-and-smart-tasks/)

Wenger, Etienne. *Communities of Practice: Learning, Meaning, and Identity.* New York: Cambridge University Press, 1998.

Index

A

Acceptance Criteria
    User Stories · 70-71, 76
Adaptation · 5, 6
Agile architecture · 166
Agile Manifesto Principles · 12-21
Agile Manifesto Values · 10-12

B

Beedle, Mike · 27
Brooks, Frederick P. · 7
Brooks' Law · 165
Build-up chart
    Release · 151
    Sprint · 150
Burndown chart
    weaknesses of · 146-149

C

collaboration
    co-located Teams · 163
    communication bandwidth · 154-155
    communication modes · 159-161
    definition · 153, 154
    distributed Teams · 161-162
    physical space · 156-158
    proximity · 161
communication bandwidth · 154-156
communication modes
    convection currents · 159
    drafts · 160-161
    osmotic · 160
Communities of Practice · 177-178
complexity (software) · 7

Component Team · 167-170
    example · 169
Conditions of Satisfaction
    User Stories · 70-71
Conflict modes · 56
context switching · 41
continuous integration · 173

D

Defined Process Control · 1-5
Definition of Done · 71, 112-114, 117
Deming, W. Edwards · 4
Derby, Esther · 107

E

Empirical Process Control · 3-7
Enterprise Agile
    architecture and design · 166
    Communities of Practice · 177-178
    Component Teams · 168-170
    continuous integration · 173
    coordinating Teams' work · 173
    Product Owner role · 175-176
    Scrum of Scrums · 173
    shared Product Backlog · 167
    stagger Daily Scrums · 170
    synchronize Sprints · 171-172
Epic (User Story) · 67
    estimating · 100
estimates
    Epics · 100
    modified Fibonacci sequence · 100
    problems with traditional · 90
    relative · 91-95
    Story Points · 93
    Team ownership · 97

estimating techniques
    affinity grouping · 98, 100
    Planning Poker · 95, 97-98

F

feedback
    product · 25, 103- 105
    Team · 26, 106-108
Fibonacci sequence (modified) · 100
Fist of Five · 186
Ford, Henry · 2, 18
Forming
    Tuckman Model · 54-55

G

Garbo, Greta · 55
Greenleaf, Robert K. · 32
Grenning, James W. · 95

I

IEEE-830 requirements format · 65
impediments · 88
Inspection · 5-6
INVEST
    User Stories · 74-76

J

J-shaped curve · 60

K

Kernighan, Brian · 20

L

Larsen, Diana · 107

M

McKenna, Jeff · 89
measurement
    suited to mass production · 145
mini-waterfall · 114
Model T · 2-3
multitasking · 141

N

Norming
    Tuckman Model · 58

O

optimism bias · 91

P

pair programming · 140
Performing
    Tuckman Model · 59
Plan-Do-Check-Act (PDCA) · 4
Plan-Do-Inspect-Adapt · 4, 25
Plan-Do-Study-Act (PDSA) · 3
Planning Poker · 95, 97-98
potentially shippable product increment · 112, 132
Product Backlog · 26
    adaptive planning · 63-64
    business value · 63
    Product Owner responsibilities · 63
    shared across Teams · 167
    User Stories · 65
Product Vision · 184-187

R

Rawsthorne, Dan · 19, 116
refactoring · 19
Royce, Winston · 8-9

S

Schwaber, Ken · 23, 27, 33
Scrum
    artifacts · 25
    events · 24
    roles · 24
        Product Owner · 33, 51, 56, 58
        ScrumMaster · 31-33, 55-61
        Development Team · 37-38
    values · 27, 28
Scrum events
    time boxes · 81
Scrum events
    Backlog Refinement · 89
    Daily Scrum · 85-88
    Sprint Planning · 84
    Sprint Retrospective · 106-108
    Sprint Review · 103-105
    Story Time · 89
Scrum of Scrums · 173
    common problems · 174
    scaling up · 175
Servant-leadership · 32
Shewhart, Walter · 3
Sloan, Alfred P. · 3
Spike · 102
Sprint
    changes to · 120-121
    mini-waterfall · 114
    not finished · 124
    purpose · 111
    release · 124
    Technical Debt · 116-118
Sprint Backlog · 25
    managemement · 137
    management · 137
Sprint calendar · 128
Sprint Goal · 131, 132
Sprint Planning
    day and time · 127
    how to · 133-135
    Sprint Backlog management · 137
    Sprint Goal · 131-132
    Task Board · 137-140
    Tasks · 136
    Team commitment · 132
    time box · 133-135
    Velocity as a guide · 130
Stacey Matrix · 6
Storming
    Tuckman Model · 55-61
Sutherland, Jeff · 23, 33

T

Tabaka, Jean · 108, 153
Takeuchi and Nonaka · 22
Task Board · 137-142
    Task heuristic · 143
Taylor, Frederick Winslow · 1
Taylorism · 2
Team Spectrograph · 45-50
Teamlet · 58, 139, 141, 159
Teams
    communication lines · 38
    cross-functionality · 42-50
    dedicated membership · 39
    improvement · 53
    J-shaped curve · 60
    maturity · 54-61
    quality product · 51-52
    self-management · 42
    self-organization · 42
    shared membership · 40
    size · 38
    Sprint commitment · 51
    Sprint Review · 53
    sustainable pace · 52
    work estimates · 51
    working agreements · 57, 140, 143, 161
Technical Debt · 116-118
Theme (User Stories) · 68
Thomas-Kilmann Conflict Mode
    Instrument (TKI) · 57
Three C's
    Card · 68
    Confirmation · 69
    Conversation · 68
Time boxing · 81
Transparency · 4, 6
    organic · 152
Tuckman Model
    Forming · 54, 55
    Norming · 58
    Performing · 59
    Storming · 55-56, 60-61

U

User Stories
    Acceptance Criteria · 70-71, 76
    Conditions of Satisfaction · 70-71
    Epics · 67
    Estimable (INVEST) · 75
    focus on the customer · 65
    Independent (INVEST) · 74
    Negotiable (INVEST) · 74
    Small/Sized Appropriately (INVEST) · 75
    specific role or persona · 66
    Splitting · 72
    Testable (INVEST) · 76
    Theme · 68

Three C's · 68-69
Valuable (INVEST) · 74

V

Velocity · 101, 122, 123, 130
Velocity Certainty Principle · 123

W

Wake, Bill · 74
Waterfall (process) · 5, 7, 8
working agreements · 57, 140, 143

Made in the USA
Middletown, DE
30 August 2019